GENDERING CITIZ
WESTERN EUROPE

New challenges for citiz
research in a cross-national context

Ruth Lister, Fiona Williams, Anneli Anttonen,
Jet Bussemaker, Ute Gerhard, Jacqueline Heinen,
Stina Johansson, Arnlaug Leira, Birte Siim and
Constanza Tobío, with Anna Gavanas

First published in Great Britain in 2007 by

The Policy Press
University of Bristol
Fourth Floor
Beacon House
Queen's Road
Bristol BS8 1QU
UK

Tel +44 (0)117 331 4054
Fax +44 (0)117 331 4093
e-mail tpp-info@bristol.ac.uk
www.policypress.org.uk

British Library Cataloguing in Publication Data
A catalogue record for this book is available from the British Library.

Library of Congress Cataloging-in-Publication Data
A catalog record for this book has been requested.

ISBN 978 1 86134 693 3   paperback
ISBN 978 1 86134 694 0   hardcover

Cover design by Qube Design Associates, Bristol.
Front cover photograph kindly supplied by Getty Images.
Printed and bound in Great Britain by Hobbs the Printers, Southampton.

Contents

List of authors

Anneli Anttonen is Professor in Social Policy at the University of Tampere, Finland.

Jet Bussemaker is a political scientist working at the Free University, Amsterdam and is also a Member of Parliament for the Dutch Labour Party, and junior minister in the Dutch government.

Ute Gerhard is Professor Emeritus of Sociology (Gender Studies) at the University of Frankfurt/Main, Germany.

Jacqueline Heinen is Professor of Sociology at the University of Versailles-St-Quentin, France.

Stina Johansson is Professor in Social Work at Umea University, Sweden.

Arnlaug Leira is Professor in the Department of Sociology and Human Geography, University of Oslo, Norway.

Ruth Lister is Professor of Social Policy, Loughborough University, UK.

Birte Siim is Professor in Gender Studies at the Institute for History, International and Social Studies, Aalborg University, Denmark.

Constanza Tobíio is Professor and Vice-Dean in charge of Sociology at Carlos III University in Madrid, Spain.

Fiona Williams is Professor of Social Policy, University of Leeds, UK.

Introduction

Citizenship links the individual with the collective. This book too is the work of individual researchers who have worked collectively as an international team. The outcome is therefore not the more usual edited collection in which authors of individual chapters work with an editor. Rather it is the product of a collaborative process of iteration in which authors responsible for individual chapters have drawn on material provided by the whole team and members of the team have discussed and commented on each chapter. This process has helped to illuminate some of the challenges faced in researching citizenship in a cross-national context.

The introduction begins with an explanation of why it is necessary to understand citizenship in context. This is followed by a brief account of the meanings of citizenship and of feminist interpretations of them and, finally, an overview of the volume.

Citizenship in context

Citizenship can be understood both as an academic and political concept and as lived experience (Lister, 1997, 2003; Siim, 2000). Our analysis highlights three key elements of citizenship: rights and responsibilities, belonging and participation. The starting point for the volume and central theme running through it is that *context matters*. Although, as a concept, citizenship is typically constructed in abstract, universal terms, the universal nevertheless is interpreted and articulated in specific national social and political contexts, reflecting historical traditions and institutional and cultural complexes. Thus, for example, the British literature on citizenship has traditionally tended to focus on the relationship between individual citizens and the state, central to its liberal tradition; in contrast, the Scandinavian literature has been more likely than the British to emphasise the relations between citizens as a collectivity, reflecting the feelings of solidarity emanating from a long history of social democracy.

As lived experience, citizenship cannot be divorced from its context – temporal and national. Diverse aspects of gendered citizenship are salient at particular periods of time in different countries (see Chapters One and Two). Indeed, understandings of what it means to be a citizen, and the vocabularies used to capture these meanings, are likely to differ to some extent between European countries, as discussed in

Chapter One. Moreover, within countries people may experience citizenship differently depending on factors such as age, class, ethnicity, religion, gender, sexuality and (dis)ability. These factors interact to weave the texture of lived citizenship for individual citizens (see also the Conclusion). The main focus here is gender, in particular from the perspective of women, and the intersections between gender and 'race' and ethnicity with reference to immigration, asylum and multiculturalism. These intersections are important both theoretically and politically, yet they have too often been the subject of separate areas of study (Williams, 2001, 2004a).

Regimes

The notion of 'regimes' has been one way of trying to make sense of context so as to enable countries to be grouped together in the search for both common and differentiating patterns. The idea of a regime conveys a sense of clusters of countries around dominant institutional patterns and policy logics. It thus provides the basis for cross-national comparison and also for making sense of both stability and change over time. The best-known use of the notion of regimes in social policy is that of 'welfare regimes' associated with Gøsta Esping-Andersen, who explains that 'to talk of a "regime" is to denote the fact that in the relation between state and economy a complex of legal and organizational features are systematically interwoven' (1990, p 2). His three-way classification of welfare states into liberal, corporatist/conservative and social democratic is typically used as a starting point for cross-national welfare state analysis (with the frequent addition now of the 'Latin Rim' or Mediterranean regime).

However, the limitations of this classification, particularly from a gendered perspective (see, for instance, Sainsbury, 1996; Daly and Rake, 2003), have led to modifications of the original specification of welfare regimes and to the development of alternative forms of regime analysis. One approach, following Jane Lewis (1992, 1997), has been to analyse welfare states with reference to the strength of the male breadwinner policy logic governing the relationship between paid work and family/care responsibilities. A key development from this perspective has been the displacement in some countries of the male breadwinner by an increasingly individualised universal breadwinner model. All adults capable of paid work are regarded as 'adult workers' or at least potential adult workers (even if part-time in the case of many women).

Another source of criticism of the initial welfare regime analysis was that it largely ignored the provision of welfare services and thus did not provide a satisfactory account of differences in the organisation of the care of children and adults, which is critical to any gendered analysis. This prompted an attempt to develop an alternative analysis around the idea of 'social care regimes', further developed by a number of feminist analysts (Anttonen and Sipilä, 1996; Daly, 2001a; Bettio and Plantenga, 2004). Care regimes differ according to the extent and nature of the role played by the state in the provision of care for children and older people and the extent to which care remains the responsibility of the informal family sector.

More broadly, and with implications for care regimes, it is possible to identify 'gender regimes' (Walby, 2004). These represent the combination of culture, institutions, power relations and social practices within which gendered citizenship operates and constitute 'the key policy logics of welfare states in relation to gender' (Pascall and Lewis, 2004, p 373). 'Gender regimes can be seen as systems through which paid work is connected to unpaid, state services and benefits are delivered to individuals and households, costs are allocated and time is shared between men and women in households as well as between households and employment' (Pascall and Kwak, 2005, p 33; Einhorn, 2006). These distributional processes reflect dominant gender cultures, or the understandings of and meanings attached to gender and generational relations (Pfau-Effinger, 2002, 2005). Gender cultures also shape the everyday social and cultural practices that are part of the lived experience of citizenship. Culture is thus important in linking 'from above' institutional regime analysis with 'from below' understandings of everyday lived citizenship.

The lived experience of gendered citizenship in any particular country is heavily influenced by the dominant gender regime as well as by the nature of the welfare and care regimes, which govern social citizenship – the nexus of rights and responsibilities underpinning individuals' welfare, broadly understood – in particular. Citizenship is also lived within specific 'citizenship regimes' 'with unique structures of internal inequality and forms of inclusion and exclusion' (Saraceno, 1997, p 27). Jenson and Phillips (2001, p 72) explain that:

> because citizenship is an historical construction, its form will vary. Particular political struggles, particular trajectories of development, and institutional legacies underpin the forms of citizenship as well as the timing of acquisition of rights. The result is that one may speak of citizenship regimes, just as one can speak of social-welfare regimes. We can say that the concept of citizenship regime denotes

the institutional arrangements, rules, and understandings that guide and shape concurrent policy decisions and expenditures of states, problem definitions by states and citizens, and claims-making by citizens.

Finally, the notion of 'migration regimes' captures the combinations of formal/legal rules and political/cultural practices that govern the terms of entry to nation state citizenship for migrants (see Chapter Three). Migration regimes cannot be divorced from experiences of racialisation and multiculturalism (although analytically and politically they too often are). Together they represent the internal and external *intersecting* aspects of nation and nationhood, operating within and at the borders of nation states (Williams, 1995, 2001, 2004a).

These various forms of regime – welfare, care, gender, citizenship and migration – dovetail together to constitute formal citizenship and to frame the lived experience of gendered (and racialised) citizenship in different ways. We therefore refer to various forms of regime in later chapters, particularly in the policy studies chapters in Part Two. However, because country clusterings may differ according to the form of regime discussed, it is not appropriate to classify the countries in our study according to any kind of overarching regime analysis.

Levels

Welfare, care, gender, citizenship and migration regimes represent a helpful device for setting citizenship within specific national contexts. It is not, however, only the national context that frames the lived experience of citizenship. Sub-national differences are also important to varying degrees. Thus, for instance, in the UK devolution has meant the development of differences in some aspects of the regimes which frame citizenship in its constituent nations; and in Germany and Spain regional governments have considerable autonomy. Moreover, gender cultures can vary even at neighbourhood level, as demonstrated in Duncan and Edwards' study (1999) of the 'gendered moral rationalities', which influence lone mothers' navigation of their citizenship responsibilities as paid workers and mothers.

Above the nation state, the European Union (EU) plays an important role in framing how citizenship is experienced within and at its borders. As a law-making and regulatory supranational body, the European Commission (EC) has influenced the development of the various citizenship, welfare, care, gender and migration regimes within member states. Despite limitations, which place constraints on the EU's impact on gender inequality, initiatives such as equal treatment directives in the areas of employment and social security and resolutions addressing wider questions such as the gendered distribution of care responsibilities, have strengthened women's citizenship in a number of member states (Hobson and Lister, 2002; Walby, 2004). In theory at least, accession to the EU should strengthen the framework of gender equality in the accession countries of Central and Eastern Europe, although observers are divided as to what the reality is likely to be in practice (Heinen and Portet, 2004; Pascall and Lewis, 2004; Pascall and Kwak, 2005). It should be remembered that from the perspective of Scandinavian welfare states the EU has sometimes appeared more as a threat to women's rights as citizens than as an opportunity for their advancement.

The EC has promoted European citizenship as complementary to nation state citizenship in order to encourage identification with the EU. While, for many, European citizenship appears still to be a fairly abstract notion, some commentators suggest that its significance lies in its potential (Bellamy and Warleigh, 2001, cited in Hoffman, 2004). In order to develop that potential the EC has promoted the idea of rights at the European level, for instance through the Charter of Fundamental Rights (adopted in 2000 following the earlier report of the Comité des Sages [1996]) and has emphasised the importance of integration through citizenship practice in informal cross-EU networks (Zippel, 2004; Gerhard, 2006). It is a potential that some groups, such as the European Women's Lobby and the Black and Migrant Women's Project, have exploited, 'creating solidarities and opening spaces for the articulation of challenges to the dominant meanings of citizenship which inscribe' the marginalisation of women and in particular, black and migrant women (Williams, 2003, p 142; see also Pudrovska and Ferree, 2004). These challenges represent 'an attempt to redefine the gendered and racialized contours of European citizenship, emphasizing the importance of a citizenship in which people have a voice which is both participative and representative, connecting the local to the international' (Williams, 2003, p 142).

Changes

The EC is placing increasing emphasis on the global dimension of its economic and social policies. This global dimension is one aspect of a number of demographic, economic and social changes, which provide the final contextual element for the study of gendered citizenship in Europe. Growing fears about the impact of declining birth rates in much of the EU on future European competitiveness and prosperity (not detailed in this volume) mean that women's labour market position and their (in)ability to combine paid work with family responsibilities, with implications for the provision of child and elder care, take on a new policy salience (Esping-Andersen, 2002a; Knijn and Komter, 2004; Dixon and Margo, 2006). Countries such as Finland, France and, most recently, Germany (but not the UK) have responded with policies favouring larger families (see Chapter Four). The issue of migration is also viewed partially through the lens of demographic change, as (some) migrants are seen as potential labour power, needed to make good the demographic deficit, while others are to be kept out by exclusionary asylum and immigration policies. The increasingly ethnically diverse complexion of Europe is giving rise to debates about the implications for citizenship, with reference in particular to multiculturalism (discussed in Chapter Three). (The diversification of family types is another important issue in the demographic debate but is not addressed explicitly in this volume, which is not concerned with family patterns as such.)

Demographic pressures are also one factor in the emergence of 'a social policy for children' in Europe (Daly, 2004, p 146). Children as citizen-workers of the future are key assets in the social investment model of the EU (Lister, 2004), with childcare in particular emerging as an important policy tool (see Chapter Four). This is a double-edged development (Ruxton, 2005). On the one hand, a higher place for children on the European policy agenda opens up new possibilities for policies to promote children's well-being and to realise the full potential of the UN Convention on the Rights of the Child (reflected in the EC's [2006] document, *Towards an EU Strategy on the Rights of the Child*). On the other hand, the social investment model runs the risk of treating children (and also women and migrants) in largely instrumental terms. Counter discourses, stronger in some countries than others, position them as rights-bearing citizens – *de jure* or *de facto* – with voices that need to be heard in political debate.

The meanings of citizenship

We have argued that citizenship must be understood as a contextualised concept and lived experience. We turn now briefly to introduce the main traditions of thinking about citizenship, clarify its key elements and summarise the insights that feminist theorising has brought to the topic (see also Lister, 1997, 2003; Voet, 1998; Siim, 2000).

The main traditions of thinking about citizenship (developed in more depth in historical and contemporary context in Chapters One and Two) can be represented in the form of a citizenship 'family tree' (see Figure 0.1).

The civic republican and liberal traditions form the two main branches of the tree. In civic republicanism, which has its origins in classical Greece, the essence of citizenship is the fulfilment of civic virtue and duty, primarily through participation in collective self-government. Two important offshoots of this branch, which prioritises the interests of the wider citizenship community, are communitarianism and maternalism. Communitarianism places great emphasis on belonging and on common cultural identity, values and norms; like civic republicanism it prioritises duties and responsibilities over rights. Maternalism represents an explicitly feminist offshoot of the civic republican tradition. It identifies motherhood as a specifically female contribution to citizenship, for it is mothers who are responsible for raising the next generation of citizens. In different guises, maternalism argues for improvements in the material conditions of women as mothers (sometimes drawing on rights discourses) and the projection of maternalist values of nurturing, care and compassion into public life. A contemporary, more universalist and less gender-specific version of this can be detected in arguments for the recognition of an ethic and practice of care as an expression of citizenship responsibility, not confined to either mothers or women but nonetheless embedded in recognition of gender and other inequalities (Sevenhuijsen, 1998; Williams, 2001).

Figure 0.1: Citizenship 'family tree'

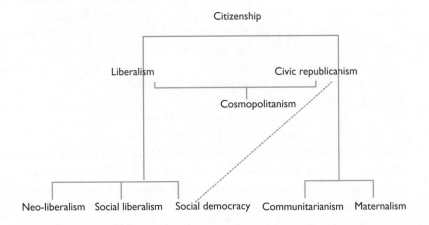

In the other main branch of the liberal tradition, it is the rights of the individual, which are key to citizenship. The 20th century was dominated, at different times, by two offshoots of the liberal tradition: social liberalism and social democracy on the one hand and neo-liberalism on the other. Social liberalism and social democracy broadened the domain of rights to embrace social rights, which, through the state, guarantee citizens a degree of economic security irrespective of their position in the market so that citizens are not totally dependent on selling their labour power to survive (see Dwyer, 2004). In its Nordic form, social democratic citizenship has also emphasised participation (denoted in Figure 0.1 by a dotted line connecting it to the civic republican branch of the tree). The neo-liberal offshoot represents a late 20th-century reassertion of classical liberalism, which challenges the validity of social rights and prioritises civil rights (particularly market rights such as the right to own property) over political rights (Faulks, 2000).

Both civic republican and liberal models feed into cosmopolitan citizenship, which transcends the boundaries associated with nation state citizenship. Although cosmopolitanism can be traced back to ancient Greece, it tends to be associated with the philosophers of the Enlightenment, notably Immanuel Kant (Hutchings and Dannreuther, 1999; Linklater, 2002). Cosmopolitanism's belief that citizenship can be inscribed as both a status and practice at global level has received renewed impetus with contemporary processes of globalisation.

Individual citizenship regimes can be characterised according to where they sit on the citizenship family tree. However, this statement needs qualifying in two ways. First, the leaves on the branches take on different hues, reflecting the particular historical circumstances within which they have grown. Second, in reality citizenship regimes draw on both of the main branches of the tree, in varying combinations of branches and offshoots. Whatever the citizenship regime, the different elements of citizenship emphasised in the two main citizenship traditions are present (Bellamy, 2004).

At its most basic, citizenship provides individuals with a legal status deriving from membership of a citizenship community, in this case typically the nation state. In the words of T.H. Marshall, 'all who possess the status are equal with respect to the *rights and duties* with which the status is endowed' (1950, pp 28-9, emphasis added). Marshall's own exposition of citizenship is remembered primarily for his classification of civil, political and social rights. Marshall's analysis has been criticised by feminists particularly for its failure to see how gender (and not only class) divisions structure denial of and access to citizenship rights (see also Chapter One). Nevertheless, as this volume attests, his tripartite classification has proved of enduring use, including in recent analyses of gendered citizenship in post-communist societies (Heinen, 1997, 2006).

Contemporary citizenship struggles in Europe have, on the one hand, involved the defence of rights, particularly social rights, in the face of the neo-liberal challenge to their validity and of welfare state retrenchment. On the other hand, they have represented claims for new categories of rights such as reproductive, sexual, disability and cultural rights. This has led to new formulations of citizenship such as 'sexual citizenship' (which both articulates sexual rights claims and promotes the citizenship status of groups whose sexuality is stigmatised [Richardson, 1998, 2000; Weeks, 1998; Lister, 2002]); 'intimate citizenship' (which relates citizenship to people's intimate lives, embracing but not confined to sexual citizenship [Plummer, 2003]); and 'cultural citizenship' (which involves 'a right to full cultural participation and undistorted representation' [Pakulski, 1997, p 83; see also Stevenson, 2003]). Disabled people have framed citizenship claims for civil, political and social rights in terms of access, self-determination and recognition of their contribution (Morris, 2005) and have challenged the dominant image of 'the active, fit and autonomous citizen' (Marks, 2001, p 170).

Dominant political discourses, however, have increasingly prioritised citizenship obligations and responsibilities over rights in many Western societies. In particular, paid work is now treated as a primary citizenship obligation for women as well as men in the 'adult worker' model discussed earlier. At the same time, however, in some countries this has been balanced by new rights to help parents (in practice usually mothers) to stay at home to care for very young children (see Chapter Four).

Membership of a citizenship community (which in this instance is not necessarily confined to the nation state, as explained later) is not just a question of rights and obligations. It also involves a set of social and political relationships, practices and identities that together can be described as a sense of belonging. Belonging is not a fixed state, nor just a material one; it involves also emotional and psychological dimensions. Young people, immigrants and marginalised groups, in particular, have to negotiate belonging and different groups experience belonging to the citizenship community in diverse ways. An important element of belonging is participation. Nancy Fraser (2003, p 36) posits 'parity of participation ... [that is] social arrangements that permit all (adult) members of society to interact with one another as peers' as a core social justice ideal. This requires a fair distribution of material resources so as to ensure independence, voice and equality of respect. From a specifically citizenship perspective, *political* and *civic* participation, underpinned by political, civil and social rights, is typically regarded as pivotal to the understanding of citizenship as a practice.

Membership and belonging are also *multi-layered*, as indicated previously. Thus the citizenship community meaningful to individuals is not necessarily confined to the nation state. Increasingly citizenship is theorised and experienced at a number of levels – from the intimate, through the local, national and regional (the EU being a prime example) to the global, where it is sometimes represented in the language of cosmopolitanism and of human rights (see Chapter Two). Jones and Gaventa (2002) ground such a multi-layered understanding in a concern with the concrete 'spaces and places' in which citizenship is practised. They point out how citizenship as an identity and practice 'is likely to differ across the spaces in which people's lives are played out: the home and personal relations, local and national politics, to the global arena' (2002, p 19).

The policy studies in Part Two of this volume move between these different spaces and places. While our approach to citizenship highlights the three elements outlined earlier – rights and responsibilities, belonging and participation – it also takes seriously Marshall's starting point of *equality*. Feminist and other strands of critical citizenship theory have demonstrated the ways in which citizenship has, in different societies, failed in its promise of equality. Rather than citizenship's traditional 'false universalism', which has perpetuated inequalities, feminist/critical citizenship theorists have argued for a conceptualisation and practice of citizenship rooted in a 'differentiated universalism in which the achievement of the universal is contingent upon attention to difference' (Lister, 2003, p 91). Genuine equal citizenship, it is argued, has to embrace diversity. Contemporary citizenship politics are in part a politics of recognition – claims for recognition of status and identity – which, in turn, means they are also a struggle for political voice (Phillips, 2003). Citizenship is thus not static but develops in response to the exercise of the agency of women and men, individually and collectively through political and civil society associations (Lister, 1997, 2003; Siim, 2000).

The heart of the now well-developed feminist critique of mainstream citizenship theory lies in its challenge to the public–private dichotomy that underpinned it. We refer here to the gendered divide between the public sphere of the *polis* and the economy on one side and the private domestic sphere on the other, rather than to the distinction between state and market (although the latter is also relevant to the analysis in Chapters Four and Five). This dichotomy has not only served to exclude women from full citizenship in practice, but it also defined them as essentially incapable of citizenship, for they were deemed to lack the 'male' qualities and capacities necessary for citizenship in the public sphere. (It should be noted, however, that for some women the public–private divide has represented a bulwark against racist oppression or, in the former socialist regimes, a refuge from a totalitarian state.) Out of this critique has developed a re-articulation of citizenship, which problematises the gendered domestic division of labour and the status accorded to unpaid care work in relation to the rights and responsibilities of citizenship (Lister, 1997, 2003, 2007; Sevenhuijsen, 1998). It has done so in particular citizenship contexts, reflecting 'national and culture-specific understandings of what care is about' (Leira and Saraceno, 2002, p 57). One result has been to put childcare at the heart of debates about social citizenship and also gendered citizenship more generally.

Two underlying themes emerge in this volume, representing different facets of citizenship's Janus-faced quality. The first is the ways in which citizenship operates as a force for both inclusion and exclusion. Whereas mainstream citizenship theory tended to focus on its inclusionary promise, critical citizenship theory has highlighted its exclusionary tendencies both for marginalised groups within nation states and for those trying to move between nation states as migrants or asylum seekers. Second is citizenship's simultaneously emancipatory and disciplinary quality. The same policies can represent both. Thus, for example, paid work has represented an emancipatory path to citizenship for many women, providing them with more or less economic independence and access to social citizenship rights. Yet where lone mothers and carers are required to seek paid work as a condition of social security rights it can be experienced as a disciplinary force for some of those who wish to provide full-time care. Or, policies that require immigrants and refugees to learn the language of their new country as a condition of legal citizenship may be experienced by many as disciplinary, but in some instances could be emancipatory, opening up access to public citizenship, especially for women who might otherwise be isolated in the domestic sphere.

Overview of the book

As already noted, this book is a collective endeavour. The authors have collaborated for many years as part of the wider European Network for Theory and Research on Women, Welfare State and Citizenship. In 1998, some members of the group produced a special edition of *Critical Social Policy: Vocabularies of Citizenship and Gender in Northern Europe*. In further discussions, we became more aware of the salience of the different national contexts in which we each work and of the need to interrogate these in any cross-national study of citizenship. This book is an attempt to do this.

It does not claim to be a systematic comparative study. Instead, it explores the challenge of studying gendered citizenship in a cross-national context and from a number of different perspectives. It illustrates its arguments with material from a range of Western European welfare states, representing a variety of welfare, care, gender, citizenship and migration regimes: Denmark, Finland, France, Germany, the Netherlands, Norway, Spain, Sweden and the UK. In addition, it makes some reference to Central and Eastern Europe. Members of the team have taken responsibility for specific chapters, drawing on material provided by the team as a whole, as follows: Introduction and Conclusion – Ruth Lister; Chapter One – Ute Gerhard; Chapter Two – Jet Bussemaker; Chapter Three – Birte Siim with assistance from Fiona Williams; Chapter Four – Anneli Anttonen, Stina Johansson and Arnlaug Leira; and Chapter Five – Fiona Williams, Constanza Tobío and Anna Gavanas. Jacqueline Heinen has provided the information on Central and Eastern Europe. Ruth Lister and Fiona Williams have edited the volume as a whole with editorial assistance from Lisa Hunt and Steven Mosby. The team has met on three occasions to discuss the contents and draft chapters; it is grateful to the Swedish Council for Working Life and Social Research for funding these meetings. It is also grateful to the Hessian Ministry of Science and Art, which supported two preliminary workshops under the auspices of the Cornelia Goethe Centre in Frankfurt.

The book is divided into two parts. Part One provides a framework for the cross-national analysis of gendered citizenship. It aims to clarify the various ways that the concept of citizenship has developed historically and is understood today in the European welfare states represented. Chapter One takes a historical perspective so as to contextualise citizenship through elaboration of its legal and theoretical roots. Chapter Two elaborates on the contemporary framing of debates and struggles around citizenship and looks at citizenship beyond the nation state. Both chapters pay particular attention to gendered exclusions and the struggles of women's movements for full and equal citizenship.

Part Two comprises three interrelated policy studies, which throw light on critical elements of gendered citizenship in 21st-century Europe and which make more concrete some of the issues raised in Part One. They foreground different aspects of the meanings of citizenship: belonging and participation in Chapter Three, social rights (in relation to childcare) in Chapter Four and its multi-layered quality in Chapter Five. The topics, which span private practices and public policies, represent areas of significant change in terms of policy and lived experience. They are likely to become increasingly salient, especially in the context of EU enlargement, the societal shifts outlined earlier and contemporary debates around the meanings and responsibilities of citizenship.

Chapter Three considers the challenges for gendered citizenship posed by asylum and migration and the potential tensions between ethnic diversity and gender equality as new forms of citizenship develop as a result of migration and integration policies. In addition to analysing such policies in the context of different migration regimes, the chapter addresses debates around the headscarf and diverse marriage arrangements in order to explore the meanings of lived gendered citizenship in increasingly ethnically diverse societies. It raises important questions around the nature of belonging in such societies.

Chapter Four discusses the care of young children. As noted previously, care and the division of care responsibilities between women and men has emerged as a key issue in the theorisation and politics of gendered citizenship. It has implications for the citizenship of women and men and (although not discussed here) for the well-being of children (see Lewis, J., 2006b). The development of policies around the care of young children has meant a radical extension of the meaning of social citizenship particularly in the Nordic welfare states and has been a significant element in the development of EU social policy.

Acting as a retrospective bridge between Chapters Three and Four, Chapter Five brings together the issues of care and migration through a study of the transnational dynamics of care, sometimes referred to as 'global care chains'. In some European countries, migrant women from the global South are providing the care of young children so as to enable European mothers to access citizenship through paid employment. This is one way of addressing the emergent 'care deficit', which has been identified in contemporary European welfare states that are moving towards the 'adult-worker' model. It represents a privatised solution to gaps in public childcare provision and to rigidities in the gendered domestic division of labour. It also renders many women without citizenship status vulnerable in the undervalued grey economy of household labour. This policy study differs from the others in that it introduces original empirical data from research conducted by Tobío, Gavanas and Williams in Madrid, London and Stockholm and does not include the other countries covered in this volume. As well as integrating the study of care and migration as elements of gendered citizenship, the chapter illustrates citizenship's multi-layered nature in the 'spaces and places' of the domestic and the global and locates the experience of citizenship squarely at the intersections of the public and private spheres. It develops further the notion of lived citizenship.

A brief conclusion reflects on some of the challenges faced in researching gendered citizenship in a cross-national context and highlights what we believe are the fresh perspectives gained by bringing together the issues of childcare and migration in a global context.

Part One
Historical and cross-national perspectives

ONE

Historical perspectives

Introduction

As context matters, a cross-national European study of the meanings of the concept of citizenship must, first of all, take the distinctive historical backgrounds into account. Understandings of citizenship have not only changed over the course of time, but its multifaceted, different meanings also reflect both varied political and social histories and legal traditions and cultures in the respective European countries. When, in this chapter, special attention is paid to legal traditions and cultures as characteristic of particular trajectories of development, this is not intended as a reduction to a legal discourse; on the contrary, it is an attempt to be concrete and extend our view of political ideas or conceptualisations to what is called 'lived experience'. For the notion of 'legal cultures' comprises more than norms, doctrines or institutions of a legal system, it also includes attitudes towards the state and the practical experiences of those who were excluded from citizenship rights or became involved with the law. Since citizenship is not only a legal status but also a practice and lived experience (Lister, 2003), the awareness of the significance of legal cultures, therefore, may contribute to an understanding of 'citizenship regimes' as 'historical constructions' (Jenson and Phillips, 2001) and may explain specific barriers to equal citizenship or particular trajectories of inclusion respectively. These legacies, different historical roots and legal cultures, political struggles as well as particular institutional trajectories, still shape today's discourses and have an impact on citizenship theory and practice. Of special interest are the 'overlapping vocabularies' of the different discourses and debates with respect to female citizenship that impeded the possibility of gender equality (Landes, 1996). This means that the history of women's citizenship has deviated from the development usually depicted in the traditional citizenship literature.

In this chapter, however, the attempt at exploring the different historical and political contexts cannot be complete; it must be restricted to an exemplary or ideal type of argumentation. Since ideal types are always theoretical exaggerations, which in reality never exist in pure form, they will be illustrated by exemplary historical features. After introducing the terminology of the legal tradition and the models of the modern concept of citizenship, the second part of the chapter will discuss the delays and the impediments to women's citizenship in the different dimensions of political, civil and social citizenship rights. While in the first two parts the focus will be more on the exclusionary aspects of the historical theoretical and political construction of citizenship, the third part discusses the role played by feminist interventions − nationally and internationally − in opening up citizenship to women. The conclusion highlights a number of insights that can be gleaned from this historical overview of the concept of citizenship from a gendered perspective.

Legal traditions

Terminology

When examining the etymology of the term 'citizenship', we find similarities in the European tradition with regard to a double meaning of citizenship: on the one hand, the legal status of an inhabitant of a community, city or state in the mere sense of being situated or '*belonging to*' and on the other, inhabitants who are recognised as full members of a city or state and are entitled to *participate* in authority or sovereignty. Citizenship therefore represents a legal status and is also used as a term to include or exclude certain groups. The English language, which also used the notion of 'subject' to describe the relationship between the individual person and the state (until the 1948 British Nationality Act), made this distinction as well. Both before and even after the parliamentary reforms of the 19th century, which introduced partial, gender-based and property-based voting rights, the regulations distinguished between 'ordinary subjects', who had no right to participate directly in government decisions, and those privileged by rank or property. Only the latter owed allegiance, including military or jury service and the payment of certain taxes (Oliver and Heater, 1994, pp 58-60).

Several other European languages have also employed different terms to distinguish those who merely belong to a city or state − such as 'denizen', 'inhabitant', or 'national' − from those who are entitled to political participation and representation. The French language clearly distinguishes between the terms 'citoyen' and 'bourgeois' and thus reflects the clear-cut distinction between public and private law of the Roman law.[1] The Spanish Constitution of 1812 drew a similar distinction between 'Spaniards' and 'citizens'.[2] Thus, 'being Spanish' did not automatically mean access to political rights such as the right to vote and to be elected, which were reserved exclusively for 'ciudadanía', or citizens (Closa, 2004, p 131).

A similar double meaning of citizen can be found in the Scandinavian language with regard to the terms 'Statsbürger' and 'Mitbürger'. It seems to be the same differentiation that dominates the German legal discourse with its distinction between 'Staatsbürger' (citoyen) and 'Stadtbürger' (bourgeois or citizen of the city) (Riedel, 1975). Immanuel Kant, as a contemporary of the French Revolution, used the French terms to provide us with a systematic explanation: 'Only who is entitled to vote and to take part in legislation is called a citizen ('citoyen', i.e. citizen of the state, not only of the city/'bourgeois') (Kant, 1793/1922, p 434). In drawing a sharp line between the 'bourgeois' as the private individual who is enjoying civil rights, and the 'citoyen' as the person who is entitled to participate in elections and to exercise political rights, these definitions were generally acknowledged in 19th-century continental Europe and governed jurisdiction. The distinction between 'bourgeois' and 'citoyen' also reflects the separation of the public sphere from the private sphere, which has been critical to the exclusion of women from the public sphere.

The variety of meanings attached to the English term 'citizenship' is not only a question of language or of translation, it also reflects different legal systems and traditions of thinking that follow different logics, notably those in Roman and common law.[3] Roman law shaped jurisprudence in most of continental Europe, whereas the English common law tradition resisted this influence and thus formed a legal circle of its own (see the Appendix at the end of this chapter).[4]

Despite many variations in European history we also find certain common attributes of citizenship. Everywhere the personal concept of citizenship that indicates the relationship between sovereign and the individual preceded the development of a territorial or national affiliation. But only 'full' citizens enjoyed a certain balance of rights and duties towards the community. Aliens, serfs, children *and* women were regarded as 'passive' subjects rather than 'active' partners. This was true for the Greek '*polis*' and also for ancient Rome, where the notion of *civis* and *civitas* was originally founded on individual status, not on domicile or residence. Only the later Roman Empire extended these membership rights to the whole empire. In a long process, which lasted from the Middle Ages to the 19th century, the citizenship of male landlords and householders in the cities and estates developed.

First defended against feudal interference as a privileged status, then, in the era of absolutism, it was extended and transformed into subjecthood – a development from 'the manifold allegiances of medieval man into a single but comprehensive bond of national citizenship' (Brinkmann, 1959, p 472). The group of citizens comprised a rather small number of property owners, exclusively male, who fulfilled the social prerequisites of 'possessive individualism' (Macpherson, 1964). Or as John Locke (1970/1690, p 87) put it: only those who are 'proprietors of their own capacities' and 'can provide for themselves', who are thus 'free from the will of others', are 'man born ... with a Title of perfect freedom, and an uncontrolled enjoyment of all the Rights and Privileges of the Law of Nature'.

The modern concept of citizenship as a legacy of these developments represents not only a combination of but also the tension between the two elements: membership and participation in a political unit *and* a personal status, legitimised by the notion of 'liberty', the 'rights of man' and secular natural law. However, in the different social and political contexts of the emerging nation states, we must be aware of different strands of argumentations and uneven developments in the 19th and 20th centuries.

Models of the modern concept of citizenship

The modern concept of citizenship emerged in the political and societal transformations resulting from the American and French Revolutions and was accompanied by the radical changes of the Industrial Revolution. As noted in the Introduction, two models of citizenship and schools of thinking have vied with each other for dominance: the *civic republican* and the *liberal* versions. These, together with liberalism's social liberal and social democratic offshoots, will serve as a basis for a discussion of the gender of citizenship and the question of how much room historically the different models allowed for the participation of women.

The French concept of citizenship can be regarded as the model for the civic republican tradition. France and, in our sample of countries, Spain – with a break in the nation's history by the Francoist dictatorship (Closa, 2004) – have been decisively influenced by the republican model of citizenship. Its defining features are good civic behaviour and a republican form of state, hence the term 'civic republican' (Heater, 2004, p 4; see also Habermas, 1996). The most important virtue of a citizen is participation in collective self-government. Following Rousseau's (1947) theories about the Social Contract, this means participation in the General Will, which casts the people of a state as the sovereign. First and foremost, citizenship spells the right of political participation as well as the duty to contribute to the common good. Citizenship rights are conceived of as 'positive' civil rights and liberties in contrast to so-called 'negative liberties', understood as rights of the individual against the state. The latter are at the core of a liberal concept of a citizen who as a human being is entitled to enjoy these civil rights and liberties as fundamental freedoms from governmental force and interference. The French concept of citizenship was predominantly attached to the language of democracy and political participation, motivated by the ideal of 'active involvement in a self-governing community of equals' (Laborde, 2004, p 51; see also Siim, 2000, pp 44ff). Although the radical republicanism of the French Revolution was built up on 'solidarity' as one of the key notions, the citizens' social rights were not provided for. Social reform stayed underdeveloped even in the Third Republic (from 1872 to 1944) when – following Bismarck's example of introducing social insurance – the French welfare state was introduced from above. Nevertheless, state education – socialisation into a shared culture, language, and way of life – played a central role. As an inclusive strategy of cultural assimilation and civilisation and thus part of participatory citizenship, education, however, functioned not only to emancipate but also to discipline: according to the 'French republican doctrine, citizens are "forced to be free"' (Laborde, 2004, p 49).

When the French Revolution abolished the rule of the old powers and intermediary bodies and created the nation state (which functioned as the sole representative of common interest), the emergence and the conjunction of state, nationality and citizenship were supported by a catalogue of republican duties. These demanded certain attitudes towards the state. One of these duties was a commitment to patriotism as a civic virtue, which was tellingly characterised as 'civic fraternity'. Not only here does it become clear that 'the universal bourgeois subject was at the outset a gendered subject. Only male rights to full individuality were protected... Undeniably, then, liberty and equality came to be overshadowed by fraternity (the brotherhood of men) in the new order produced by the Revolution' (Landes, 1988, p 158).

The republican model for women was motherhood. It was the mother's duty to educate the children as good republicans and to instil in them the love for the republican virtues and principles of liberty and equality. Mothers were the guardians of virtues and morals. This was the reason why, during the French Revolution, they were at first allowed to participate in public debates and meetings. As 'citoyennes without citizenship' (Landes, 1996, p 305) or as 'Républicaines revolutionaries' they even demanded the right to bear arms in defence of the republic (Duhet, 1971, pp 115ff). But this and similar forms of intervention and participation suffered a quick and dramatic end, when already in 1793 the women's clubs were prohibited and Olympe de Gouges, author of *A Declaration of the Rights of Women and Citizens* (quoted in Bell and Offen, 1983; Gerhard, 2001, and to be discussed later), was executed. It is remarkable that, despite their immense contribution to the Revolution, French women did not get the right to vote until 1944 – although in the republican view the right to vote is the central right, the 'paradigm of all rights' (Habermas, 1992a, p 330). The contradiction that was already obvious in the French language, calling the women 'citoyennes' but withholding full political participation from them, was not resolved.

Women were not regarded as equal citizens in the liberal tradition either; consequently they were excluded from political participation. Even in Britain, the country with the oldest forms of parliamentary representation, women did not get full voting rights before 1928. In contrast to France's revolutionary dramaturgy, the British history of constitutionalism and democracy developed slowly over the centuries. This was called 'English gradualism' and was also characterised by 'the passive character of British civil institutions' (Turner, 1990, p 207). The development began with the Magna Carta of 1215 and the first limitations of royal absolutism. It continued with the Habeas Corpus Act of 1679, which guaranteed certain fundamental liberties to everyone (for example protection against arbitrary incarceration), irrespective of whether the person in question was a subject of the British Crown. After the Glorious Revolution in 1688, a constitutional monarchy was established, parliamentary rights were strengthened and the institution of serfdom was revoked. However, the voting reforms that were introduced after 1832, extending voting rights, for the first time explicitly excluded women from suffrage. The linkage until 1918 of even men's voting rights to the ownership of property and the exclusion of certain groups (notably women and recipients of public relief) also confirms the tight connection, as well as the gender bias, of liberal ideology to possessive individualism.

At the centre of the liberal concept of citizenship there is the individual. The gradual development of parliamentary rights was based on the fact that 'many rights and duties that in other political cultures would have been explicitly proclaimed or embodied in a constitutional code were tacitly taken for granted, embodied in every-day social practice, or they evolved through the common law' (Harris, 2004, p 75). The individual's civil rights were defended as civil rights and liberties first against the feudal lords, then against every kind of state force but also against other citizens. Behind this stands the idea of innate, inalienable human rights that are not connected to the state, and the assumption of the individual right to freedom and autonomy. But those who can participate in these rights and are the subjects of these rights in a bourgeois society – as we have already learned from Locke (mentioned earlier) – are only those who own property and can sustain themselves. According to the liberal viewpoint, the state is generally seen as a necessary evil, required to protect the civil citizenship rights of individual citizens as part of a contractual relationship between individual citizens and the state.

This is the model that also historically characterised the Netherlands in our sample of countries. However, in the 20th century an increasing 'pillarisation' of influential denominational organisations replaced the hegemonic power of the liberal parties, leading to the development of a variant of citizenship of the civic-republican branch, a more communitarian model (Bussemaker, 1998; see also Chapter Two). Britain has also integrated different elements of other citizenship regimes into its development towards a modern welfare state. Under the influence of the trade union struggle and the class conflicts of the late 19th century, Britain eventually moved from a liberal to a reformist, that is a social liberal solution (Turner, 1990, p 196). At the turn of the 20th century, in an era of migration, there was also a clear shift away from the permissive and laissez-faire citizenship philosophy of the former non-restrictive nationality legislation (in 1844 and 1870) with the introduction of immigration controls.

This period saw a lively interest in how to develop 'the habits of good citizenship' in the population. At the same time the 'new' or 'social' liberals appealed to the common good in an attempt to combine a collective notion of citizenship, underpinned by the state, with liberal ideas of rights. Their recognition of the importance of basic social rights to the exercise of individual freedom represented a challenge to the market liberalism of the 19th century (Lister, 1998). The Beveridge Report (Beveridge, 1942) finally marks the turn in social policy that introduced the British welfare state on the basis of social citizenship rights. T. H. Marshall's (1950) still influential analysis, which introduced a tripartite and thus enlarged system that reshaped the concept of citizenship, laid the foundation of a social policy that does not solve the tension between the free market economy and social and economic inequality but tries to alleviate its effects.

The Nordic states – Denmark, Finland, Iceland, Norway and Sweden

– stand as ideal-typical representatives of a social democratic model. Despite variations, they all meet the characteristics of Esping-Andersen's portrait of the social democratic regime. Although his classification mainly aims at marking the structure and institutional patterns of *welfare* regimes, these states at the same time exemplify social democratic *citizenship* regimes. Since entitlements are based on the 'principles of equality, universalism, and de-commodification of social rights' (Esping-Andersen, 1990, p 27), these welfare states work on the basis of universal citizenship. The social democratic model places greater emphasis than other models on the relations between citizens and not just between individual citizens and the state. Moreover, with less distance between the state and civil society and citizens, historically 'the state was not perceived as such a hostile and alien force to the individual as in many other countries' (Kangas and Palme, 2005, p 19).

Noteworthy too is a positive perception of active citizenship that is founded on social movements, first on the alliance between the working class and the peasant movement, then, since the end of 19th century, also on women's movements as agents of social change. Thus, citizenship was constructed as citizenship 'from below', as an 'activist, participatory and egalitarian ideal' (Hernes, 1987, p 139). The fact that Scandinavian women gained suffrage earlier than elsewhere in Europe (see Table 1.1 on p 28) has been of long-term significance. However, it was not until the middle of the 20th century that other elements of women's citizenship were achieved. For instance, in Sweden women's organisations allied with the Social Democratic Party successfully campaigned not only for 'the married woman's right to work' but fought 'for the employed woman's right to marry and to have children' (Myrdal, quoted in Leira, 2002, p 22). In Denmark women's organisations together with peasants' and workers' movements began to influence the state apparatus by democratic struggle, but 'the fundamental shift in the discourse and practice of social and political citizenship happened in Denmark after 1960' (Siim, 2000, p 113). Two decisive steps were subsequently taken to change the 'old' social democratic governance tradition of corporate decision making by parties and labour unions into a more 'women-friendly' welfare state: the move from a male-breadwinner to a dual-breadwinner model, accompanied by an expansion of publicly funded childcare and the intrusion of women into the labour market, particularly into the public sector, as well as 'a dramatic increase in women's participation and representation in decision-making bodies' (Siim and Skjeie, 2004, p 150).

In contrast to the universalism of the social democratic Nordics, the patterning of social entitlements for specific social groups (Therborn, 1995) is a distinctive feature of the German welfare state and citizen regime, which has also been held up by its supporters as representing a social democratic achievement. The early introduction by the Bismarckian state of social insurance, health insurance and accident insurance (1883-89), tied to work record and paid contributions, and the first legal protection of expectant and nursing mothers (1878/1883) made the German Empire, followed by the Austrian–Hungarian Empire, the forerunner of governmental social policy. It was a typical 'ruling class strategy' and serves as an example of where citizens' rights were granted 'from above' (Turner, 1990). While this social policy was intended to ease the living conditions of the industrial workers, it also served to pacify the strong workers' movement. General voting rights for men after the founding of the German Empire in 1871 allowed the rise of the Social Democracy Party and the extension of social security rights. When, after the First World War, the democratic Weimar Republic was established, the 'central agreement' between 'labour and capital' paved the way for the German corporatist welfare state. This social compromise was celebrated as 'a triumph of democracy' and 'victory of parity'(Neumann, 1978/1935), yet it was at the cost of women's social citizenship (Gerhard, 1988). Although women and their organisations had been pioneers in social reform since the end of the 19th century and had been recognised as equal political citizens since 1918, the renewed exclusion of women from this agreement signalled a defeat of the feminist movement at the very moment when the first democratic Weimar Republic was established.

In the breaks and collapses of the German nation state the comparative security of workers' social entitlements stood in contrast to the long-time insecurity of political citizenship rights. Over nearly two centuries the concept of German citizenship was burdened with the separation of nationhood and statehood (Preuß, 2004). The absence of a unified nation state up to 1871 was one reason why German national identity formed around common language and culture (Brubaker, 1994; Gosewinkel, 2001). The fragmentation of German citizenship in the sense of belonging and membership was reproduced after 1945 by the competition of two German states that both claimed the exclusive right of representation in foreign and domestic policy. Dissociation from the socialist system with its propagation of women's employment and collective childcare was also one of the reasons why family and women's policy in Western Germany remained conservative.

Historical experiences discredited any nationalist consciousness in the post-war era. As a result, the West German constitution, the 'Basic

Law' of 1949, that established the Federal Republic as a democratic and social state under the rule of law, placing the guarantee of basic rights as the binding norm for all institutions of the state, played a critical role in the formation of attitudes towards the state. Together with the jurisdiction of the German Constitutional Court these basic rights 'sharpened the awareness of both public actors and the citizens that fundamental rights constitute directly applicable law' (according to a former Chief Justice of the German Constitutional Court, Limbach, 2001, p 177). This is why Habermas (1992) talks of a 'constitutional patriotism' to characterise the post-Second World War political generation. However, social rights in particular, although guaranteed in the Constitution, are not automatic but have to be claimed and asserted through the law. As in all Western countries, the civil rights movements, the students' movement and new women's movement of the 1960s and 1970s broadened the space of civil society and invented new standards of justice that changed the understanding of citizenship in the broad sense of political, civil and social rights.

Women's delayed and impeded citizenship

What is indeed most striking in the history of women's citizenship are the 'overlapping vocabularies and political practices of seemingly distinctive orientations to democratic politics' with regard to female citizenship (Landes, 1996, p 295). From the gender perspective there is a remarkable degree of common ground within republican and liberal discourses. The republican as well as the liberal model converge in the basic differentiation between public and private spheres and the firm appointment of women's place in the private sphere. The liberal approach has regarded the private sphere as a space of personal freedom that must be protected against all governmental interference. The bourgeois male assumption was that the private sphere allows people to be themselves, to care for others, and to follow their interests as private persons while at the same time the patriarchal power structure was totally ignored, although unanimously defended and restored in family and marriage law (discussed later). The republican model, which subordinates the private sphere even more strictly to the public good, also ascribes strict gender roles for women as mothers and guardians of republican virtues. Rousseau's (1963) philosophy of gender roles, which was founded on assumptions about the 'nature' of women but also cast them as the 'moral' gender, was subsequently quoted more or less literally in the juridical literature (Gerhard, 2001).

For an overview of women's delayed citizenship (see Table 1.1) we will follow T.H. Marshall's (1950) differentiation of the dimensions of citizenship. Marshall's account of citizenship opens up the possibility of analysing more closely the exclusion and partial inclusion of women into the group of legal subjects, of citizens. For a variety of reasons, Marshall's approach has been criticised especially by feminist scholars on grounds of his gender blindness or androcentrism; the assumption of a disembodied public citizen (Hobson and Lister, 2002); and his evolutionary, Anglo-centric, male-oriented perspective on the development of citizenship and his neglect of the impact of social movements (Giddens, 1983). The value of his study as a point of departure, however, lies in the fact that it uses citizenship as a category to analyse society, especially from the perspective of governmental social policy, and it explores its meaning for the social structure and political order of democratic industrial societies. Thus, not only is a necessary connection between the social and political preconditions of successful citizenship established, it also becomes clear that in a civil and democratic society social justice and the agency (Lister, 1997, 1998, 2003) of all citizens is of primary importance. Marshall presents a sociological approach that understands individual action as social action that is integrated within the social structures of society, but it also understands these structures – similar to the institutions of the law – as subject to historical change. These connections as well as the demand for autonomy and participation provide the link to feminist analyses and policies.

> Agency provides a link between an active, participatory citizenship and demands for equal civil, political and social rights. Finally, the focus on women's agency points to the importance of women's activities as mothers, workers and citizens and of the interconnection of different arenas of state, market and civil society. (Siim, 2000, p 2)

The exclusion from political participation

More than anything else, in the context of the bourgeois revolutions in Europe and the US, women demanded political rights, since they were 'de facto' participants of the revolutionary movements (Godineau, cited in Landes, 1996, p 305). The common point of departure was the experience of exclusion, of exclusion from the group of active citizens and thus the 'broken promise' of the bourgeois revolutions. This is true first and foremost for the collective protest of the women of the French Revolution who not only demanded bread but also

Table 1.1: Steps to women's equal rights

	Denmark	Finland	France	Germany	Netherlands	Norway	Spain	Sweden	UK
Age of majority for unmarried women and widows	1857	1864	1804	1794 (ALR)[e] 1804 (Cc)[f] 1820s and 1830s in various German states	1810	1863	1812	1863	As 'feme sole' with many rights[a]
Property rights of married women, mostly limited to own income or reserved property[b]	1880/99	1889	1907	1794/1896	1956	1888	1889	1874	1870/82
Equality in marriage[c]	1925	1929	1938/42	1953/57–1977[d]	1956	1927	1933-39/1975	1920	1935–69[d]
Maternity benefits	1915	1937	1913	1883	1913	1909	1933	1931	1911
Alimony for illegitimate mothers and/or children	1763/1908	1734/1922	1912	1794 (ALR) 1896	1909	1763/1915	1888 (with distinction between natural and unnatural children)	1734/1915	1926
Women's access to university	1875	1901	1863	1908	1876	1884	1910	1873	1869
Male universal suffrage	1918	1906	1848	1871	1917	1897	1869–1974 1890	1907	1918
Female suffrage	1915	1906	1944	1918	1919	1913	1931	1919	1918/28
Self-determined abortion within a trimester	1973	1970 for strict reasons	1975, since 2001 without obligatory counselling	1976 for strict reasons, 1996, but with obligatory counselling	1981 with obligatory counselling	1978	1985 for strict reasons	1974	1967 within 23 weeks for strict reasons

Notes:

[a] A 'feme sole' (as spinster or widow) was a legal individual in many customary laws also on the continent, especially as woman in small business.

[b] Property rights that might also include personal earnings from gainful employment.

[c] This is a broad category since it may refer only to the end of legal incapacity and marital guardianship (e.g. in France or the Netherlands), but also to different steps of equal rights as regards legal custody of children, equal disposal over matrimonial property or equal rights in divorce (the Nordic model of marriage).

[d] Removal of fault-based divorce.

[e] *Allgemeines Landrecht für die Preussischen Staaten* (ie the Prussian Code of 1794)

[f] *Code Civil Français.*

human rights and political participation, submitted petitions, founded political clubs and yet – as mentioned earlier – were despised for their impertinence, excluded from all political decisions and persecuted. The most important document of this time, the *Declaration of the Rights of Women and of the Citizen*, written by Olympe de Gouges in 1791, subverted the *General Declaration of Human Rights* by replacing 'men' (either in the sense of 'human being' or 'male') with 'women' in the text (Gerhard, 2001, pp 223-6). The feminist counter discourse insisted upon the equality of the sexes and at the same time pointed to gender difference. In the seemingly minor deviations from the 'General Declaration' the specific female experiences of injustice were made visible and a path was opened up for the radicalisation of democratic principles, linking demands for political, civil and social rights (Siim, 2000, p 54; see also Gerhard, 2001). With the drafting of a new 'social contract' (Bell and Offen, 1983, pp 108-9) – one of several political writings – Olympe de Gouges already tried to overcome the two-tiered structure of the liberal legal order that separated the private and political spheres on the basis of gender. Thus, she put her finger on the contradictions that were inherent in the civil society's gender relations (see also Scott, 1996).

The fact that the process of democratisation for men at the same time led to the explicit exclusion of women shows that gender became a primarily political category in civil society. Just at the moment when others were brought in, women were explicitly written out (Harris, 2004, p 82). As soon as in the process of gradual democratisation, the corporate privileges of landowners and property rights were converted into rights of political representation, the adjective 'male' was added to the right to vote. This is true not only of the English voting reform in 1832 but also, for instance, of all revisions of the ordinances in the cities and communities of the German Alliance throughout the 19th century (Frevert, 1995, pp 62ff; Gerhard, 1997, pp 515ff).

The female experience of exclusion and disappointment in their revolutionary comrades was repeated in the course of the European revolutions of 1830 and 1848. In several European cities, women who had participated in bringing about democratic movements and who had taken a stand for liberty, democracy and the unity of their country, were forced to admit that the political sphere had been established as a male domain and as men's concern only.

The exclusion of women from the political sphere was effected not only by withholding from them the right to vote but also by a multitude of restrictions such as a ban from participation in political meetings and a prohibition on founding political groups or clubs. Nevertheless, these bans were handled differently in the European countries. At first, repression was strongest in France. The intense use and 'misuse' of the right of assembly by women was given as the reason for the drastic ban and the persecution of women's clubs by the Jacobins that occurred already in 1793. The French parliamentary assembly argued in republican manner: 'If women were allowed to participate in heated public debates, they would teach their children not love for their country but hate and prejudices' (quoted in Ostrogorskij, 1897, p 166). The presumed dangerousness of women's clubs for public peace also infused a later French decree of 1848, as well as a ban inscribed in 1850 into the law of association in the German Alliance, which was effective in Prussia until 1908. The press laws issued around 1848 in the context of the revolutions were gradually liberalised in Germany (after 1874), as well as in France (after 1881). Remarkably, Spain introduced explicit censorship of married women in 1870 that prohibited them from publishing or working as an artist or literary figure (Scholz, 1982, p 607), and Russia and thus Finland (which was under Russian rule) kept a ban on female editors until the end of the 19th century.

One of the few public rights benevolently conceded to women was the right to submit petitions. It was used extensively by women in all countries throughout the 19th century. It was regarded as the right of those who were excluded from all other political rights. The French National Assembly argued against infringing this right in 1851: 'Women are allowed to keep the right to submit petitions without being drawn into the current of political debates, and they have to keep it if only because of the role that society ascribes to them outside of the political sphere (Ostrogorskij, 1897, p 165).

Denial of civil rights, individual autonomy and rights of property to women

The denial of citizen status for women and their exclusion from the social contract was closely connected to the special role of women in and for the family assigned to them by most of the theoreticians of bourgeois society (notably Fichte, Hegel, Kant and Rousseau). In their political theories a fundamental role for society was assigned to the family, be it as the 'germ cell of the state' or as an institution that was both protected and regulated by the state. The exclusion of women from the bourgeois public sphere and their inclusion in the private sphere by marriage contract or 'sexual contract' (Pateman, 1988) with its exactly defined 'order of the sexes' was not just a remnant of a feudal past but also an 'invented tradition' (Hobsbawm, 2000). It was constitutive of the functioning of bourgeois society and of a 'liberal model' (Habermas, 1989; for critique, see Fraser, 1985). However, in contrast to the patriarchal unanimity concerning the denial of political rights for women, the arrangements concerning civil or private rights were quite diverse. The reason for this lies in the fact that private rights, especially marriage and family law, are deeply traditional. They are founded on traditions and habits and are defended against modernisation and thus against the principle of equality.[5] Therefore, it must be noted that in nearly all European countries, the decisive step towards really equal marriage rights was taken after 1945 and as a rule not before the 1960s and 1970s. And we have to bear in mind that legal restrictions and gains are experienced differently according to diversities among women with regard to class, religion, ethnic origin or sexuality. Finally, it should be noted that, as a rule, unmarried women gained equality before the law when they came of age.

In his commentary on the draft of the French *Code Civil*, the civil law passed in 1804, Jean E. Portalis (1844) insisted that families were not only the 'nursery of the state' but also that the power of husband and father was a republican invention. It seems that the reaction of French revolutionaries to the idea of freedom and equality of women, the return 'to the orthodoxy of new bourgeois values' (Vovelle, 1982), was stronger and more despotic than in the rest of Europe where contemporary conditions were still pacified with paternalistic goodwill. The French *Code Civil* is usually praised in legal history as a first realisation of liberal principles in private law and as a 'masterpiece of the art of legislation' (Holthöfer, 1982, p 884). Regarding marriage law, it was, nevertheless, unique in terms of its contradictions and rigid patriarchalism. The leading rule, in force until 1938, reads: 'The man owes his wife protection; the wife owes the husband obedience' (Art 213 Cc). This means, although a wife could formally own property, she was absolutely subjugated to her husband's will and needed his authorisation to enter into contracts (Art 215 to 217 Cc). These rules were even more significant since the *Code Civil* had a great impact on all countries subjected to French rule by the Napoleonic wars and even left its mark after those countries or regions had become independent of French rule. This is true for Italy, the Netherlands, Spain and some parts of the German states, for instance the left bank of the Rhine and the Duchy of Baden, as well as for the Duchy of Warsaw (between 1815 and 1918 the Polish Kingdom under Russian authority). Despite several legal reforms in the post-Napoleon era, for instance, the Netherlands kept the principle of legal incapacity of wives until 1956 (Holthöfer, 1982, p 929). Spain, after a long process of debating her own Spanish codification, in 1888, passed a civil code, *Código civil*, that with regard to family law followed the French code and even strengthened the rules concerning divorce due to the influence of the Catholic church (Scholz, 1982). In Spanish legal history during the Second Republic of 1931-39, married women had already gained equal rights and equal political citizenship. Both were lost again under the Franco regime and were only regained in 1978 and 1981.

In France divorce was impossible until 1884. The unrestricted authority of the husband as head of the household also included his supremacy as a father. A mother had no entitlement to bring up her child or any appeal if the father took a child above six years of age away from her. The more remarkable then is a particularity of the Spanish law that since the 1870s, confirmed in 1888, entitled a married mother to take over paternal authority in case of the absence of the father (Scholz, 1982, pp 609-10). The high esteem of women as civic republican mothers here led to totally different consequences than in France. However, children born out of wedlock in Spain, as in other countries under French law, had no father, since investigation of fatherhood was forbidden (Art 340 Cc). Neither mother nor child had any claim against a man as long as he refused to acknowledge the child voluntarily as his until 1912 in France and 1909 in the Netherlands. To sum up: in the words of an early feminist scholar, Marianne Weber (1907, p 318), the Napoleonic Code, in contrast to other codifications of the time, 'preserved the traits of medieval patriarchy the longest and in its purest form'.

While the leading rule in the French law was obedience and subordination of the wife under her master's command as a republican virtue, legitimised by the superior interest of the public good, in the English common law the regime of community of property of the spouses, the so-called *couverture*, remained the dominant paradigm under which lawyers ruled out women's identity as legal subjects. The single identity of a married couple was encapsulated in William Blackstone's formula in his commentary on English common law: 'In law husband and wife are one person, and the husband is that person' (Vogel, 1990, 2000). The contradiction between this dictum and the concept of a liberal society lies in the relevance of the property right for economic independence, agency and citizenship. The strong emphasis on rights of property, however, also explains why the Married Women's Property Acts, starting in the 1870s, together with the first suffrage campaigns, were a decisive step for English women's citizenship rights. The new arrangements, however, were not so much to secure the wife's independence from her husband as to prevent him from overriding the interests of the succeeding generations (Cornish, 1982). The wife acquired contractual capacities only with regard to, and to the extent of, her separate property. As another step of gradual and reluctant concession to social change the Matrimonial Causes Act of 1857 granted divorce *a vinculo*, if 'the matrimonial offence of adultery on the part of a guilty wife' was proved. In a case of desertion a wife was to be treated as owner of the property and earnings she thereafter acquired (Cornish, 1982). The invocation of marriage as an indissoluble institution – in contrast to marriage as a private contract – and the fiction of a 'spiritual community' aside from economic dependence survived until the 20th century. The treatment of married women in law as entirely independent persons was achieved only in 1935 (Kiernan et al, 1998; Vogel, 2000).

The legal landscape in Central Europe before the enforcement of the German Civil Code in 1900 was multi-coloured and complex, because it was fragmented into a variety of legal sources, jurisdictions and systems of law, which did not necessarily coincide with state boundaries. Particularly with regard to the legal status of women, the lack of legal unity and legal clarity – for example more than a hundred different legal systems of marital property – caused legal insecurity (Gerhard, 2000).

In roughly comparing the different systems, the Prussian General Code, a 'model of enlightened government planning' (Koselleck, 1975, p24) and populations policy, seems to have been the most woman-friendly. It enabled women in a marriage contract to reserve their own property from their husbands' administration and it granted unmarried mothers a claim to maintenance for the support of their children. This was the reason why commentators very soon denounced these provisions as spoiling moral standards and making the Prussian state 'a true paradise of women' (Schlosser, 1970, p 279). By the middle of 19th century, however, jurisdiction and legal reform had changed these regulations in favour of men who now were allowed to refuse payments on grounds of the woman's bad reputation. The *ius commune* [German 'common law'] (see the Appendix at the end of the chapter), which was in use in at least one third of the German territory, proved favourable to women for different reasons. In the late Roman tradition of marriage as a 'free union', marriage had no impact on the legal status and the property relations of the spouses. Consequently, separation of property was the rule, so that the married woman could enter into contracts and administer her fortune. In contrast, the Saxon law, which preserved the Germanic legal traditions of the *Sachsenspiegel* and other medieval texts, declared married women subject to gender tutelage, a form of guardianship on the basis of gender. No wonder that the German women's movement, at the end of the 19th century, when campaigning against the different drafts of the Civil Code, would have preferred a reform based on the principles of the Roman *ius commune*, but their mass protest failed completely. Enforced in 1900, with its family and marriage regulations in force until 1953 and 1957 respectively, the German Civil Code reaffirmed the husband's right to decide in 'all matters affecting communal life of the couple' and also re-established paternal authority. Moreover, the husband – unless separate property was agreed in the marriage contract – was granted the exclusive right to manage marital property and to intervene in his wife's labour contract.

In this context, the Scandinavian development of women's private legal status is highly interesting, because it was not only a question of the different timing of legislation but also of the different speed in the transition from agrarian to modern society, skipping the bourgeois phase. Although also here a gender-based guardianship for all women, both married and unmarried, was formally abolished only after the middle of the 19th century, married women's capacity to act was connected to a rather early granting of property rights to all women. We find legal capacity granted to the wife with regard to her separate property and her own earnings in Sweden in 1874 (Regner and Hirschfeldt, 1987), in Norway in 1888 (Sandvik, 1987) and in Denmark in 1899 (Dübeck, 1987). Married Women's Property Acts did not necessarily signify equality between the spouses. Nevertheless, Scandinavian women were among the first to get the right to vote (as mentioned earlier, and see Table 1.1) and, even before that, were already involved in initiatives for law reform in women's organisations and political parties. This enabled them to take part in preparatory work, in public debates, in family law committees and in Parliament. Enacted in 1920 in Sweden, 1925 in Denmark, 1927 in Norway and 1929 in Finland, marriage reform was also a result of intense cooperation among the Nordic legislators. These Acts provided for equal property rights, divorce liberalisation and complete abolition of male authority as well as equal custody of children. This rather early gender equality in marriage based on individual rights of the spouses and at the same time on an understanding of gender roles and gender difference (together with social control by medical expertise grounded in eugenic thinking) is characterised as the 'Nordic model of marriage' (Melby et al, 2006). The *Danske Lov* of 1763 already granted a maintenance claim against the father of illegitimate children, which was extended and confirmed in all Scandinavian countries at the beginning of 20th century (see Table 1.1).

In sum, the different stages and dimensions of equality in marriage are not just a question of economic equality but concern also equal rights with regard to discretionary power in all marital affairs, the right to take up employment, the custody of children and divorce. As heated moral debates and a broad literature in legal history signify, regulations concerning the rights of illegitimate children and their mothers also seem to be a touchstone of gender justice or – more often – injustice, comparable to contemporary concern over reproductive rights. The history of family law in the 19th century is one of gradual and reluctant concessions to social change, although with different timing and impediments. If, as in the liberal citizenship regimes, the strongest emphasis was on property rights, without doubt married women's disposal of their own property, which might also include the disposal of their own earnings from paid employment, already had an impact on women's social status and agency. However, since marriage law in the 19th century retained the husband's discretionary power, the value of these gains was limited so long as care and household duties were part of the wife's marital duties. Thus, failure to fulfil these duties because of gainful employment could be cited as reason for fault-based divorce.

The liberal citizenship regimes, as well as the civic republican statutes concerning marriage and gender relations, thereby retained a principle of dominance and hierarchy vis-à-vis married women. They secured this principle at two levels: by requiring the wife's obedience and subordination to the husband's 'right of command' and by her economic dependence, anchored in the husband's right to administer her property and the earnings from her work. The Scandinavian countries were the only exceptions to this development. After a comparatively late emancipation from paternal authority even of unmarried women (only in the middle of the 19th century), the tight connection between achieving political and civil citizenship rights provided Scandinavian women with a better starting position for a citizenship practice that paved the way also for social citizenship.

Social rights and activities

The different timing of the achievement of women's citizenship rights in comparison to men's can also be seen with reference to social rights. In contrast to the sequence T.H. Marshall (1950) developed using the example of the British male citizen, for women an opposite order seems to have been true: first, women were covered by some highly restrictive and disciplinary social rights under the Poor Laws[6] and then gained some social rights as mothers in the early 20th century; then, second, after the turn of the 20th century or the end of the First World War, in a number of countries women gained suffrage and gradually achieved political rights, generally after men; and third, only as late as the 1960s and 1970s were they recognised as full equal partners in civil law.

When it came to the first socio-political measures of the industrial states of the 19th century that were aimed at women, or, more exactly, at working mothers and their children, in most European countries these regulations had an important impact on women's role and the gender order in the emerging welfare states, reconfirming a gender-specific division of labour (Scott, 1995; Hausen, 1997). For the protective regulations for pregnant women, introduced first in Switzerland in 1877 and in Germany in 1878, were, above al,l work restrictions and prohibitions on women. Indeed, Marshall (1950, p 24) observed that 'women were protected because they were not citizens'. They were not really concerned with women's well-being or health but with their reproduction duties, which were endangered by the poor conditions of factory work – as shown by numerous social surveys. These work restrictions under the pretence of protection, allegedly also aiming at securing moral standards, were a reason why working-class women and feminist movements campaigned at the international level against protective legislation of women workers only, rather than for humane working conditions for both sexes. The effect of legal labour protection for women workers was and is ambiguous. Although its

> indirect impact was to reinforce women's dependency on husbands who benefited from the welfare measures, and hence to reinforce the gender gap in terms of income and (relative) poverty, on the other hand, certain welfare provisions [...] were aimed directly at women and contributed to relieving some aspects of female misery and poverty, particularly those related to maternity. (Bock and Thane, 1994, p 4)

In most countries, measures such as maternity leave emerged as an appendix to male-oriented social insurance or health insurance and covered only insured working mothers or wives of insured men, granting no or only very small benefits (see Table 1.1). The different approach of the Maternity Insurance Act of 1910 in Italy and of the Sheppard-Towner and Infancy Act of 1921 in the US, which offered direct claims for mothers and their children, was a victory for women's movements and the very first step towards individual social citizenship rights focused on women. A next step was the introduction of child or family allowance systems in the interwar period in almost all European countries and after the Second World War in Britain (see Bock and Thane, 1994; Bock, 1995). In spite of national differences in social security systems the overall results were rather similar structures of 'a double standard of welfare provision for men and women' (Gordon, 1990, p 11) or a 'two channel welfare state' (Nelson, 1990, p 124). These were characterised by a systematic split between labour market-related social security programmes with primarily male recipients and family-based means-tested social assistance schemes, granted primarily to female recipients, thus stabilising a system based on the gender-specific division of labour.

However, as feminist scholars emphasise (Sarvasy and Siim, 1994; Lister, 2003), social citizenship is not only a question of entitlement, it also involves participation in all realms of public and societal life: not only in political institutions or bodies but also in neighbourhoods, at workplaces, in charity work or voluntary organisations and social movements. In this respect, women were and still are pioneers of social work and social citizenship. Thus, women's active contribution to welfare reform, not only as recipients but also as campaigners and as social and political actors, comes to the fore. As agents of civil society, women have formed a 'reservoir of active citizenship' (Leca, 1992, p 21) or as Viola Klein (1971, p 17) put it: their 'humanitarian interests which formed the starting-point of social research, and practical social work itself, actually provided the back-door through which women slipped into public life'.

Feminist interventions

Women have both initiated and contributed to social and political change. In everyday life and particularly within the family they took over responsibility for others and thus decisively contributed to the common good or, as we say today, to the production of welfare (Kaufmann, 1994). This means that even before being formally recognised as equal citizens, women, as 'de facto participants', acted out various possible roles for female citizens (Landes, 1996) and thus practised social citizenship, reflecting their 'conceptualisation of the duties of citizenship' (Lewis, 1994, p 50).

These interventions were not only the individual acts of single, courageous women but were also collective actions based on networks, voluntary organisations, political and religious associations and a variety of socio-political projects invented and organised by the women's movement. For example, the establishment of employment agencies, vocational counselling and legal aid offices, where movement activists provided other women with advice and support in all legal matters and disputes free of charge, were institutional models that were later taken over by the welfare state. With the launch of professional associations and self-help projects to train, advise and protect women, especially in the health sector and community care, women developed concepts of social reform and established schools and curricula for an education in social work that combined social practice and experiences with expertise and scholarship. They were thereby initiators and forerunners of social work as a profession.

In some cases, their actions accentuated class and racial divisions. When the women's movement emerged in the late 19th and early 20th century and entered the political sphere mobilising for political participation, suffrage and civil rights as well as for welfare issues and the resolution of social problems, the differences between women became even more apparent. Defining common interests and needs was particularly difficult for women from different social classes, political, religious or cultural backgrounds and for women with different sexual orientations. Therefore, when women's movements in most European countries reached their peak in the two decades around the turn of 20th century and when gender became the point of departure for common organisations and political interventions, controversies arose over political priorities, strategies and conflicting loyalties. While the proletarian women's movement fought for equal pay for equal work, the extension of protection of maternity rights, and employment protection for women, middle-class women first of all struggled for access to education and professional training (see Offen, 2000; Paletschek and Pietrow-Ennker, 2004). In fact, they regarded access to higher education for girls, to universities and to special women's professions as a prerequisite for active citizenship and self-determined action, while for others the struggle for equal wages or against racial discrimination was a question of sheer survival.

Just as diverse as the political contexts and opportunities were the splits and forms of coalition building in the respective countries. Similar to the dominant class conflicts in German society, where an orthodoxy of 'pure division' (Clara Zetkin) between the proletarian and middle-class women again and again hindered common political intervention, a strong organisation of women within the political party structure framed women's activities in the British case (Thane, 1993). The Scandinavian women's movements also succeeded in forming alliances with men, for instance with the Radical Liberals, but in addition they achieved cooperation between the feminist movement, the peasant movement and/or the Social Democratic Party. Spain saw only isolated instances of demands for women's rights by individual writers, and did not have a general social movement until the early 20th century. These writers emphasised the fight for education, since 'women were defined as mother educators with a significant role in civilizing Spanish society' (Nash, 2004, p 249). In France, a section of the women's emancipation movement hesitantly supported women's suffrage and advocated only moderate measures, whereas others invented the term 'feminism' and were radicals, 'tied to moments of revolution', who preferred to shock in order to convince others of their cause (Rochefort, 2004, pp 79, 97).

Whether the different wings of the women's movements were moderates or radicals, middle-class or proletarian feminists, nationalists or pacifists, so-called egalitarians or maternalists, the key dividing line was the use of difference or equal rights arguments. One example of this division was the polarisation with regard to the question of labour legislation. The controversy was between those who approved special treatment for mothers with regard to their different, particular role and needs, drawing on maternal values and an alternative maternal caring practice – described as 'maternalists' or 'welfare feminists' – and those who demanded equal rights on the grounds that gender-specific protection would lead to discrimation against women – characterised as 'egalitarians' or 'equality feminists' (Banks, 1986; Lewis, 1991; Bock and Thane, 1994; Sarvasy, 1994).

The concept of 'organised motherhood' had already been developed by the international suffrage movement before 1914 as the rationale for their demands: they wanted equality and participation to counteract a male politics, to make it human. It was an attempt to transcend the limitations of traditional femininity and at the same time a programme 'to place women not only in nurseries, kindergardens and schools but in ministries and parliaments' (von Zahn-Harnack, 1928, p 76). The focus of feminist activity on social questions in the 1920s, labelled as maternalism and 'welfare feminism' was therefore a pragmatic strategy with ambiguous success. On the one hand, it proved to be possible to take a maternalist approach to increase equality for women at a time when patriarchy still dominated the private and the public sphere (Blom, 2001). On the other hand, in this version of feminist politics, which privileged rights of mothers and children, maternalism served as an alternative pillar of the welfare state (Skocpol, 1992). In effect, the claim to equality was annulled by the many welfare provisions defining women's difference: a position linked to demands for a family wage and rather conservative visions of marriage and family.

At the international level, bitter disagreement reigned between those who emphasised gender difference and called themselves 'new feminists', and those protesting against protective legislation for mothers. The middle-class women's movement in continental Europe formed a rare alliance on this issue even with social democrats and socialists, all of whom felt that protective legislation for mothers, maternal stipends and insurance constituted an important strand in social politics. In contrast, representatives of the Anglo-American and most of the Scandinavian movements as well as some radical egalitarians on the continent feared that protective legislation would anchor gender specificity in law and inevitably lead to discrimination. Maternalism also tended to reduce women's contribution to the common good and social citizenship practice to a question of gender difference without considering inequalities and differences in class, religion, nationality and race which split women's groups (Sarvasy, 1994; see also Koven and Michel, 1993).

It is significant that all these women's mobilisations for the 'betterment of the world' transcended state boundaries and were organised as international movements with international bodies. This is, for example, true for the movement for women's political rights, particularly suffrage; the movement for moral reforms, the crusade against the regulation of prostitution by the state and against the international trafficking of women; as well as the campaign for international protective labour laws mentioned earlier (see Berkovitch, 1999). The significance of the international suffrage movement for the development of women's position as citizens is shown by the far-sighted decision made by the International Woman Suffrage Alliance in 1926. When in the aftermath of the First World War women had gained the right to vote in several countries, the organisation decided to continue their work even though it seemed as if their goal had been achieved. 'The organization would continue to work to secure suffrage and such other reforms as are necessary to establish a real equality of liberties, status, and opportunities between men and women' (Rupp, 1998, p 23). The organisation took on the new name of International Alliance of Women for Suffrage and Equal Citizenship.

The new 'wave' of women's movements that spread almost simultaneously in various European and North American countries in the late 1960s also had an international orientation from the very beginning. Prior to the second wave, since in most European countries after the Second World War decisive steps were taken towards more equal rights for women by way of new legislation or constitutional guarantees, for many the 'woman question' seemed to be answered. In most Western countries the return to normalcy after the sufferings and political breaks of the war meant re-familialisation, restoration, even re-masculinisation (Moeller, 1998). To evoke the silence of women's movements during the post-war period, while at the same time indicating its continuity, scholars used the term 'doldrum' to describe the situation (Rupp and Taylor, 1990). The Scandinavian women's movements were best prepared as a result of 'feminisation from below' since the 1930s, coalition building with the labour movement or left and liberal parties and an increase in women's representation in decision-making bodies. This enabled them to create a more 'woman-friendly state' (Hernes, 1987) that laid the ground for developing more equal citizenship for men and women than in other European welfare states, including all dimensions of citizenship rights necessary for agency and social and political participation.

Even where women's movements were not as successful, second-wave feminism everywhere had a great impact on gender relations and acted as a catalyst for social and cultural change. With their protests, their criticisms and their demands, the various women's movements of the 19th and 20th centuries brought the contradictions of civil society and their lived experience of injustice onto the political agenda and constituted a driving force for social change and societal reform. However, as illustrated also in later chapters, women's influence and representation in the political realm remains weak, since the problems of a gendered division of labour and care are not yet solved in either the public or private sphere.

Conclusion

When trying to summarise the results of almost 200 years of political history of the concept of citizenship from a gendered perspective, this review of a cross-national study provides us with several insights. First, in the international comparison, the variety of terms used and the different legal systems point to the complexity of the issue. The variety of legal cultures and traditions, political and social contexts, which have changed over time, frame the distinct relationships between the individual citizen and the state.

Different models of citizenship regimes are the background to the gendered understanding and experience of citizenship. But both civic republican motherhood and liberal property ownership used the model of a traditional marital guardianship to legitimate women's exclusion. Despite differing citizenship regimes, similar vocabularies and forms of argumentation are used when it comes to the gender of citizenship. Thus, at the same time, when the concept of citizenship was developed as a legal status and in its political meaning as an indicator of a democraticisation process, the female gender became a political category. Beyond the different contexts and conditions and the different citizen regimes and political opportunity structures, the reasons given for excluding women from the political sphere and for their responsibility for the care of children and family have been very similar. Here, the core of the contradictions within modern civil rights becomes obvious: a gender-specific division of labour, which apparently seemed to be incompatible with the principles of freedom and equality of all men. Thus, women's equal citizenship was not only delayed but impeded as long as possible.

During the long period from the 19th century to the end of the 1960s, although women were victims of discrimination and excluded from politics and citizenship rights, they were also actors, participants and promoters of social movements and political change. Their interventions and counter-discourses referred to the universal promise of democracy: freedom, equality and solidarity. Especially in times of radical political and social change, many women already were de facto citizens, performing a social practice of citizenship that was indispensable for the welfare of individuals and the common good. Both in terms of these practices and the exclusions against which they resisted, there were similarities as well as differences in the 'lived experience' of gendered citizenship across European nation states.

We also learned that the interplay and interdependence of the three dimensions of citizenship – political, civil and social – is crucial for the agency of the individual as well as for a democratic practice. The historical comparison of different national legal systems has shown that the acquisition of the right to vote alone does not make women participants with equal rights in politics and society. In the face of a gendered division of labour the right to have rights and to contribute to legislation can only come into effect when women have equal rights also in the area of private law, particularly family law, and when they have their own resources and economic security. The relatively early civil law equality of women in the Scandinavian countries, also closely connected to the relatively early achievement of suffrage, provided Scandinavian women with a better starting position, particularly with regard to political rights. In other countries, equality in family law was often achieved only a generation later. Thus, the anchoring of male, patriarchal prerogative in the private sphere undermined the political ability to act and to take part in politics and decision making.

At the beginning of this history of impediments, Olympe de Gouges' declaration of women's human rights (quoted in Gerhard, 2001, pp 223-6) exposed the paradoxes and contradictions in the vocabulary of male political theories, both republican and liberal. But she insisted upon equality that acknowledges difference in a variety of respects. The controversy about the question as to how far equality has to embrace difference and which differences matter, runs like a thread through the history of women's claims for citizenship. Since equality is not an absolute principle but a dynamic concept pregnant with historical struggle and bound up with 'the historicity of gender difference' (Fraisse, 1995, p 33), the realisation of equal citizenship of women in their diversity remains a major task. Chapter Two takes up the story in the 1970s and widens it to include other actors in contemporary citizenship debates.

Notes

[1] As a legacy of the Roman law the distinction between public and private law structures the whole legal material in continental Europe. Following a definition of one of the most famous legal scholars in the Roman classics, Ulpian: public law contains all acts and relationships between an individual and the state or a representative of the authorities respectively. It is characterised by hierarchies or subordination. In contrast, private or civil law governs the relationship between individuals, who are considered as equals. A contract is the paradigmatic legal form. The distinction roughly corresponds to the differentiation between political and civil citizenship rights (see Wiethölter, 1972).

[2] Spaniards were 'all men free born and living within the Spanish territories [including the American colonies] ... [they] enjoy the condition of being Spanish, and hence are entitled to civil freedom, rights of property and other legitimate rights' (Closa, 2004, p 131).

[3] Roman law influenced the Central and Western European legal systems through several waves of reception following the 12th century with the exception of English law. It was based upon the civil law of the classical era of the Roman Empire. The legal sources were first

communicated and transferred by a codification of the Byzantine emperor Justinian, then again transformed and commented on by legal scholars of the Renaissance, the Italian law schools and in the 16th century collected in the so-called *Corpus iuris civilis*. Its characteristics are an abstract terminology and a clear systematic that shaped European jurisprudence more or less until the 20th century. It was called '*ius commune*' (which needs to be distinguished from English 'common law').

[4] Common law rests on a body of judgments and commentaries, complemented by statutes. Law was not written by code, but as a sum of procedures and precedents interpreted by judges and legitimised by a long tradition of customs and embedded in the guarantee of certain basic freedoms (Cornish, 1982).

[5] That was even the case in the Scandinavian states, which, in the second half of the 19th century, agreed on cooperation in the 'nordic jurisdiction' and unified the contract and trade laws but first postponed a modernisation of the family laws because of national peculiarities (Tamm, 1987).

[6] Marshall pointed to the ambiguous and shifting status of the British Poor Law with regard to citizenship. By the 1834 Act 'it treated the claims of the poor, not as an integral part of the rights of the citizen, but as an alternative to them – as claims which could be met only if the claimants ceased to be citizens in any true sense of the word', for they forfeited civil and 'any political rights they might possess' (Marshall, 1950, p 24).

Appendix: Legal circles and legal families

1. Areas influenced by Roman law

All over Europe – with the exception of England, Wales and Ireland – in the period between the 12th century and the 16th century, Roman civil law was adopted as the fundamental system, and by different ways of combining it with local law, local statutes or customary rights it became the so-called common law (*ius commune*). 'Roman law was laid out like a net over one's own (native) law, the holes were very wide but provided the whole with a structure' (Wesel, 1997, p 362). From this, in Western and Southern as well as in Central and Northern Europe there developed three 'legal families' after the end of the 18th century:

1.1   French law, orientated towards the French *Code Civil*, was valid from 1804 in almost all of the Romance countries, not only in Europe, including Belgium, France, Italy, the Netherlands, Romania, Spain and parts of Poland. As a result of the Napoleonic Wars the *Code Civil* was valid in the German territories west of the Rhine as well as in Baden and Westphalia until 1900.

1.2   The Central European legal family is strongly influenced by Roman law and by a jurisprudence trained according to it, which, however, is also orientated towards German legal sources and codifications in the German language. A number of civil laws and legal codes were standardised in 1896 in Germany under the *Bürgerliches Gesetzbuch* (Civil Code). Until then there was also a so-called *common law*, strongly based on the tradition of Roman law (it was valid everywhere in Central Europe where neither local statutes, the laws of free cities, nor codifications were valid – to be strictly distinguished from English common law). Moreover, the *Schweizerische Zivilgesetzbuch* (Swiss Civil Code) of 1907 was also adopted by countries such as Albania, Bulgaria, Greece and Turkey and in parts of Poland because of its mature system and clear language (Wieacker, 1967).

1.3   The Scandinavian civil law is recognised as a distinct legal family mainly because, although influenced by continental jurisprudence, it has not adopted Roman law to the same degree as the Central European legal family; indeed it resisted the trend towards the scientification of law. Furthermore, Denmark, Norway and Sweden – joined by Finland in 1917 when it gained independence – started the project of Nordic cooperation at the end of the 19th century, aiming at standardising law most of all in the field of civil and commercial law. A less formal kind of legal thinking is considered typical in Scandinavian civil law, showing a concrete-practical approach (Tamm, 1987).

2. English common law
The core countries of the Anglo-Saxon legal circle are Australia, Canada, the UK (although there are some variations within the UK, for example the closer following of Roman law in Scotland) and the US, as well as all Commonwealth states except so-called mixed jurisdictions (for example Louisiana, South Africa, or Montreal and Quebec).

TWO

Vocabularies of citizenship since the 1970s

Introduction

In this chapter, we describe and analyse the range of actors involved in contemporary citizenship debates. These actors include left-wing and right-wing politicians, feminist movements, trade unions and social movements more generally. They may adhere to more dominant and powerful discourses on citizenship or struggle with alternative formulations, attacking mainstream or defending former interpretations. For all these reasons, it is not clear a priori whether citizenship is a liberating or a disciplinary concept; in fact, as stated in the Introduction, it can be both, depending on who is using the concept, in what context, and with reference to which kinds of vocabulary. From a gender perspective, such a contextualised analysis is especially important, since binaries such as public/private, dependence/independence, needs/rights, individual/community, may also be highly gendered, as well as context driven.

We focus here on those contextual issues concerning citizenship that have emerged within the European welfare states since the 1970s. We will start with asking why citizenship has become such a key concept. Then we will describe various contemporary vocabularies and feminist critiques of citizenship. In the next section, we examine some striking citizenship issues and debates in contemporary welfare states. Finally, we analyse the consequences of international developments for these vocabularies of citizenship, with a special focus on both European citizenship, and the framing of citizenship in former communist countries.

Social and political developments and the rise of the concept of citizenship

Within recent decades, citizenship has become an influential concept used in various spheres. Among academics it is used as a central concept to describe and explain developments within social and political transformation processes. In politics it is used to reformulate both the relations between citizens and the state, and relations among citizens. Within social movements and activist groups, it refers to questions of inequality, social cohesion and community life. In international organisations, such as the European Union (EU), the concept of citizenship appears to name and frame a shift in the position of the nation state and its citizens.

The main reason behind the popularity of the term 'citizenship' seems to be that so many contemporary issues and problems can be related to it. New questions have arisen as to the distribution of citizenship rights as a result of demographic developments, changing family and gender relations and welfare state reform. The process of individualisation, for example, raises questions about the basis for relations of solidarity, about social control and about public life, while the restructuring of European welfare states has led to new debates about social rights, benefits and citizenship obligations.

The growing number of migrants and asylum seekers in Europe has generated important questions about their citizenship and their entitlement to social and political rights. When and how do migrants become citizens of a nation; what are the conditions (for example concerning territory, language, work, partnership); and to what extent is dual citizenship accepted? Welfare states with well-developed and inclusive social rights for 'insiders', such as Denmark, Norway and to a lesser extent the Netherlands, may face particular problems with migrants, since the national welfare state is exclusive and migrants might be regarded as a threat to existing social rights, especially by right-wing political actors (see Chapter Three).

More generally, social pluralism, migration and individualisation have elicited debates on belonging and communitarianism. These may take place at the local level, referring to social cohesion in the neighbourhood, or at the national or even European level, where the question of shared values is the subject of debate. The increasing importance of the EU as the provider of citizenship rights, the fall of the Berlin Wall and the development of civil and political citizenship in Central and Eastern Europe, the questionable status of the nation state, increasing democratic disengagement and the call for more participation at the local level, all raise new questions concerning citizenship in terms of rights and practices.

In what might be called the 'Post-socialist Age' (Fraser, 1997), citizenship is not only a matter of social rights or socioeconomic redistribution, but also a matter of recognition and belonging. Whereas rights and redistribution refer to socioeconomic (in)equality, recognition and belonging refer to cultural identity and to unity/ diversity. This can be the recognition of identity and identity politics or of cultural or religious traditions. The awareness of belonging to a group and sharing an identity and values can have a strong liberating effect, since it may help in finding a voice that can argue for participation and social rights. On the other hand, belonging can also be used in a disciplinary way, for example when it excludes people who do not share the dominant values, or do not belong to the dominant ethnic group. As we will see in this and subsequent chapters, justice requires both redistribution and recognition. Due to developments such as globalisation, migration and the fall of the Berlin Wall, claims for recognition and belonging have become increasingly important since the 1990s, especially in European welfare states. People might feel excluded from their country's main community (for instance, migrants who are unemployed and experience discrimination) or feel threatened because traditional communities are falling apart (as longstanding inhabitants of big cities may experience). In the 1990s, following the Islamic Revolution in Iran and the consequences it had for Western European welfare states with sizable Islamic communities, the politics of religion acquired a significance it had not enjoyed in Europe since the late 19th century (Stuurman, 2004, p 177). Since the 9/11 attack by Muslim radicals on New York's World Trade Centre in 2001, the political relevance of these questions has increased.

Contemporary vocabularies of citizenship and feminist critiques

Building on classical traditions of citizenship (see Chapter One), different contemporary vocabularies of citizenship have been developed, containing various forms of feminist critiques. Following the metaphor of the citizenship 'family tree' (see the Introduction), within the liberal branch we can distinguish a social liberal or social democratic vocabulary, neo-liberal interpretations and rights-based feminism. The republican tradition has inspired vocabularies of participatory citizenship, and explicitly feminist vocabularies of maternalism. The communitarian branch on the civic republican side of the citizenship family tree is also inflected by neo-conservative, religious and Christian democrat, and maternalist or care-based feminist vocabularies. In addition, new vocabularies have been developed that are difficult to classify, such as cosmopolitanism (and see also the Introduction).

Liberalism

Social liberalism builds strongly on the distinction made by Marshall (1950) (see Chapter One), focusing on social rights as a product of 20th-century welfare states. The extent to which social rights have been developed in welfare states, making people less dependent on the market, varies among welfare states, as shown by Esping-Andersen's (1990) influential welfare states regime typology. From this perspective, social democratic regimes create the most generous social citizenship rights, since many benefits and services are universal, and access is relatively easy for legal residents. However, citizenship is not gender neutral. Just as the independent male householder serves as the typical ideal citizen in classical and democratic theory, the male worker serves as the typical ideal citizen in the literature on social rights (Orloff, 1993, p 308). The social democratic citizen still tends to be represented as the citizen-worker, as Hernes (1987) put it.

Feminists have extensively used and criticised the social liberal tradition to reframe citizenship. First, by extending the idea of citizenship to the relations between the family, the market and the state, they have revealed that citizenship does not bear solely on rights (and duties) in the domain of economic activity and the realm of democratic politics, but also on the private sphere of the family and on the tasks of care. As observed in the Introduction, feminists have raised the critical question as to whether, and to what extent, care excludes women from social citizenship, especially in the private sphere. Second, they have asked whether care work should be recognised as a basis for (inclusive) citizenship rights, by creating both the right to give and the right to receive care (Knijn and Kremer, 1997; see also Chapter Four). Such an approach demands new social provisions and new social rights, such as public childcare and parental leave. However, there are striking differences between welfare states when defining the care needs of specific groups of citizens, varying from pro-natal notions in France, labour market- and equality-oriented arguments in the Nordic countries, and traditional notions about female caring at home in the Netherlands and Germany (see Chapter Four). In countries like Britain, with poorly developed care rights and with strong breadwinner traditions, since the 1960s, a progressive social rights citizenship vocabulary has been used as a tool to demand individual citizenship rights for women, and an expansion of social welfare in order to increase equality between men and women. Nordic countries come closer to inclusive citizenship since extensive leave schemes and public childcare were interpreted as a solidaristic discourse of social rights, which offers citizen-parents new possibilities to care for children, thus expanding the caring dimension of the welfare state. A rather recent phenomenon in the field of care and work is that now fathers, too, are laying claims to fathers' rights to their children. In several countries, fathers' groups are criticising the gendered character of divorce regulations, asserting that these grant more rights to mothers than to fathers to see and look after their children (see Hobson, 2002).

Beside feminists (and recently fathers), other social movements started to use the social liberal vocabulary of citizenship to argue for citizens' rights in the 1960s and 1970s. In all countries, different groups struggled for full citizenship rights, emphasising the vocabulary's emancipatory and liberating meaning. These groups include indigenous people or minority ethnic groups, such as the longstanding ethnic group of the Lapps in the Nordic countries, defending their ownership of land, resources and language, and disabled people, lesbians and gay men, and migrant organisations. In Britain, for example, the demand for the realisation of disabled people's full civil, political and social rights is represented as 'the continuing struggle for citizenship' (Barton, 1996, p 187; see also Morris, 2005). Gay and lesbian rights movements have used this vocabulary as well, to frame anti-discriminatory demands in terms of individual rights, such as the Citizenship 21 campaign launched by Stonewall, to challenge homophobia and to empower lesbians and gay men. The Gay Pride Marches that nowadays take place in many countries also in their early days utilised notions of empowerment.

Migrants have used the vocabulary of citizenship to demand full access to education, labour market participation and political participation in their new home country. In Denmark, for example, migrants campaigned together with social workers against a benefit provision adopted by the Liberal Conservative government in 2002, which stated that non-citizens gain the right to full and equal social benefits only after living in Denmark for seven years. The citizenship movement claimed that this policy represents a breach both of the general principle of universalism in Danish social policies, and of the equal treatment principle in human rights conventions (see Chapter Three). Other examples are the movement of the '*sans-papiers*' in France, or the '26,000 faces' in the Netherlands, focusing on the right to citizenship through their demands concerning the '*droit d'asile*', and the right to be treated as a human being.

More generally, the point needs to be made about the collective organisations of permanently settled minorities who are not migrants but second and third generation individuals. Many minority ethnic groups, including those who are settled, have their own associations, websites and networks, usually closely connected to notions of active citizenship, whether the focus is more on group identity or on individual freedom. Some of them also seek culturally sensitive services from the welfare state together with full and equal access. One example is the Swedish Cooperation Group for Ethnic Organisations, which successfully lobbied to increase the supply of care services for older members of different ethnic groups in Sweden. More than anywhere else, the suburban revolts in France, during the autumn of 2005, illustrate the feeling of marginalisation and exclusion among the young of foreign origin and their demands for recognition and respect. This throws up new issues for the topic of citizenship.

The mainstream post-war welfare state discourse on citizenship has also been criticised from quite another angle, the neo-liberal point of view. Neo-liberalism claims a minimal state and maximum freedom of the market economy. The neo-liberal rhetoric of citizenship focuses on consumerism and obligations. Whereas the social liberal vocabulary argues for an expansion of social rights, neo-liberalism rejects such rights. It argues that citizens have their own responsibility to insure themselves against social risks. Neo-liberalism contains a firm critique of welfare statism and a positive appraisal of individual autonomy and active citizenship. It has attempted to break down the relation between social and political citizenship. Furthermore, it focuses strongly on the obligations citizens have towards themselves and other citizens. Neo-liberal social policies tend to have strong gender implications. Hence, just as the notion of independent social rights of women started to gain acceptance, the very concept of social rights was challenged. In such a context, a more socially oriented liberal vocabulary such as Marshall's is the opposite of neo-liberalism, offering an important basis from which to defend citizenship rights.

Central and Eastern Europe, before and after 1989, provides a different perspective on contemporary (social) liberal citizenship. Deduced from the very fact of the original communist framework (the abolition of private property, the negation of freedom of expression, of organisation, of circulation and so forth), the essence of civil rights had a purely formal character in Soviet-type societies, as did political rights, to the extent that all organs of power were pervaded by the all-powerful Communist Party. Nevertheless, some social rights did exist; these ensured a minimum of protection for the individual (for example, employment guarantees, subsidies for food and housing and extremely modest pricing for an array of services such as childcare). Even though one could not speak of citizenship in its full sense, up to a point these rights constituted a social dimension of citizenship, with particular importance for the status of women (Heinen, 2006). Since 1989, parallel to the retraction or suppression of a number of the existing social rights, new forms of civil and political citizenship have emerged (discussed later).

Altogether, (social) liberal vocabularies of citizenship still have a strong contemporary relevance, particularly with respect to the development of civil and political rights in new democratic states, the protection of social rights in welfare states, the relation between political and social rights, the development of new rights such as sexual rights and the shift from a discourse of rights to one of obligations, as well as questions concerning care, paid work and equality.

Civic republicanism

The other main branch of the citizenship family tree is civic republicanism. It has attracted renewed attention, in particular in relation to questions concerning democracy and the political community, and participation and political rights. In addition, this tradition has some contemporary relevance with regard to the separation of the private and public sphere, the relation between rights and virtues, and the meaning of participation and active citizenship. It has inspired research on women and the feminist movement as actors, on democracy and the political community (among others Phillips, 1991; Mouffe, 1992).

Starting from the civic republican tradition, in several countries, new debates have been developed about active citizenship in relation to various disadvantaged groups. It has been used to argue for active participation as a core aspect of citizenship, which is especially important in countries where women's political representation is still low. Nevertheless, the philosophies underlying pleas for more equal participation vary. The French demand for parity, for example, is often simultaneously based on the philosophical principles of both citizens' equality and sexual difference, while in Scandinavian quota systems, taking a more pragmatic stance, the main argument emphasises women's historical marginality in politics on the basis of gender equality. Parity refers to the legal right to equal representation of men and women in politics, with the object of replacing the 'rule of brothers' with a real democracy (Siim, 2000, p 67). It means that women should make up 50% of all political bodies by law. According to Joan Scott (2005), the struggle for parity has begun influencing representations by criticising French universalism, and by putting into question the definition of the citizen as an abstract person. Yet, it is too soon to predict the concrete effects of this influence on political and social life, for

> conceptions such as the universal abstract individual are more likely to be changed by practical experience than by theoretical pronouncement. The slow entry of women into the political system, from the bottom up, may eventually have a desymbolising effect, making sexual difference an irrelevant consideration for politics, and so alter the political field of force in ways we cannot yet foresee. (Scott, 2005, p 149)

The French case for parity demonstrates the ambiguities of a sexually differentiated citizenship, which recognises sex as a basis of citizenship (Fassin, 2002; Lépinard, 2007). The argument for parity is built on radical notions of equality ('perfect equality'), but on notions of sexual difference as well, challenging traditions of republican universalism. For on what basis should women be represented in Parliament – as mothers or as citizens?

In other countries, too, the republican key word of participation has gained renewed attention since the 1980s, often under the rubric of 'active citizenship'. As explained in the next section, in Britain active citizenship was used by Conservative politicians in the 1980s not as a call to political participation, but to volunteer work and charitable giving, and more recently by New Labour to encourage community participation and consumer choice in welfare. In Finland, the idea of active citizenship has become popular in recent years. Here, it has been reinvented as a remedy for welfare state crisis and a 'dependency culture', and has been related to notions of self-reliance and obligations of citizens towards civil society. In the Netherlands, the concept of active citizenship dominates debates on political and civil society participation. In Denmark and Norway, political debates about the new roles of citizens as users of social services arose during the 1980s. Both motherhood and parenthood have become potential areas of active citizenship. During the 1990s, the emphasis fell on the active role of *parents* as user-citizens in the boards of schools and childcare centres. Nowadays, the good citizen is still perceived to be the active citizen, and the number of men and women organised in voluntary organisations has continued to grow (Torpe, 2003).

Communitarianism

Some of these notions of active citizenship reflect the influence of communitarianism. As explained in the Introduction, communitarianism represents an influential contemporary offshoot of civic republicanism. If liberalism is about the politics of rights, communitarianism is about the politics of the common good (Sandel, 1982). Communitarianism focuses on common values and norms as a central issue in people's lives, and on people's duties towards one another as citizens. In addition, communitarian notions offer strong arguments for the organisation of welfare on a small-scale, interpersonal level, analogous to the village. This is particularly true in relation to care: within communitarianism there is a tendency to revert to traditional patterns with respect to issues of morality and care. In practical recommendations arising from such a communitarian vision, the emphasis quickly comes to lie on the importance of a caring attitude and affectivity within family life. However, the ways in which communitarian notions are linked to specific cultural identities are diverse, varying, for example, from the notion of the 'common good' connected with the policies of social democracy in the Nordic countries, to respect for very different religions and social organisations in public life, as in the Netherlands.

Recently, communitarianism is also presented as an alternative to a strong welfare state. Indeed, it assumes a shift from abstract and bureaucratic state authority towards community responsibility, although the gendered aspects of community care are often neglected. Communitarianism has gained political influence in various countries since the late 20th century. In Britain, already in the 1990s, Labour was inspired by communitarian principles. In the Netherlands and Denmark, too, there has been an increased emphasis on voluntary work, on the social responsibilities of citizens in general, and on the responsibility of the family for the education and behaviour of children in particular. In Denmark, for example, a new agreement, reached in 2005, makes it possible to punish families when their children prematurely drop out of school or commit a serious crime. These measures primarily target migrant families.

Maternalism

There is also an explicit feminist vocabulary, which has much in common with communitarianism: maternalism. In maternalist discourse, it is suggested that interpreting womanhood or motherhood in terms of citizenship could bring care as a value into the public domain (Dietz, 1985). It shares with communitarianism values such as compassion and care, as well as the notion of culture and identity, in this case the female identity. Maternalist thinkers such as Jean Elshtain (1981) and Sarah Ruddick (1989) have influenced European debates about the ethics of care and 'caring citizenship,' that refer to the transformation of private virtues into public values (see, among others, Sevenhuijsen, 2000). In the Netherlands, such notions have contributed to a reformulation of equal opportunity policies, from a focus only on women's economic independence towards a concern with the relation between economic responsibility and daily caring responsibilities. Notions built upon maternalist-communitarian ideas of citizenship have been used in a liberating way by feminists in the Nordic countries. In Finland the concept of maternalist citizenship seems to have made a comeback through the introduction of a children's daycare allowance. Cash grants for childcare have often been interpreted as a resurfacing of maternalist undercurrents, for instance by the left-wing parties, in public debate, and by some researchers, whereas parties to the centre and right – including the Christian Democrats – have proposed the cash grant as supporting traditional family values (Leira, 1998; see also Chapter Four). Not surprisingly, therefore, such demands are highly contested among feminists.

Citizenship issues in changing welfare states

The overview of citizenship vocabularies is complicated, since the various traditions and vocabularies are influenced by local and national circumstances (see Chapter One). As a result, there are also notable differences between countries in their present way of conceptualising citizenship. In the British literature, for example, traditional analysis reflected the Marshallian approach, with a particular emphasis on social and civil rights and a generalised duty to respect the law (Commission on Citizenship, 1990). Yet, more recently, citizenship is conceptualised more in terms of obligations and responsibilities, most notably in the political discourse of New Labour. In Scandinavian countries, as observed in Chapter One, the emphasis on the relation between citizens as a collectivity and active citizenship refers to a broad perception of democratic politics, which has created opportunity structures for people to influence political institutions from 'below'. In France, debates on citizenship are strongly influenced by republicanism, while in 1970s' Spain and more recently in Central and Eastern Europe, the focus has been on civil rights, freedom and political participation.

The country-by-country overview, which follows, illustrates how, in the current context of change, the relations between the rights and obligations of citizens vis-à-vis the state are being reframed. Some developments have strengthened citizenship's emancipatory potential, for instance with regard to rights of sexual citizenship; others have reinforced its disciplinary qualities, particularly in countries such as Britain and the Netherlands where neo-liberalism or neo-conservatism became influential in the 1980s and 1990s.

Britain

In Britain, both the retrenchment of the welfare state and the politics of successive Conservative governments have left their mark on discussions on citizenship. The Conservative governments of Margaret Thatcher and John Major deployed depoliticised notions of citizenship around the figure of the 'active citizen' (who was supposed to give money and time as an act of charity) and the consumerist 'Citizen's Charter'. Under Conservative rule, the welfare state underwent a major restructuring, the result being the strengthening of its liberal elements, while its more social democratic elements were weakened. The aim was to reduce the role of the state through a greater emphasis on private and means-tested provisions. At the same time, citizenship also provided a key intellectual and political tool for those defending the values of the welfare state against the new right.

New Labour's 'Third Way' draws on the new right, its own social democratic traditions, and on communitarianism. New Labour frequently speaks the language of citizenship, especially that of citizenship obligation and responsibility. In addition, echoing communitarian notions, Tony Blair's Third Way describes duty as an essential New Labour concept. The former Home Secretary David Blunkett, in particular, promoted active citizenship as part of his agenda for 'civil renewal', arguing that active citizens make strong communities (Blunkett, 2003). He set up a virtual Centre for Active Citizenship, while the Home Office established a biennial Citizenship Survey. Earlier when Education Secretary, he was instrumental in the introduction of citizenship education in secondary schools. New Labour concentrates on investing in public services, yet these services are to be delivered in partnership with other agencies, with a larger role for the private and voluntary sectors (with implications for citizenship accountability). Central to social security policy is the emphasis on responsibility, particularly through paid work, which has meant a more stringent conditionality attached to benefit entitlement. Responsibility is also at the heart of the government's 'respect' agenda, designed to tackle antisocial behaviour and to promote civility. New Labour has been criticised on the centre left for the depoliticisation and consumerisation of citizenship (Finlayson, 2003; Lawson and Leighton, 2004; Marquand, 2004).

Alongside more disciplinary policies, the government has extended the civil rights of gay man and lesbians, thereby strengthening their sexual citizenship, and there is greater acknowledgement of the diversity of partnership relationships. In New Labour's family policy a moral and economic imperative of the importance of paid work for fathers and mothers has brought together support for working parents, investment in children's opportunities and parental responsibilities (Williams, 2005). Investment in children, education, childcare, and anti-poverty policies is part of a new design of the social investment state in which children represent 'citizen-workers-of-the future' (Lister, 2004; Williams, 2005; see also Chapter Four). From a gendered perspective, New Labour's approach can be broadly characterised as an example of what Nancy Fraser (1997) calls the 'universal breadwinner' model. In this model, the citizenship responsibilities associated with the breadwinner role are universalised, so that women can be citizen-workers alongside men. Jane Lewis (1992) has dubbed this an 'adult-worker' model, albeit one which, in practice, involves one-and-a-half workers, given the tendency for mothers to work part time.

As in most other countries, asylum has become one of the key political issues in Britain. Both the Conservative and the Labour governments have introduced very restrictive policies with regard to both the entry of asylum seekers and their treatment once inside the country. Politicians and the right-wing media have talked of 'bogus' asylum seekers. In addition to changes to the laws with regard to entry to the country, the government is reforming nationality law and the rules governing the acquisition of a formal citizenship status (see Chapter Three). It is also encouraging debate on the substantive meaning of 'Britishness' and of British citizenship.

The Netherlands

In the Netherlands, citizenship played a role, too, in legitimating neo-conservative and new social democratic policies towards the welfare state. Here, citizenship is located in civil society, not in the state, and a good citizen is one who cares for others (Stuurman, 2004). Dutch debates on citizenship have for some time been dominated by the communitarian tradition of citizenship, in which moral behaviour and civic spirit are central notions. In the 1980s, Christian Democrats in particular used the concept of citizenship as an alternative to state responsibility. They emphasised duties, moral obligations, common values and a restoration of communities, such as families and neighbourhoods, framed in a communitarian perspective on citizenship. The very invention of the vocabulary of communitarian citizenship has been a way to disguise the failure of policy to respond effectively to new developments in society, and to challenges for the national government since the 1970s (Bussemaker and Voet, 1998).

During the 1990s, the liberal notion of citizenship was dominant, as various groups argued for the strengthening of individual civil rights, especially with respect to issues such as euthanasia and abortion. Their campaigns also resulted in civil rights for gay men and lesbians, through the introduction of same-sex marriage. But market-oriented governments also increasingly formulated citizenship in terms of consumerist and market-oriented values (Bussemaker and Voet, 1998). Since the return of Christian Democrats in the government in 2002, citizenship is back at the heart of the political debate, but more as a moral issue. Prime Minister Balkenende is a great admirer of the communitarian Amitai Etzioni, and argues for a revaluation of morality, respect and social values.

At the same time, attention has shifted largely from issues of redistribution, such as social security, to social-cultural issues of recognition. Already, this shift is reflected in the new policy instrument of the 'citizen's contract' for migrants and accepted asylum seekers, established in 1995, which has recently taken the form of a compulsory exam. Ayaan Hirsi Ali, a Muslim woman and a former employee of the social democratic think tank who became an MP for the Conservative Liberal Party until 2006, played an important role in the public debate. She criticised Islam as an oppressive religion for women – harsh criticism in a country where religion has historically played such an important social and political role. Her film about women in Islam was directed by filmmaker Theo van Gogh and led to his murder in 2004, plunging the country into a political and social crisis. Ever since, there has been an ongoing debate between those, conservatives mostly, arguing for the protection of traditional Dutch culture, and their opponents, predominantly non-governmental organisations (NGOs) and the radical left, arguing for the recognition of various cultural identities.

France

Where we may call the Dutch model liberal communitarian, the French model can be understood as liberal republican. As observed in Chapter One, the French notion of citizenship is singularly political, and strongly related to the state, not to society. A good citizen is a person investing in the Republic and civic virtue (Stuurman, 2004, p 181). Despite the central notion of lawful equality in the public sphere, gender differences are frequently articulated within debates on citizenship, as shown by debates about family policies, migration and – as we have already seen – parity. Indeed, the struggle for parity in politics presented a critique of French republicanism and universalism. Those arguing for parity point out that the French inclusive vocabulary of citizenship for men is in contrast to women's historical exclusion from the public domain (Siim, 2000).

French social and family policies are highly gendered, since mothers are regarded as especially good citizens if they give birth to new French citizens. The combination of republicanism in the public sphere and maternalism in relation to family policies has continuously resulted in contradictions within these policies, from the 1970, when the emphasis was on the paradigm '*égalitaire*', to the 1980s and 1990s under the socialist government of François Mitterrand, and the current right-wing government (Jenson and Sineau, 1995, 1998). Despite these shifts, the republican ideology persists in the story of the '*citoyenneté des femmes*', and family politics have been characterised by pro-natalism, for instance, granting special rights to families with three or more children (Chauvière, 2000). Family associations defending traditional values have been able to exert much influence on laws relating to women's status as citizens. This is shown over the last decades by various examples: the limitation of the right to abortion for under-age women in 1975, under pressure from the French Medical Association and conservative organisations (this clause was abolished only very recently); the reasons adduced for a number of measures adopted in the field of childcare, which refer to the discourse of conservative thinking as opposed to the discourse of emancipation (Commaille, 2001); or the restrictive clauses on adoption and succession concerning non-married couples (whether hetero- or homosexual) as defined by the PACS (*Pacte civil de solidarité*), adopted in 1999 (Fagnani, 2001). On the other hand, the programme of Gender Opportunities launched by the Jospin government in 2000 aimed at insisting on equality among men and women through various measures (for instance encouraging young women into male-dominated educational paths; mixed juries; and gendered statistics). But these had a limited impact in a situation where traditional representations concerning family duties remain dominant (Heinen, 2004).

Gender dimensions are also very present in the French debate on migration. The vocabulary of citizenship was the French solution to developments of mass migration, identity politics and European integration. In the 1980s, Mitterrand campaigned with traditional notions of 'Frenchness', and republican themes played a major role in the 1988 elections. In the 1990s, migration policies moved further from policies of recognition, towards policies of adaptation to French culture. Current debates in France about the headscarf (*affaire du foulard*) are strongly influenced by the civic republican tradition. This debate has divided feminists between those arguing for the recognition of cultural diversity, and those arguing for French universalism and state regulation (developed in Chapter Three).

Germany

Whereas citizenship in France historically has been state-centred, the German understanding has been community- or *Volk*-centred. It is historically characterised by an organic, cultural or racial community related to the notion of *Volksgemeinschaft*, although it moved from an ethno-cultural orientation towards a territorial orientation, which has been carried into the new German nation state after the Reunification in 1990, and the new Immigration Act of 2004 (see Chapter Three). But long before, the emergence of social movements in the 1970s changed West Germany's civil society in fundamental ways. Because, given the two German states, national self-determination and any hint of national consciousness were discredited in the light of the German past, political and legal discourses were highly committed to basic rights. In this way, the concept of 'constitutional patriotism' (see Chapter One) became the credo of the generation of 1968. Since the 1970s, 'citizenship' was promoted among left liberal or social democratic jurists under the heading of '*Bürgerrechte*' (citizenship rights) (see the Committee for Civil Rights and Democracy (www.grundrechtekomitee.de) and the journal *Kritische Justiz* (*Critical Justice*). Although at that time, this approach was not consonant with the dominant opinion of the legal profession, it was very influential within the Greens. From the 1990s onwards, feminists also re-engaged in these issues, not only as part of the academic discourses of citizenship, but also within NGOs involved in the new international women's human rights movement.

The civil rights movement, having emerged in Eastern Germany to unleash a 'silent revolution' after 1989, built up a coalition with West German lawyers, feminists and civil rights activists, in order to claim a new constitution and intervene in the debate about it. In the end – apart from technical improvements with regard to positive action for women – the constitutional movement was not really successful. The process of unification ended up as an unparalleled staging of masculine, patriarchal and economic interest politics, in which the representatives of the West German corporatist and conservative party-state obstructed the participation of the women's movement and that of the civil rights movement (see Young, 1999).

German reunification has led to high costs and has faced immense challenges in attempting to amalgamate two totally different socioeconomic systems. Together with demographic trends and an expensive social security and generous health care system, welfare state retrenchment is widely seen as unavoidable but has nevertheless met with large protests especially from traditional trade unions, as both the progressive Schröder government and the Merkel coalition have discovered.

The Nordics

In the Nordic countries of Denmark, Finland, Norway and Sweden (Iceland is not discussed here), the concept of citizenship has appeared only recently in public debate, but implicit notions of the Marshallian approach to social citizenship can be traced far back. As explained in Chapter One, in the Nordics, the citizen's relation towards the state is a friendly one. The Swedish concept of the 'Peoples Home' illustrates how the Swedish state is rooted in a collectivist tradition, where the protection of collective rights is given priority over individual rights. Citizens trust public authorities and rely on universal social benefits and services. In the Nordic countries, gender seems to be acknowledged as integral to citizenship, which is influenced by social democratic norms and embedded in social and political institutions. The women's movement did not meet with the tough resistance encountered in other countries. In Sweden, for example, Social Democrats forestalled many demands from the women's movement through a relatively progressive policy of gender equality. The expansion of the welfare state and of gender equality policies in the late 20th century has been a very important factor in the inclusion of women as active contributors to and receivers of welfare. All Nordic countries, and Sweden in particular, developed a coherent system of social services, which were, at least in principle, universally based on social citizenship rights. Women's home-based care went public, and their dependency on the income of husbands and partners decreased. However, even in this model, women have more responsibility for the informal care for older people, and are working part time more often than men when there are small children. On the other hand, immigrant women represent something of an anomaly in the organisation of care work, as some follow patterns no longer common in the Nordic countries (see Part Two).

As in other countries, during the 1990s, neo-liberalism grew in influence, with demands that individuals and families take more responsibility including for care. The political right has used the concept of citizenship to argue for less state responsibility, and the replacement of the welfare state by private initiatives and individual responsibility. Here, active citizenship means that citizens have not only rights, but also obligations towards one another. Yet, leftist commentators and scholars close to the Social Democratic Party use the concept of active citizenship, too, emphasising the need for a society in which civic virtues and social bonds between people are respected. Citizens are expected to take on an active role in society, in the economy and civil society alike. These ideas strongly resemble Britain's Third Way policy.

In most of the Nordic countries, gay men and lesbians have been and still are very active in demanding the right to marriage and establishing partnerships on a par with heterosexuals. As explained in the Introduction, their demands can be interpreted as claims to sexual citizenship. Their lobby was not without result: in the Nordics gay men and lesbians are now allowed to register their partnership and have rights similar to those established for marriage among heterosexual couples. There is one important exception: no country's legislation gives them the right to adopt a child as a couple, although in recent years this issue has been much debated. Moreover, the entitlement of gay men and lesbians to artificial insemination, and to public funding for it, is still a controversial political issue in Finland and Denmark. And in Norway, the marriage ceremony for gay men and lesbians is only civil, not religious, because the Lutheran State Church objects. In Sweden, the issue of licensed marriage between same-sex partners is still being discussed.

Spain

In Spain, during the 1970s and 1980s, the concept of citizenship appeared only seldom in public debate; framed as it was around 'liberties', a term representing the absence of political rights during the Franco dictatorship, and universal human rights. Citizenship appeared in the next decade, linked, on the one hand, to feminist theory and political discourse (García Guitián, 1999; García Indo and Lombardo, 2002), and on the other, to immigration issues (Cantó, 2003). Some authors have pointed out the tensions between citizenship as expressed through sub-state nationalisms, like those in the Basque Country or in Catalonia, and a gendered approach (Del Valle, 1997). The question at issue is which is more important: regional identity, leaving gender issues aside, or gender sensitivity towards equality? Others have criticised the citizenship concept for its narrow meaning, linked to a specific political community, as opposed to human rights, which are inclusive towards all human beings (Sánchez Muñoz, 2003).

The current socialist government, led by Zapatero, made the improvement of the rights of women, particularly the equality of women and men, one of the main distinctive characteristics of his government. For the first time in history, there is complete parity in the Cabinet (eight women and eight men). The new law on violence against women was the first one to be proposed to Parliament; it was passed with the approval of all parties. Another law, passed in 2005, changed the Civil Code to accept gay and lesbian marriages on the same basis as heterosexual marriage. Two other important laws on gender equality and care for older people, which seek to extend citizenship rights were, in 2006, under discussion in Parliament.

Overview

To summarise, we may conclude that despite the historical differences between these countries, contemporary debates on citizenship also show common features. In many countries, citizenship has been articulated at different times by social movements, including women's movements, arguing for the extension of civil and social rights, participatory democracy and social well-being. Within this perspective, notions of 'rights' and participation have been central.

Since the 1980s, citizenship rights have been criticised by neo-conservative and neo-liberal political parties. They criticised post-war social democratic conceptions of social citizenship, replacing these with moral and consumerist conceptions instead. Women's groups argued for more inclusive citizenship, focusing on the issue of care, beside the need for equal access to the labour market and equality within the labour market. Other important citizenship issues refer to welfare state reform. Here, there is great tension between the social movements' and women's organisations' arguments for the extension of citizenship rights, for example to include care as a public responsibility, and the neo-liberal and communitarian argument that more private responsibility is needed to reform social policy.

A third recurrent issue in citizenship debates concerns the migration and asylum policies that have appeared in almost all countries since the 1980s. Anti-immigrant groups have criticised citizenship rights for immigrants, arguing for a more exclusive citizenship. Others have called for more attention to be paid to identity and the gendered character of immigration and integration policies (see Chapter Three).

A fourth issue relates to sexual citizenship. New living arrangements and family policies have been developed, extending civil and family rights to gay and lesbian couples (with the common exception of the right to adopt). In some countries, the right of abortion has been limited, as in Poland, for, as we shall see, sexual citizenship rights have not been extended in the accession countries of Central and Eastern Europe.

Citizenship in Europe and beyond

As explained in the Introduction, due to supranational developments, in particular the EU, the role of the nation state as the first and foremost community of citizenship has come under question. Although citizenship might also be developed on a local and regional level (varying from communities to neighbourhoods), as in the UK, Germany and Spain, we will focus here primarily on the international levels of citizenship. First, we will focus on the European aspect, then on global and human rights aspects.

European Union

Since the start of the EU in the 1950s, a social liberal vocabulary on citizenship has dominated EU legislation. Until recently, however, the term citizenship was not used. Equal treatment in EU terms was strictly limited to the common market, and thus to the labour market. Nevertheless, despite the fact that, therefore, EU policies have traditionally largely been tied to paid workers, EU regulation in the 1980s and 1990s resulted in the strengthening of a range of social rights for women. Recently, debates arose about new citizenship rights formulated in the European constitution, but since the 'No' vote in the referenda held in 2005 in France and the Netherlands, the public's Euro-optimism seems to have been replaced by Euro-scepticism, even in some traditionally pro-European countries. The notions of belonging and identity play a crucial role here, and are closely linked to the notions of nationalism, migration and ethnicity.

From the beginning, gender was at the heart of the European integration process. Unequal pay for men and women was one of the first topics to be debated in the EU, when France and Germany revealed fundamentally different views on women's paid work. The conflict had nothing to do with gender as such; the main issue was France's concern about its competitiveness, since social protection was integral to wages in France, but not in Germany. Yet, it gave rise to Article 119 of the EC Treaty on equal payment, and thus heralded gender-related EU social policy. Although supportive of women's labour market participation, the EU has been rather hesitant in paying attention to issues concerning care work.

Nevertheless, the 1970s were a very active period for European Commission women's policy. During this period of the EU's enlargement with the accession of the UK, Ireland and Denmark, the Commission started to broaden the employment agenda to include aspects of quality of employment, improvement of worker health and safety conditions, and gender equality as well. The Council of Ministers passed five equality directives between 1975 and 1986. Indeed, most countries have been compelled to adjust their social security legislation and labour legislation in this respect, as a result of the directives of the European Union and the binding decisions of the European Court of Justice with regard to equal treatment. Although the concept of citizenship was still not mentioned at the European level, this period of EU legislation echoes the vocabulary of social liberalism, with its strong focus on equal rights and equal opportunities (Hantrais, 2000; Heinen, 2003).

In the mid-1990s, Ostner and Lewis concluded that social policy had not developed much further at the EU level and that progress was slow and unlikely to continue (1995, p 165). They referred to the shift from 'hard' European laws towards 'soft' law and Employment Guidelines. Within the Guidelines, common goals are formulated by the Open Method of Coordination leaving implementation to member states. European policy, as in the 1986 Single European Act, dealt above all with the free movement of trade and labour, while social policy was seen at best as a tool for economic policy. Care was not regarded as a public responsibility. Bleijenbergh (2004), analysing European social policies on care issues since the 1990s, arrived at a more optimistic conclusion 10 years later. She argues that, with the introduction of new European measures on childcare (1992), parental leave and part-time work (1997), care-giving became a significant issue within European social policy. In her view, the attention to European social care rights served the same purpose that Marshall (1950) attributed to national citizenship rights. She argues that the principle of equal opportunities served as a bridge to reconcile the contradictory claims of the development of a European capitalist market with the call for European involvement with social equality.

> The concept of citizenship was referred to less often in the part-time debate than in the childcare debate, but the same issues were nevertheless at stake, i.e. citizens' inclusion in European society, the guarantee of a minimum level of social equality and European responsibility for providing social rights. (Bleijenbergh, 2004, p 153)

Following Meehan (1993), Bleijenbergh argues that citizenship rights (especially the reconciliation of work and care) at the European level appeared to compensate for the perceived breakdown of national (gender) regimes. Concerning care issues, the women's movement and female officials ('femocrats') in particular, played an important role in reformulating feminist ideals on social citizenship in terms of the European logic of the internal market and equality. However, as Maria Stratigaki (2000) (one of these officials) underlines, concepts initially formulated in terms of gender equality were often used in supranational texts as an incentive for encouraging reconciliation of work and family life for women, not for men:

> The social partners managed to agree on parental leave as a reconciliation rather than an equality measure [...] The directive specified that 'men should be encouraged to assume an equal share of family responsibilities' by taking parental leave, but without further specification on how this could be achieved. (Stratigaki, 2000, p 43)

Furthermore, there is a clear distinction between European leaders. The activism on gender equality was particularly high under the leadership of Jacques Delors (1985-95), achieving success on the issues of childcare, of part-time work, but also of parental leave. Since 1995, the European Commission has drawn back from its earlier activism and the focus is much more on the European Monetary Union. The Commission has done less to challenge member states to take the Open Method of Coordination really seriously. The vocabulary of social rights in the EU was replaced by a more neo-liberal vocabulary on economic competition and the need for cutbacks.

We may conclude that, at the EU level, care is incorporated in social policy only in so far as it is linked to employment policies; in a labour market where dual breadwinners are becoming more and more common, and women are needed to make the welfare state affordable in the future, this will become a more usual practice. Increasing women's labour participation has proved to be a strong driving force for the development of the vocabulary of social rights and social citizenship in Europe. The 1997 Treaty of Amsterdam stipulated non-discrimination in Article 13 as a basic principle of the EU, thus expanding the scope of competence much further than equal pay and labour market-related issues. Article 13 forbids discrimination in relation to sex, 'race', ethnicity, religion, age and disability. The intervention by the European Women's Lobby – especially the mobilisation of black and migrant women – has been very important in shifting this framing of European policy. It challenged almost every dimension and meaning of citizenship within EU policy discourses. The articulation of the interests of black, minority ethnic and migrant women challenged the close connection between nationality and access to the social rights of citizenship, and in doing so challenged how nationality is constructed in both material and symbolic ways (Williams, 2003).

The recognition of multiple inequalities in the Treaty of Amsterdam has inspired national debates about institutional measures to combat discrimination. For instance, in Norway – with its strong tradition of gender equality – the Equality and Ethnic Discrimination *Ombuds*(men) merged to one single institution. Similarly, in the UK, the three existing commissions dealing with gender, 'race' and disability are to be merged into a single Commission for Equality and Human Rights, which will also address discrimination on grounds of sexual orientation, religion/belief and age and will support human rights legislation. The European Constitution of 2004 – rejected by French and Dutch referenda – stresses equal rights and fundamental social rights for everyone in Europe. Nevertheless, there are also countervailing forces within Europe, arguing simultaneously for less involvement in social issues at the European level and enforcement of the internal market, and for more national autonomy. Within such a context, gender equality and full citizenship rights are still under debate.

Beside social rights and care, integration, migration and ethnicity have become important European issues as well. There is a strong relation between nationality legislation, regulating entrance to the territory, and 'integration' legislation. The Treaty of Amsterdam sought to enhance and accelerate the harmonisation of asylum and migration policy, and set the general structure for action towards a common EU asylum policy. The spirit and the objectives these measures should follow were expressed at the European Council Meeting in 1999 in Tampere, Finland. Since then, the recognition of gender-specific issues within the EU has been growing, especially concerning grounds for protection in asylum law and the requirements for family unification. Whereas no reference at all was made to gender-specific grounds for asylum in the 1990s, the European Commission's proposal for a Council Directive 2001 and the final Directive of 2004 (discussed in Chapter Three) refer to gender-specific grounds for asylum, such as sexual violence, female genital sexual violence or other acts of a gender-specific nature.

It is likely that in the EU, the relation between migration/asylum policies on the one hand, and social policies on the other, will become more and more interrelated in the near future. As explained in the Introduction, demographic developments, such as the ageing society and low fertility rates, point to a shortage of labour. The need for cheaper labour for the health and care sectors suggests that the gender dimension might become more explicit in debates about labour migration (see Chapter Five).

Enlargement

The recent big step in European Enlargement, the accession of Central and Eastern European countries, complicates the future of gender and citizenship in the EU, since it brings together rather different regimes on welfare, citizenship and gender, reflecting different ideologies. In Central and Eastern European countries, since 1989, civil and political rights have been developed, while existing social rights and legal provisions have been dismantled or called into question. The protective laws of the old regime, which provided special entitlements for mothers of young children (childcare leave for parents, leave to care for a sick child) and for lone mothers (priority access to childcare and preschool for toddlers, and twice the standard family or childcare benefits) were among the first to be questioned. Thus, the notion of public care that did exist under the previous regime has de facto disappeared from the political agenda (Heinen and Portet, 2002).

Despite the existence of what we might call social rights in Central and Eastern Europe (mentioned earlier), a social rights vocabulary was less developed there than in Western Europe. Within the former, social rights often were interpreted negatively, due to the coercive nature of the state (in discourse, for instance, the obligation of all women to work was stressed far more than the right to employment). Since the early 1990s, any decisive role for social rights in the definition of citizenship has de facto been denied. This process has often been reinforced by the strong pressure of international bodies, encouraging these governments to reduce public spending.

The picture is even more complicated if we not only focus on care and labour issues, but also include sexuality. Although gender equality, acknowledgement of homosexuality, and the rejection of violence against women are formally part of the so-called Copenhagen criteria that a country must meet in order to enter the EU, we know that homosexuality is still not accepted in a country such as Romania. We also know that in Poland the right to abortion is almost completely prohibited (Nowicka, 2004). The right to abortion is being denied, to the detriment of women's civil, political and social rights as well as their reproductive rights (Marques-Pereira, 1998). The prohibition of abortion demonstrates – in Poland better than anywhere else – that the liberal concept of the separation between the public and private realms is less than absolute, and is applied differently to men and women. The denial of the right to abortion is emblematic of the politicisation affecting the private sphere in numerous areas. This form of politicisation, however, does not extend to issues of domestic violence or the sharing of household tasks, subjects presumed to be purely private matters. Despite the efforts to restore civil rights formerly denied or effectively gutted of any real meaning under the Soviet regime, women's personal liberties are denied and their citizenship effectively curtailed.

The prospect of integration into the EU creates a framework for the articulation of women's citizenship rights, social, political and civil. The new member states are obliged to integrate the '*acquis communautaire*', which often means a qualitative step forward in legislation, as well as an obligation to eradicate formal discrimination against women (specifically in the field of work). But at the same time, this process inevitably meets a number of limits: the changes in law do not automatically change the practices; economic interests appear to be far more important than social concerns; the gender mainstreaming logic suffers from the weakness, if not the total absence, of the means of control and of penalties to enforce such a dynamic; and the question of gender discrimination does not involve any substantial parliamentary debate on the subject, whereas in most cases powerful actors in NGOs are absent as well. Thus, the integration of European directives appears more as an obligation or a formality than anything else. What is more, in order to satisfy the conditions of entry into the EU, the new member states are simultaneously pushed to implement drastic cuts, which affect women's status as citizens. The renegotiation of the public sphere is based on a concept of citizenship from which women are largely excluded, even though it supposedly is an inclusive form of citizenship involving all individuals.

Overall, we may conclude that gender issues, including issues not directly linked to the labour market, have increasingly become political issues within the EU. The feminist liberal vocabulary on self-determination as a basic citizenship right is slowly entering EU language. At the same time, gender equality is still rather controversial, especially in former Communist and traditionally Catholic countries such as Poland. Abortion, in particular, is such a difficult issue that a compromise on the supranational level hardly seems possible.

Human rights

Apart from at the European level, citizenship is also developing at the global level. This might refer to notions of cosmopolitan citizenship, alluding to either international rights or to more global communities (see Introduction). Here, we will primarily focus on human rights from a gendered perspective (for a discussion of the relationship between citizenship and human rights, see Lister, 2003).

The vocabulary of international and global citizenship concerning gender has been developed particularly within the United Nations (UN). Within the UN, a broad notion of human rights dominates, which includes social and cultural rights. The Human Development and Gender Development Indices have been of great importance in developing gender-sensitive frameworks, as shown by a number of documents (UNRISD, 2005). But most important was the explicit definition of the principle of non-discrimination in gender terms, in the 1978 International Convention on the Elimination of all forms of Discrimination Against Women (the CEDAW), 30 years after the Universal Declaration of Human Rights was established. The CEDAW strongly focuses on a broad notion of (individual and social) human rights, as is clearly stated in Article 1:

> For the application of this Convention, the 'discrimination of women' is understood to mean any form of distinction, exclusion or restriction on the basis of gender that leads to or is intended to harm or nullify the recognition, the benefit

or the exercise of women's human rights and fundamental
freedoms in political, economic, social and cultural fields,
in the field of civil rights or any other area, regardless of
marital status, based upon the principle of equality between
men and women.

Within the international forum, the classical liberal tradition strongly
dominates the vocabularies on gender and citizenship. At the same
time, women as global actors have succeeded in extending the feminist
approach within the liberal vocabulary to domains other than work
and politics, as happened in the 1980s with the issue of violence against
women. During this period, many initiatives were taken by UN
member states to combat violence against women, although the
Convention originally did not specifically refer to violence. At the
1993 World Conference on Human Rights in Vienna, member states
went one step further, acknowledging that existing measures to protect
women were inadequate. In the same year, the Declaration on the
Elimination of all forms of Violence against Women was adopted.
Two years later, moreover, the sexual rights of women were recognised
for the first time at an international level, in Beijing. Step by step, in
response to pressures from international women's networks, the UN
accepted women's rights as human rights. As a consequence, violence
against women is now recognised as a war crime, and genital mutilation
and bridal immolation can be tackled as a human rights and citizenship
issue. Thus, women's rights are formulated both in terms of human
rights, and in terms of rights of women (Molyneux and Razavi, 2002).
Women have organised across national frontiers to develop transnational
networks and alliances, principally to promote women's human rights
at an international level and to challenge neo-liberal economic policy
(Moghadam, 2005). Thus, they have contributed to the development
of cosmopolitan citizenship.

Conclusion

In all European welfare states, as well as at EU level, citizenship has
been an important concern, centring on various issues, including the
questions of care and paid work, migration and ethnicity and the
development of civil, political and social rights together with new
forms of rights such as sexual and reproductive rights.

Progressive, social rights-based vocabularies of citizenship had their
origins in post-war developments and the 1960s, and were reconciled
in the 1980s and 1990s, to defend the values of the welfare state against

ideological attacks from the right and to extend social rights to oppressed groups. The philosophy of citizenship provided a means for reconciling the collectivist tradition of the left with notions of individual rights, and provided a key intellectual tool for defenders of the welfare state, as is demonstrated particularly clearly by the British case. At the very moment that independent social rights for women slowly gained acceptance, the content of social rights itself became the object of discussion, especially in countries where welfare state retrenchment has been significant. Republican and communitarian notions of citizenship have returned in current debates as well, especially in combination with participation and belonging. Political debates about parity, as in France, or quotas, as in the Nordic countries, show that gender equality is still something that cannot be taken for granted.

Overall, we may conclude that citizenship is a strong liberating concept that has been used by many groups to fight for rights, participation and inclusion, as well as to defend rights that were won in previous struggles. However, it appears that citizenship is also increasingly being used as a disciplinary mechanism, which regulates what people should do or how they should behave in order to be correct or 'normal' citizens. Rather than the 'natural' extension of citizenship envisaged by Marshall (1950), citizenship is the object of contemporary struggles around its locus (local, national, global), and around the meaning of its core elements (rights and obligations, participation and belonging).

Although these debates are not all gender specific per se, they often have a strong gender subtext. This is especially relevant in relation to ethnicity and the role of caring and care work in society. The following chapters will focus in more detail on the relevance of gender for specific citizenship debates on migration and ethnicity, care work and paid labour, and the internationalisation and globalisation of care work.

Part Two
Policy studies

THREE

Gendered citizenship: migration and multiculturalism

Introduction

Globalisation, European integration and migration pose new challenges for understanding citizenship from a transnational perspective. Since the 1990s the increase in migrants and refugees has sparked new political debates about multiculturalism and multicultural policies across Europe, debates which have, increasingly after 9/11, been coloured by Islamophobia.[1] These debates follow both similar and diverging paths in different European countries, all of which carry different legacies of colonialism, imperialism, and different histories of migration. In some, the debates about multiculturalism are new; in others, such as the UK, they revive and reshape debates of the 1960s following post-war immigration. Along with these differences, the heterogeneity of groups and the policies and lived experiences also constitute aspects of recent and past migration. With increasing immigration restrictions in Europe, the only way to gain legal access to enter many countries has been through family unification or as refugees or, to a lesser extent, as workers with designated and required skills. Since the early 1980s female labour migration has increased along with a growing stratification between different migrant groups, according to qualifications and skills (Kofman et al, 2005).

The overall objective of this chapter is to explore the meaning of these challenges of migration and multiculturalism for gendered citizenship. The focus is on the intersection of gender with (minority) ethnicity, in terms of the rights and claims of minority ethnic women, in those nine European countries which are the subject of this book, taking into account their differing citizenship, migration and gender regimes. Multiculturalism is an ambiguous term that refers to principles that either respect minority rights or defend special rights for minority groups. The debates point to how public policies deal with difference and diversity, as well as normative visions about diversity, and strategies for achieving these visions. Multiculturalism is also highly complex because, as Chapter Five shows, policies and public discourses often differ from the lived practices of citizens.

Migration and multiculturalism represent a double challenge for the classic framing of citizenship in that they force us to analyse the tension between equality and recognition of diversity and the relationship between national and transnational arenas. Citizenship is about the inclusion and exclusion of individuals and social groups in societies where struggles over rights have been closely linked to the nation state. The context of European integration has heightened the supranational/external dimensions of national policies while the European Union (EU) has gradually become a provider of citizenship rights (see Chapter Two).

Asylum and naturalisation policies express a transnational dimension to the framing of citizenship (Soysal, 1997) that creates further tensions between citizenship and human rights (Turner, 1993; Lister, 2003). One way to set out cross-national differences and explore the tensions between pluralist integration and assimilation in Europe is to look at this relationship between migration and citizenship. A crucial distinction here is between the external dimension of migration and the internal dimension of integration policies (Brochmann and Dölvik, 2004, p 161). The former regulates legal access to enter the country while the latter designates rights and obligations of those who enter legally and includes migrant groups as well as permanently settled minority ethnic groups.

Bringing gender into the frame poses a further challenge. Feminist scholarship has analysed the link between male domination and the oppression of minority groups along with different strategies to include women and marginalised social groups in society, through either mobilisation 'from below' (Young, 2000) or representation 'from above' (Phillips, 1995). Group rights (Young, 1990) have been proposed as one way to empower marginalised social groups, while the notion of a multicultural citizenship (Kymlicka, 1999) has been presented as a means to protect the rights of minority groups and indigenous peoples against the majority. However, often debates about multiculturalism have been gender blind. One interpretation of this is found in Susan Moller Okin's (1999) influential article, which challenged the multicultural paradigm by arguing that it was against women's rights. While Okin is surely right to identify a tension between gender equality and the protection of minority rights, her conclusion that multiculturalism is always bad for women because it protects religion and patriarchal families and cultures is far too abstract. The meanings that family and religion have formigrant/minority (indeed, non-migrant/minority) women are not universal and this chapter illustrates the point that 'context matters' by looking at migration, multiculturalism and women's rights in a comparative cross-national context.

In fact, while comparative research has identified different welfare and citizenship regimes (Turner, 1992; Siim, 2000; Bellamy, 2004), it has only recently started to analyse migration and multiculturalism. Ruud Koopmans' and Paul Statham's (2000) model compares the political opportunity structures that different institutional frames give to minority organisations in different European countries. In this approach citizenship is perceived both as a form of membership and 'as a specific cultural imprint of nationhood functioning as a form of symbolic closure restricting the ability of migrants to join the national community' (Koopmans and Statham, 2000, p 19). The model operates with four ideal-type regimes: (1) ethnic segregation, (2) ethnic assimilation, (3) republican monism and (4) pluralism or multiculturalism (Koopmans and Statham, 2000, pp 18-29). This model informs the overview of public policies and political, cultural and social rights and obligations in the nine countries (summarised in Tables 3.1 to 3.3 on pp 83, 89 and 96).[2]

As already suggested, migration research has been gender blind, and feminist research has discussed how to include a gender dimension to research on migration regimes. Fiona Williams' (1995) comparative framework addresses the tensions between race/ethnicity, gender and class in welfare states. The focus is on three interrelated dynamics underpinning the development of welfare states: the family, work and nation (Williams, 1995, pp 149-54). Williams' article informs the frame for the study of *gendered* policies and debates about migration and multiculturalism.

In these ways, the chapter explores the interconnection between the logic and dynamics of migration, multiculturalism and gender through a cross-national approach focusing on the interplay between institutions, discourses and the meanings of lived citizenship, discussed in the Introduction, for minority groups in the nine European countries. Its guiding hypothesis is that lived culture is dynamic and contextual – not static – and the interaction between minority families and the dominant institutions, culture and norms often creates new mixes of cultures, norms and identities (Siim, 2003; Williams, 2004b).

The first part of the chapter, 'Conditions for acquiring citizenship', explores the interconnection between two dimensions of migration: the *external* dimension regulating territorial conditions of access; and the *internal* dimension regulating the rights and obligations of persons living legally in the country. The external dimension refers to migration and the internal dimension examines the tensions between pluralist integration and assimilation of minority ethnic groups. The second part of the chapter, 'The framing of gendered debates', explores the ways in which public regulation of and debates about multiculturalism and 'integration' are gendered, focusing on two issues: forced and arranged marriages and the headscarf/*hijab*. We show how these point to tensions between gender equality and the rights of minorities, and between the public and private arenas, both critical to the experience of gendered citizenship. These issues also demonstrate how regulation in these areas is influenced by national perceptions of citizenship, of migrant/minority women and of different public–private relationships; they further illustrate the gap between policy and the lived experience of citizens. The conclusion raises new research questions about how we understand the relationship between migration, multiculturalism and gender from a cross-national perspective.

Conditions for acquiring citizenship

This section provides a short overview of migration and asylum legislation with examples from the selected countries. This is the legislation that regulates the access of so-called 'aliens' to enter the country legally as well as the rules for acquiring citizenship. Two sets of tensions are explored. First, as noted above, is the dilemma between, on the one hand, a human rights regime that requires the EU to accept refugees and, on the other, EU realpolitik that blocks migration to the EU for reasons of economic, social, welfare and political costs ('Fortress Europe') (Brochmann and Dölvik, 2004). This also involves different needs of deregulating economies for cheap labour and of welfare states for qualified workers such as doctors. Since the increasing restrictions on 'guest workers' in most European countries, these two elements have become increasingly intertwined, with the largest group of migrants now entering as refugees or through family unification. Recently there has also been an increase in 'selective' migration that allows specific categories of workers to enter on a 'green card' targeted to the needs of the labour market. The second tension explored here is that between pluralist integration, in the form of multicultural policies, and assimilation. We can see this in the gradual harmonisation of restrictive asylum and migration legislation expressed in EU Directives and guidelines in Europe since the 1990s (see Chapter Two)[3] and in the accompanying intensification of integration policies.

Key elements and trends in European migration policies

National histories, institutions and political cultures influence the balance between an open and restrictive migration policy. Citizenship is tied to the nation state and only a few countries in Europe, including the UK, Sweden and Finland, currently accept dual citizenship. One of the main motives behind the move towards restrictive European migration legislation of both Left and Right during the 1990s has been to limit immigration from Third countries (that is, non-EU countries). During the 1990s European migration regimes have in effect moved closer together, combining the two principles: *ius sanguinis* and *ius soli*. We look briefly at this, focusing mainly on the changes in the rules to obtain citizenship through naturalisation[4] (summarised in Table 3.1 below).

Germany and France are examples of countries with different migration models which have moved closer together (Koopmans and Statham, 2000). Germany has moved from the ethno-cultural pole – *ius sanguinis* – towards the territorial pole – *ius soli* – whereas France has moved from the territorial towards the ethno-cultural pole. For example, only children of German nationals could previously acquire German nationality by birth. After a new law in 2000, children *born* in Germany may be granted German nationality by birth if the parents have lived in Germany for more than eight years.[5] There is also a legal right to naturalisation for all who have stayed in Germany for more than eight years depending on further requirements. France[6] has moved in the other direction. Children born in France to parents of foreign nationality no longer automatically acquire French citizenship at the age of 18 if the child has residence in France. Since 1993 individuals have actively to declare that they want to acquire French nationality.

Spain has, like Germany, emphasised nationality through birth and descent, although the Spanish *Código civil* also has elements of *jus soli*. The *Código civil* was modified in 2002[7] to make it easier to regain and maintain Spanish nationality for Spanish citizens of origin, and for Latin Americans to obtain nationality within a relatively short period. In addition, legislation has become less restrictive in the sense that nationality can be obtained on the condition that a list of requirements is met, for instance prolonged residence (10 years). Spain has witnessed three recent regularisations of illegal migrants, but in spite of this the country generally remains restrictive towards refugees.

The UK and the Netherlands represent a second group seen to represent plural or multicultural migration regimes (Koopmans and Statham, 2000), with relatively liberal five-year residence requirements.

The Dutch Nationality Act dates back to 1985 with only minor amendments, except for new requirements such as passing a nationalisation test, and keeping Dutch nationality if one is abroad.

The Nordic countries[8] represent a special case. Although they belong to the same categories of welfare and gender regime, they have recently moved in opposite directions in terms of migration due to different national histories, institutions and nationalisms. Denmark has changed from a relatively liberal towards a restrictive immigration regime. Arguably, Sweden has moved in the opposite direction by accepting dual citizenship in 2001, followed by Finland in 2003. The Swedish government argued for dual citizenship as a tool for integration in accordance with Swedish policy of pluralist integration. While this was supported by an overwhelming majority of Parliament, the population was divided on the issue (46% for and 42% against the proposal) (Gustafson, 2005). However, Norway's 2005 Citizenship Act does not accept dual citizenship.

Generally, the most important requirement for naturalisation is length of residency[9] but there are variations in this, as many countries have increased or decreased the residence requirements between 2000 and 2002. At one end, strict residence requirements include 10 years in Spain, nine years in Denmark (from seven), eight years in Germany (from 15) and Finland, and seven years in Norway. At the other end, with five years, are France, the UK, the Netherlands and Sweden (less if you are stateless or a refugee).

Most European countries have some kind of language requirements, with a trend towards a more demanding language or naturalisation test before you apply for naturalisation. According to the Dutch Nationality Act of 2003 you must be able to show that you are sufficiently integrated in Dutch society and are able to speak, read, write and understand the Dutch language reasonably well. Finland and Denmark have also adopted language tests, in the UK there is a combination of language and citizenship test, and in Denmark you have to document a minimum skill in Danish language and knowledge of history, culture and society.[10]

Migration is gendered, and many women migrate via family unification (or as refugees or workers, especially in the care field – see Williams, 2004a, and Chapter Five). The universal right to family life is protected by international conventions. At the same time, family unification has become politicised because it is one of the most important migration gates to Western Europe. The European guidelines emphasise the right to family unification, and most countries have more liberal requirements for spouses.[11] There is now an EU Directive

Table 3.1: Nationality acquisition

	Denmark	Finland	France	Germany	Netherlands	Norway	Spain	Sweden	UK
Length of residency	9 years	8 years[a]	5 years	8 years	5 years	7 years	10 years	5 years	5 years
Language requirements	Yes	Yes	Yes	Yes	Yes	Yes	No	No	Yes
Citizenship courses and/or test	Yes	No[b]	Yes for test, no for courses	No	Yes	Yes	No	No	Yes
Loyalty statement or test	Yes	No	Yes	Yes	Yes	No, voluntary	Yes	No	Yes
Dual citizenship	No	Yes, since 2003	No	No	No	No	No	Yes, since 2001	Yes
Access to social security	Yes	Yes	No	Yes[c]	No	Yes	No	Yes	No

Notes:

[a] Six years if continuous.

[b] Except for language skills test.

[c] Since the liberalisation of the nationality law of 2000, receiving welfare/unemployment benefit does not prohibit naturalisation if the applicant cannot be held responsible for this situation (see Koopmans et al 2005, p 35).

on Family Unification for Third country nationals (EC, 2003: Council Directive 2003/86/EC) and most European countries have adopted policies about the right to family unification according to this Directive. One exception is Denmark, which has opted out of the EC Directive.[12] The 'age 24 provision' in the Danish Alien Act §9[13] (from 2002) requires that both spouses must be aged 24 for a non-citizen marrying a Danish citizen to get a residence permit.[14] Although this has been widely criticised,[15] there have been similar proposals and debates in Norway (Bredal, 2005). Family unification and asylum therefore provide an interesting example of the gendered aspects of migration and of the problems for the European Community of navigating between realpolitik and humanitarian principles (Brochmann and Dölvik, 2004).

Gender-related persecution has increasingly been recognised in a growing number of states as falling within the scope of the 1951 Refugee Convention's definition of refugee status, but domestic violence by family members in certain situations is less widely accepted as a basis for refugee status.[16] In the EU context, the Qualification Directive also recognises that acts of a gender-specific nature can constitute persecution. The new German Immigration Act from January 2005 follows the EU guidelines in accepting gender-specific grounds of asylum due to persecution. This is also reflected in moves to adopt gender-specific rights to asylum by Ireland, the UK, and more recently, Norway and Spain.

Spain is a recent example of more humanitarian policies that enable asylum seekers lacking state protection from domestic violence to be recognised as refugees.[17] In a precedent-setting decision in 2005, the Spanish Inter-ministerial Asylum Commission granted asylum to a woman victim of domestic violence in a forced marriage arguing that the continuous abuse violated a number of her fundamental human rights not to be subjected to torture, inhuman or degrading treatment and the right to life, liberty and security of person. This was found to be a direct result of her gender and her status as a married woman, and was thus seen to constitute gender-specific persecution. It was the first time Spain has granted refugee status to a woman who could not find protection from serious domestic abuse in her country of origin.[18] It is an example of how gendering citizenship means addressing the public–private divide.

The tensions between pluralist integration and assimilation

In the context of the tendency within Europe to both restrict 'entrance' to the territory and to intensify 'integration' of those living legally in their country this section documents national variations in integration, highlighting the growing tension between policies close to assimilation as against pluralist integration. Integration policies, norms and discourses specify the rights and responsibilities of people who plan to live in a country and contribute to, construct or change the boundaries between 'citizens' and 'non-citizens'. As such, integration is a contested and contradictory concept; policies may be inclusive, stressing pluralism and respect for diversity, as well as exclusive, emphasising assimilation to national cultural values and norms in disciplinary ways. Integration refers to normative questions about what constitutes a good citizen and concerns a broad range of policy areas from social, political, cultural and civil rights to anti-discrimination legislation. Integration is janus-faced and policies may often have a double effect of supporting and disciplining citizens, for example in the demand to learn the native language and pass a language test. Learning the national language may in itself be a valuable resource (particularly for women), but may also be subject to compulsion. There is often a gap between good intentions, practical implementation and social consequences of policies that makes it difficult to evaluate the practical effects of integration legislation. In the UK, for example, political discourse treats language lessons as an obligation of migrants to ensure integration, but at the same time, the provision of language classes is underfunded and oversubscribed in many areas, therefore not universally available as a right (NIACE, 2006).

In relation to the development of social rights, many modern welfare states have adopted proactive policies in order to promote 'integration' and improve migrants' opportunities to realise their rights. They go beyond formal rights by encouraging participation and a sense of belonging, for example through labour market schemes, social care and general welfare, education, language training, and support for non-governmental organisations (NGOs). In all nine countries studied in this book, participation in the labour market is today perceived as the key to integration for migrants generally, and women in particular, who have a weaker attachment to the labour market and higher unemployment than the indigenous population (Ministry for Refugees, Immigration and Integration Affairs, 2004). While there are large variations in requirements for labour market activation, there is a general trend from voluntary to more disciplinary schemes, from a 'soft' cultural-oriented approach towards a more economic and instrumental approach. For example, the Dutch 'citizenship contract' for migrants and accepted asylum seekers, established in 1995, has since 1996 gradually become more punitive.

It is therefore not surprising to find significant disparities in how migrant and citizen households fare across European welfare states. Morissens and Sainsbury's (2005) study of migrants' social rights in the UK, Denmark, France, Germany and Sweden concludes that migrants and minority ethnic groups are much less likely to enjoy a socially acceptable standard of living compared to majority ethnic citizens, even when the market is the main source of their income. They are also less likely to be pulled out of poverty by transfers, and where benefits are their main source of income, they run a greater risk of poverty (Morissens and Sainsbury, 2005, p 654). Thus, both immigration status and ethnicity/'race' are associated with higher risk of poverty across welfare states.

In most European countries the 1990s saw a general trend in cutting back social provisions and benefits and a tightening of control and supervision of migrants. Provision of social rights can be a vehicle to manage and monitor marginal groups, whether permanently settled or temporary. As a consequence of the moral panic about the dependency of migrant workers or refugees without work on social welfare, these groups have experienced both greater restrictions to their access to social rights (Brochmann and Dölvik, 2004, p 170) and more restrictive migration policies. One example is the UK when the 1999 Immigration and Asylum Act eroded the rights of asylum seekers by making eligibility to social security conditional upon compulsory dispersal and imposed restrictions on eligibility to work (Sales, 2002). Lack of access to public funds and resources, such as language classes, for newly arrived migrants can reinforce women's lack of independent legal and economic status, especially in the case of women with children experiencing domestic violence, widowhood or separation (an issue taken up by black and migrant women's groups at the EU – Williams, 2003).

In the Nordic welfare states, welfare is based upon universal social rights attached to citizenship, and migrants and refugees living legally in the countries generally have the same relatively generous rights as national citizens. Denmark is an exception; the Liberal Conservatives, in government since 2001, challenged the principle of universality by adopting an introductory grant in 2002.[19] This 'start-help' is lower than the amount given to people on social assistance (*kontanthjælp*), and non-citizens only gain the right to full and equal social benefits after seven years in Denmark (Ejrnæs, 2003, p 233). The policy is highly contested. The government claims that the grant is an incentive to integrate refugees into the labour market. Critics claim that it is not only a form of discrimination that reduces their economic resources but is also an attack on universalism and a breach of the equal treatment principle in the human rights conventions. Research indicates that the 'start–help' does not create jobs and has become a barrier to social integration of refugees because it increases their poverty (Ejrnæs, 2003, p 233).

Political rights, especially voting rights, are crucial for minority groups but they are not straightforward. Democratic rights refer to voting, representation in local and national elections, participation in voluntary associations and generally having a voice in public debates; there is often a gap between these formal rights and the migrants' capacity to use these rights (Koopmans et al, 2005). No European country has extended the right to vote at the national level to all foreign residents, but in the UK this right is available to resident citizens from the Commonwealth countries, as well as Ireland (Koopmans et al, 2005). Migrants are able to vote in local elections in Sweden (1976), Denmark (1981), Norway (1982), Finland and the Netherlands (1985) but not in Germany,[20] France and Spain. In terms of representation, the barriers are often lower in city councils than in national Parliaments and migrant groups are able to obtain a relatively high representation in local government, for example in cities in the UK and Denmark (Togeby, 2003; Klausen, 2006).

Most countries have advisory bodies or councils sponsored by the state that deal with immigration and integration issues. For example, the UK's most important advisory boards are the Commission for Racial Equality (which, as Chapter Two explains, will soon be part of a single equality body) and its local equivalents, the Racial Equality Councils, as well as the Race Relations Forum set up by the government in 1998. In France the two most important advisory councils are *Fonds d'action et de soutiern pour l'intégration et la lutte contra la discrimination* (FASILD) and the *Haut conseil à l'intégration*. In 2002 a national representative council for Muslims, the *Conseil français du culte musulman*, was set up. Germany has a system of special representation of foreigners at the local level with limited power (Koopmans et al, 2005, p 65; Klausen, 2006).

Cultural rights[21] may refer both to the right to be equal and to the respect for cultural diversity, including the right to practise one's own language, religion, dress and behaviour, and there is often a need to balance competing rights. As noted earlier, the move to introduce language tests is part of a general state expectation of assimilation to national values even in countries thought to be multicultural like the Netherlands and the UK. Women are usually perceived as symbols and bearers of culture and, as such, find themselves caught between different cultural norms and values, such as the gender-specific norms of marriage and dress, which are explored in the following section.

There has been a general movement towards stronger legislation against ethnic and gender discrimination illustrated by the UN Race Discrimination Convention from 1965 and the European Human Rights Convention from 1950. As Chapter Two discusses, EU Directives have been important in this respect as well. Most of the 25 member states have implemented the European Council's 2003 'Race Directive' but Austria, Finland, Germany and Luxembourg were subsequently referred to the European Court of Justice for not adhering to the requirements of the Directive.[22] Countries, nevertheless, have different anti-discrimination histories: the UK has, from the 1960s, developed relatively strong anti-discrimination laws and policies in relation to 'race' and ethnicity based upon the Race Relations Act (RRA) from 1965.[23] The Netherlands introduced a Law on Equal Treatment in 1994 that, in contrast to the RRA, covers discrimination not only on the basis of 'race' and ethnicity but also on religion. There is an anti-discrimination clause in the French Penal Code and the Labour Code offers additional protection against discrimination in the field of employment (Koopmans et al, 2005). For the Nordic countries, anti-discrimination is a relatively new policy area; in Denmark, ethnic discrimination has been against the law since 1971, while a law against discrimination in the labour market was not adopted until 1996 (Hansen, 2003) (see Table 3.2).

In summary, then, following greater regulation of migration policies, tensions between pluralist integration and assimilation have increased. It is rare that policy has moved to being generally *more* liberal towards asylum seekers and refugees, although specific instances of, for example, Sweden instituting the right to dual citizenship or Germany's shortening of residency qualifications for naturalisation, can be found. On the EU level there is a growing emphasis on 'policing of borders' and terrorism surveillance. At the same time, there is also a move towards 'managed migration' of workers, with better settlement and employment rights for skilled and professional workers. There has also been increased movement within Europe, particularly from the poorer regions of Central and Eastern Europe, with mobility rights attached to being an EU citizen. In general, this new complexity and diversity of migrant statuses has led to a greater fragmentation of citizenship rights (which Ong, 2006, calls a 'disarticulation' of citizenship) with some migrants having more or less access to cultural, social, economic, political and legal rights.

Table 3.2: Anti-discrimination rights[a]

	Denmark	Finland	France	Germany	Netherlands	Norway	Spain	Sweden	UK
Provisions against racial hatred in Penal Code[b]	Yes	Yes	Yes	Yes	Yes	Yes	Yes	National action plan against racism, 2000	Yes
Provisions against discrimination in Penal Code	Law of 1987, revised 2003	Yes	Yes	Yes	Yes	Yes	Yes	Yes	Yes
Special anti-discrimination law in Civil Code	Yes	Yes, 2004 Equality Act	Yes	Yes, Basic Law, Article 3 and 2006 General Equal Treatment Act	Yes, 1994 Law on Equal Treatment	Yes, Equality Law and Law against Ethnic and Religious Discrimination	Yes	Yes	Yes, 1976 Race Relations Act and 2000 Race Relations Amendment Act
State officers dealing with discrimination complaints	Institute for Human Rights[c]	Discrimination Board and the Ombudsman for Minorities	Commissions for Access to Citizenship (CODAC) 1996	Ombudsman and Anti-discrimination Board; 2006 General Equal Treatment Act	Commission for Equal Treatment (CGB)	Equality and Anti-discrimination Ombudsman	General Ombudsman (*Defensor del Pueblo*)	Ombudsman against Ethnic Discrimination	Commission for Racial Equality (CRE)[d]

Notes:

[a] The EC adopted two Anti-Discrimination Directives in 2000: the Directive on Ethnic Equal Treatment 2000/43/EFC and the Employment Directive 2000/73/EFC that should have been implemented by the national governments before 2003.

[b] Integration of the 1965 International Convention on the Elimination of All Forms of Racial Discrimination (ICERD) into the national criminal law. This does not cover discrimination when not accompanied by statements of racist intent (Koopmans et al, 2005, p 47).

[c] The Institute has decided to set up a Committee dealing with discrimination complaints according to the Anti-discrimination Law of 2003.

[d] To be replaced by Commission on Equality and Human Rights in 2007.

On the whole, European states' reaction has been to revert to a model of integration based on greater assimilation into the nation state and its cultural 'traditions' and less to an embrace of a multicultural, post-nationalist society, even though elements of this can be seen (for example, London's success in its bid to hold the Olympics on the basis of its multiculturalism bid). However, even this shift is not quite so determined because, at the same time, the very development of supranational governance sets in motion a notion of citizenship that exists *beyond* the nation state, even though it is still territorialised *within* the walls of 'Fortress Europe'. All of these processes have a particular meaning for women migrants, as refugees fleeing gender-specific persecution, as members of minority groups bearing, reproducing and resisting the symbols of those cultures, as family members seeking reunification, and as workers claiming a breadwinning role for their families or themselves. Some of these moves have proved contradictory for women: stricter rules in relation to family unification are negative, while a more humanitarian acceptance of gender-specific persecution as grounds for recognising refugee status is positive. We look in the following section at two examples of women as those who carry, reconstitute and resist cultural symbols and practices, and what this means in the context of moves towards integration and assimilation. (In Chapter Five we focus on women as migrant workers.)

The framing of gendered debates

The debates around the headscarf and forced and arranged marriages show how these issues are framed differently across Europe and are influenced by national histories, institutions and senses of belonging. Directly and indirectly these are gendered debates for the reasons noted above, that the women and girls are seen to 'carry' cultural difference, and often as such are deemed to be in need of 'protection' from their 'backward' and patriarchal cultures. We ask why it has become an important issue and who are the main actors? How are the political trends and patterns/logics of different citizenship and migration regimes connected to different welfare regimes and gender cultures? How do majority feminists deal with the issues?

Debates about forced and arranged marriages

Forced and arranged marriages have been the subject of highly politicised debates in some countries, for example in Scandinavia, but less so in multicultural countries like the UK. Forced marriage is a marriage arranged for a young person against their will by the parents or family members. Forcing a person to marry against their will is a violation of the Human Rights and Women's Conventions, and governments as well as women's groups have been involved in developing strategies and best practices to prevent forced marriage (see, for example, the Report on Best Practices in the UK, Norway and Germany: Center for Ligestillingsforskning ved Roskilde Universitetscenter, 2003). The issue illustrates how the discourses of integration can be both emancipatory and disciplinary, requiring measures to address at one and the same time women's equal rights and autonomy in the family, racial discrimination, and human rights violations.

Research has identified different approaches and strategies to prevent forced marriages that illuminate different citizenship regimes and gender cultures (Phillips and Dustin, 2004; Bredal, 2005, 2006). Phillips and Dustin differentiate between three different solutions – exit, regulation and dialogue. The liberal British approach[24] focuses on the protection of the individual's rights through *exit* from their group and uses international conventions as a means to secure these rights. The British case provides an interesting contrast with the more restrictive Danish approach that relies primarily on regulation, and the Norwegian and Swedish approaches based more upon prevention and possibilities for dialogue.

The prevailing philosophy in Britain has been described as a moderate version of multiculturalism, which recognises that the population is ethnically and culturally diverse, although this is gradually being overlaid with talk about national identity and social cohesion (Phillips and Dustin, 2004; Yuval-Davis, 2007). The British emphasis on individual rights is compatible with a strong tradition of NGO groups organising migrant women, for example the Southall Black Sisters (2001), an NGO organisation established in 1979 to meet the needs of Asian and African women. This organisation works from a socialist feminist perspective and tackles problems about forced marriages on several levels, through advisory groups and forming support groups for victims, advocacy activities, campaigns and political lobbying. One of the main issues for this group has been to combat domestic violence against women (Southall Black Sisters, 2001).

Phillips and Dustin (2004) notice that forced marriage is one of three gender-specific issues to emerge in recent years as the focus of media attention and government policy, together with crimes committed in the name of honour and female genital cutting and mutilation. The first two relate mainly to Asian communities, the latter to those of African heritage. The Labour government has been proactive in all three areas. It has commissioned research on forced marriage, emphasising the distinction between 'forced' and 'arranged' marriages, and created a unit within the Foreign and Commonwealth Office to handle cases and rescue girls and women abducted overseas. 'Honour' crimes are a more recent initiative where the Metropolitan Police have taken the lead after a series of murder cases in the media aroused concern. The problem of combating forced marriages is perceived as a transnational one and international conventions and transnational partnerships are used as a proactive means to combat them.[25]

In Denmark, Norway and Sweden in the 1990s, forced marriages and 'honour-related violence' became the subject of public concern expressed through gender equality, women's rights and the oppression of girls in patriarchal families (Bredal, 2005). But while Denmark adopted strict Action Plans against both forced and arranged marriages, Norway's Action Plan is directed solely against forced marriages, and Sweden has a more multicultural approach to integration, where the Action Plan does not target specific groups but is directed against the *general* oppression of girls in patriarchal families.

The official Danish approach thus focuses more on restrictive policies and negative discourses than on preventive measures and dialogue. The objective of the Government's Action Plan is to support young people exposed to force in relation to marriage and to re-enforce preventive initiatives by the authorities (Ministry for Refugees, Immigration and Integration Affairs, 2003, pp 5-10) through projects financed by special allocation funds. This includes funds granted to the *Landsorganisationen for Kvinde- og Krisecentre* (LOKK) (the National Organisation of Shelters for Battered Women and Children) to start a nationwide team of professional counsellors to offer free advice to local authorities in actual cases of forced marriage or marriages where coercion seems to have been a factor. However, this approach is problematic, because it not only intends to prevent marriages that involve compulsion, which is against the law, but also to prevent all forms of arranged marriages, including marriage between cousins. The 'problem' is constructed as a 'culture clash' between 'modern' Danish norms about gender equality in 'normal' families and the 'traditional' practices of forced and arranged marriages, which prevent self-determination for minority women. This official discourse has been challenged by a recent investigation into forced and arranged marriages based upon both quantitative and qualitative data from the five largest immigrant groups in Denmark. It found only a small minority of young people did not take an active part in choosing their own fiancé/spouse and that the influence of parents should not be exaggerated (Schmidt and Jacobsen, 2004, pp 6-7). Indeed, research from Denmark, Norway, Sweden and the UK has documented the diversity of arranged marriage practices, and indicates that it is difficult to make a clear distinction between forced and arranged marriage (Phillips and Dustin, 2004; Bredal, 2005, 2006).

The Norwegian approach[26] is somewhat different (Bredal, 2005, pp 483-4). Here the government Action Plan from 1998 focused primarily on prevention and remedy. The impetus behind the Action Plan on forced marriages was a media debate about a Moroccan girl who was abducted by her parents and sent to her country of origin, and who subsequently claimed that they planned to marry her by force. The Plan announced the establishment of a national helpline opened in April 2000. The climate changed in January 2002 when, after the murder by her father of Fadime Shindal, a young Swedish woman of Kurdish origin, a proposal to introduce an age limit of 24 for family reunification gained political support, along with other similar proposals. The Norwegian government issued their 'Renewed Initiative against Forced Marriage', a collection of 30 new measures, 10 of which cover criminal, civil and immigration law (Bredal, 2005, pp 486-8). It was accompanied by a new immigration rule requiring that a Norwegian citizen who wishes to bring their spouse to live in the country must prove that they can provide for the spouse where one of them is under the age of 23.

The Danish and Norwegian cases show the interconnection of state intervention in forced marriage with the legitimisation of stricter immigration legislation. In Sweden, policies are generally less explicitly tied to ethnicity, and the debate about honour crimes has not directly targeted minority families. In all three countries political parties have used the discourse of women's rights for racist and discriminatory purposes. In Norway and Denmark experts call for less restrictive policy regulations and argue for policies and strategies based upon intercultural dialogue sensitive to lived citizenship and to young migrants' own experiences and identities (Bredal, 2005). In the UK, Fauzia Ahmad (2006) calls for alternative conceptualisations of arranged marriage practices that remain sympathetic to cultural and religious sensibilities. This discussion suggests that, first, when public discourse focuses solely on women's emancipation, this may serve to reproduce fixed views of minority ethnic women as 'backward' or at best 'traditional'. Second, it also may minimise their agency unless the demands for the right to freedom from violence come collectively from the women themselves. However, and third, if it focuses solely on cultural rights to marriage practices, it may obscure experiences of violence. Fourth, the laws against forced and arranged marriages appear to have legitimised increased immigration controls. Finally, such discourses fuel racist ideas, rather than confront them.

Debates about the headscarf/hijab[27]

EU policy has no explicit regulation of religious practices, but new anti-discrimination Directives prohibit discrimination on grounds of religion in member states.[28] In most countries there has been an intense debate about (Muslim) women's right to wear headscarves, but the framing, the regulation of the issue, and judicial outcomes on headscarves vary considerably across Europe. In countries like the UK with an emphasis on diversity, it has not been as pressing a topic of public debate as in France, although it, and especially the *niqab* (full veil) has recently become more of an issue (Afshar et al, 2005, unpublished).[29] The headscarf is controversial and it has become simultaneously a symbol of women's oppression, their resistance to oppression, and their right to cultural autonomy and religious freedom. Two complaints of headscarf discrimination have been tried before the European Court of Human Rights, and the state decision to impose prohibition was upheld.[30] The Court stressed that it found the use of a headscarf difficult to combine with the principle of gender equality. In the Court's opinion, the choices of some women, who wear the headscarf, may put undue pressure on other women, who would prefer not to wear it (Skjeie, 2007: forthcoming).

In relation to the law in other countries, in Germany six provinces have banned teachers in public schools from wearing headscarves, but private business cannot prohibit headscarves at work. In the Netherlands there is no general ban on the headscarf, but it is forbidden for court personnel, and dress codes for students prohibit the *burqa* and *niqab*. In Denmark the issue is framed as the employer's right to institute a general dress code, although opponents interpret the ban against employees wearing a headscarf as an indirect form of labour market discrimination. In the UK the wearing of the headscarf is not, at the time of writing, legally regulated, schools are allowed to set up their own dress codes, and government guidelines allow wearing a veil for a passport photo.[31] In 2006, however, the wearing of the *niqab* became the subject of intense political debate, with feminists and anti-racists lining up on both sides (see note 29).

These differences in judicial outcomes reflect how different discourses in different countries frame the issue. In France a heated debate about religious symbols in republican schools resulted in overwhelming support for the adoption of a law, in February 2004, that forbids the wearing of 'ostentatious' religious signs. The official arguments are linked to the principle of a separation of state and Church, which has dominated discourses and politics since the Third Republic was established in 1905, and was inserted in the 1946 Constitution as one of the founding principles of the republic. This gave French *laïcité* (secularism) a different meaning from the secularism prevailing in other European states (Kastoryano, 2006). It is argued that wearing a headscarf in a republican school can be – even in the present international context – considered as a threat to the authority of the state. What is at stake is national unity and republican identity, which is different from a liberal vision of individual rights, or a liberal version of integration and state acceptance of specific group rights (see Table 3.3).

The French debate about the headscarf started as a local affair in 1989 when three girls wore a headscarf to their local school in Creil, a suburb north of Paris. It reappeared in the political arena in October 1994 when girls wearing headscarves were expelled from a public school and the right-wing Minister of Education, François Bayrou, issued a circular forbidding any ostentatious religious signs in a public school, an institution that is *par excellence* the very embodiment of national ideology as 'egalitarian, laique, inclusive' (Kastoryano, 2006). Since then it became a public affair both condemned and defended by the political class, the media and intellectuals.

The French approach expresses the dilemma between the republican principle of regulation and the liberal principle of non-intervention. French feminists, including those feminists who originated from immigrant Muslim backgrounds, were divided on the issue of the need to pass a law reinforcing the 1905 law on *laïcité*. Françoise Gaspard (2006) illustrates the feminist ambivalence: in common with the concerns of the European Court, she found that 'pure liberalism' could have negative effects on the many Muslim girls who do not wear headscarves, because they might feel pressurised to conform to their religion. At the same time, she proposed that a law banning the headscarf will mean that teenage girls wearing a headscarf will be deprived of their education.

In Germany the headscarf debate centred around the case of a school teacher in the federal state of Baden-Würtenberg, who for five years fought a legal battle over the right to wear a headscarf (Saharso, 2007). According to Sawitri Saharso, who has compared the German and Dutch cases, the teacher was an Islamic woman of Afghan descent,

Table 3.3: Cultural and political rights[a]

	Denmark	Finland	France	Germany	Netherlands	Norway	Spain	Sweden	UK
State recognition of funding of Islamic schools	Yes	No	No	Partly	Yes	Yes	No	Yes	Partly
Teachers' right to wear a headscarf to work	Yes	Yes	No	Dependent on the states	No	Yes	Yes	Yes[b]	Yes
Students' right to wear a headscarf to school	Yes	Yes	No	Yes	Yes	Yes	Yes	Yes	Yes[c]
General rights to wear a headscarf to work	Dependent on the employer	Yes	No	Yes	Yes	Yes	Yes	Yes	Yes
Voting rights in local elections	Yes, after 3 years, since 1981	Yes, since 1985	No, since 1982	No[d]	Yes, after 5 years, since 1985	Yes, after 3 years, since 1982	No	Yes, since 1976	Yes

Notes:

[a] Only voting rights in local elections are shown here: national voting and political representation are too complex across the nine countries to portray in tabular form.

[b] In Sweden, mandatory directives were issued in 2003 by the National Education Agency. These allow schools to prohibit the *burka* and *niqab*, provided they do so in a spirit of dialogue on the common values of equality of the sexes and respect for the democratic principle on which the education system is based.

[c] But see note 31.

[d] At the end of the 1980s the attempt to introduce local voting rights after the Dutch model in three northern German federal states was ruled unconstitutional by the Federal Constitutional Court, but only a few years later the Court did endorse the extension of local voting rights to citizens from other EU member states following the Maastricht Treaty of 1992 (see Koopmans et al, 2005, p 44).

who was a German citizen since 1995 and a qualified teacher in '*Grund*' and '*Hauptschule*'. When she applied for a job as a teacher the authorities refused to hire her, because she would not take off her headscarf while teaching. She brought her case before the Stuttgart Administrative Court, which, in March 2000, ruled in favour of the authorities. The Federal Constitutional Court reached a judgment in 2003 and interpreted it as a conflict between positively allowing religious freedom or disallowing the negative effects of a particular religion. While the lower courts ruled in favour of the latter, the Federal Constitutional Court came up with a different judgment: that the public law of Baden-Würtenberg was not able to support a ban on teachers wearing headscarves in school while teaching. This was followed by a change of legal provisions concerning headscarves in the 10 federal states dominated by the Christian Democratic Party. In federal states where the Social Democratic Party was in power, cases were individually subject to an examination as to the teacher's fitness to teach, whether in a public school or not. The debate, then, as Saharso argues, concerns the meaning of state neutrality about which German public and policy thinking is divided (Saharso, 2007).

In the Netherlands, following its multicultural policies, the issue of the headscarf seems less contested than in France but more so than in the UK. Saharso (2007) suggests that this is to do with the Dutch system of pillarisation where state neutrality does not involve banning religion from the public sphere, but guarantees the right of each creed to self-representation and self-organisation. She notes, first, that here the Islamic headscarf is very much accepted in public life and is only controversial when worn by public officials such as policewomen, lawyers and judges. However, it was agreed that Muslim girls who want to wear the headscarf to school could be refused admission, not for religious reasons, but on the basis that it made communication with the teachers and with their fellow students difficult.

In Spain there is no ban on headscarves but there has been a public debate about the right to wear the headscarf to school. In February 2002 a 13-year-old Moroccan girl whose family wanted a school place for her in Madrid could only find a place in a state-supported Catholic centre. Arguments arose when the centre's *Consejo Escolar* (a parent–teacher–student representative body) refused to accept the girl wearing a headscarf. The school forbade the headscarf on the basis that it was a symbol of sexual discrimination that would hinder the girl's integration. However, the Chair of Madrid's Education Committee compelled the school to unconditionally admit the girl (*El País*, 2002, 15, 16, 17 February; 2 March).[32]

Denmark, Norway and Sweden have no ban on headscarves in public schools. Here the debate is about women's right to wear a headscarf *to work*. In Denmark there have been two court cases. In the first in 1998, a young Muslim woman worker pressed a complaint against a big department store that sent her home because she would not take off her headscarf. The High Court argued that she was protected by the anti-discrimination law (of 1996) and could not be dismissed solely on the ground of wearing a headscarf for religious reasons, and that the ban was effectively indirect discrimination towards a specific religious group, and the employer was given a fine (Hansen, 2003, p 243). The second case was raised by a young girl who was fired because she did not live up to the company's dress code. Her trade union argued that she was the victim of indirect discrimination. In 2003 the High Court ruled that the dismissal was legal because the ban on the headscarves was a general ban on all forms of political, religious and cultural symbols. A Supreme Court decision confirmed this decision in January 2005. The verdict was contested by Danish human rights lawyers on the basis that only objective reasons, such as hygiene and security, could legitimise a ban on religious headscarves.

Significant in Denmark was the media portrayal of minority ethnic groups in the Danish election debate in November 2001 when the Liberal-Right government gained power, supported by the Danish Populist (People's) Party. This was highly gendered, with young Muslim men constructed as violent and young Muslim women as oppressed victims of their 'culture', often shown wearing a headscarf (even though it is only worn by a few – Andreassen, 2005). In this way the headscarf became a symbol that organises, constructs and negotiates gender, equality, nationality and identity. According to Rikke Andreassen (2005) the representation of minority ethnic groups as oppressed, symbolised by the headscarf, contributes to the prevailing myth about the Danish gender equality model, often interpreted as the right and freedom to take off your clothes. The issue divides Danish feminists and has recently fuelled public controversy about a television host who wears a headscarf and was hired to front a debate programme. One group has started a campaign against the decision to hire her, which, they argue, symbolises a public acceptance of the oppression of women, while another group approves of it as evidence of the media's acceptance of diversity.

In Norway the debate is also about a woman's right to wear a headscarf to work, but here the issue is gendered and the bans in the workplace have been ruled to be in violation of the 2000 Gender Equality Act (Skjeie, 2007). For the Norwegian Gender Equality Ombudsperson it is the discriminatory effects of the ban on headscarves for women employees that have been key, and the main argument has been the individual women's right to non-discrimination in the labour market.

Sweden has recently adopted a separation of Church and state, and within this there exists no regulation of the headscarf. The Ombudsperson against Ethnic Discrimination has stated that it is a fundamental religious right to wear a headscarf. Most political parties are split on the issue, but no Swedish party wants to forbid the headscarf, because to do so is seen as a barrier to integration that may lead to discrimination and fuel racism. In the debate, two opposing views are stressed: the individual right of a religious person and concerns for gender equality. The Swedish government plans to accept both the headscarf and Sikh turban in the police and armed forces in order to attract people from religious minorities.

These examples point to difficult questions about the representation of minority women by the majority population and about the meanings migrant/minority women attribute to their practices. There is no simple prioritising of gender equality or cultural equality. The decision to wear a headscarf may be interpreted as a symbol of oppression or as a woman's choice to practice their religion, or, in the context of Islamophobia, a form of pride and political resistance. What is important is an understanding of the political and cultural context in which women may choose to wear or not to wear a headscarf, and the meanings which women attribute to that context. For example, minority ethnic women may express a sense of belonging to more than one geographical area, social and cultural group, for example as Danish, German or British Muslims (Klinkhammer, 2003; Afshar et al, 2005; Siim, 2007).

Research across Europe indicates that Muslim women have many reasons for wearing the headscarf. For instance, Françoise Gaspard and Khosrokhavar (1995) have identified three types of women wearing headscarves in France: (1) older married migrant women for whom it represents both an ethnic and a religious signal; (2) school or college girls who wear it because of pressures from members of their family; (3) those who choose to wear it as an affirmation of their identity, often the more educated. Similarly, interviews with Danish girls (Staunæs, 2004) suggest alternative reasons of family pressure, a sign of independence, and a means to negotiate their own identity. By positioning themselves as 'honourable' – symbolised by wearing a headscarf – they may be allowed to participate in school activities that they would normally be banned from by parents, such as excursions and sports activities. Research in Germany (Klinkhammer, 2003) indicates strong generational tensions with more diversity in young women's identities. Research in the UK suggests that since 9/11, wearing the headscarf has become a political act and a sign of a new radical interpretation of their faith defined as liberating rather than constraining (Afshar et al, 2005, unpublished). In this sense, as with the issue of arranged marriages, cultural practices are not fixtures that are moved from one society to another, but are always subject to change in the local or national context within which they find themselves. The examples here show that migrant women live under different pressures, yet young women are often able to navigate between the majority norms and their own family culture, between claims for gender equality and rights to cultural respect.

Conclusion: gendering citizenship and migration regimes

This chapter has explored, from a cross-national perspective, the tensions that migration, multiculturalism and gender equality pose for understanding citizenship. Migration raises citizenship issues to do with access to the nation state and the inclusion of individuals and social groups. Arguably, all European countries today face new challenges from migration in combining the old principles of equality with a new respect for cultural and religious diversity. The tension in migration policies between realpolitik and concerns about human rights has given European integration legislation a disciplinary and a liberatory potential. The chapter has used a gendered lens to explore the connections between political institutions, policies and political-cultural norms in the policy debates about forced and arranged marriages and the headscarf. These examples illustrate how the different debates about assimilation and pluralist integration policies concerning political-cultural norms and practices are gendered. They show that women are often at the centre of the cultural conflicts that address the relationship between people's public and private lives and these affect women and men differently.

The frame of citizenship also demonstrates the tensions between equality and diversity. The gendered dimension of *the multicultural challenge* refers not only to respect for diversity of religion, culture and values but also to sensitivity to diversities in family cultures and gender equality norms. It also points to the specific *democratic challenge* to include the voices and concerns of minority ethnic women in the private and public domains. Finally, it provides a specific *gender-political* challenge to stimulate (feminist) dialogues about family forms and gender equality norms. And it indicates that policy makers and researchers need to be more sensitive to the differences within and between groups, as well as to the interaction between ethnic/cultural majorities and minorities.

A cross-national approach is helpful in revealing the close relationship between the external and internal dimensions of migration, and the various ways migration has influenced the intersections of nationality, gender, class and ethnicity. While there is some evidence for convergence of European migration regimes, there are also shifts in different directions. The republican French migration regime has moved from *ius soli* towards *ius sanguinis*, while Germany and Spain have moved towards less restrictive migration regimes. The French and German cases also illustrate the gendered tensions between multiculturalism and integration from the assimilationist pole. Thus, while they are thought to belong to different migration regimes, they have both banned the headscarf, albeit with different arguments. Spain presents a more complex case: here liberal changes in the welfare, migration and gender regimes have been possible in the context of Islamophobia (see Chapter Five).

The UK and the Netherlands, as more pluralist societies, illustrate the gendered tension between multiculturalism and assimilation, and they also show the relationship between external and internal dimensions of migration policies. They are both post-colonial countries thought to belong to the same liberal migration regime with moderate multicultural policies but with different welfare regimes. Both tend to accept the public–private divide and until recently they accepted relatively extensive civil rights for ethnic groups, including wearing headscarves for religious reasons. Today multicultural policies seem to be at a crossroads in both countries with a move away from pluralist integration towards the ethnic assimilation pole. One of the key questions is what this new trend means for people's lived citizenship and how far the two countries will go down this path.

Finally, the Nordic countries show the tension between multiculturalism and gender equality. They belong to the same family of welfare and gender regimes but recently have adopted different policies towards migration and integration with Sweden the most multicultural country. In spite of the different approaches to multiculturalism, they have all failed to integrate minorities into the labour market or society. Arguably, the universal welfare state is not morally neutral and migrants are often expected to abandon cultural beliefs and practices that violate the norms of Scandinavian solidarity, including gender equality. The key question is to what extent can the universal welfare state and gender regimes based upon 'women-friendly' policies become the basis for the inclusion of migrants, especially migrant women in society? Chapter Four now picks up the theme of 'women-friendly' states in relation to the shifting picture of childcare provision.

This chapter has illuminated the gendered implications of the different approaches to migration and multiculturalism and it has raised analytical questions about the need to develop a citizenship framework able to analyse the intersection of gender and other forms of inequality in terms of 'race' and ethnicity from a comparative cross-national perspective.

Notes

[1] The resistance to Turkey, a Muslim nation, joining the European Union (EU) is one example of this at the formal level.

[2] The model has a *formal and legal* dimension, which places a regime between an ethno-cultural – *ius sanguinis* – and a territorial – *ius soli* – pole, and a *political-cultural dimension*, which places a regime between cultural monism (assimilation) and cultural pluralism. The formal basis for citizenship addresses questions such as: how difficult is it to achieve citizenship and how many rights do non-citizens have? How extensive is anti-discrimination legislation? The political-cultural dimension address questions such as: how open is a society to cultural diversity, not only formally but also in practice? It includes the recognition of cultural diversity in the following areas: the educational system (for example, the right to a minority school and special education); the police and the military (for example, exemptions from uniforms); the media (for example, minority programmes in foreign languages); religious behaviour and other religious questions (for example, minority burial grounds, cemeteries); ethnic minority representatives in politics; the labour market (for example, affirmative action programmes); and cultural demands for achieving citizenship (for example, language tests).

[3] Asylum refers explicitly to the rules in the European Convention on Human Rights (ECHR) and migration refers to the rules for integration of workers who are Third country nationals and nationals from other European Community countries in the EU.

[4] Aliens can acquire citizenship by birth, by declaration, by adoption or by naturalisation, which is the most common way.

[5] A child becomes a German national by birth if:

- one of the parents possesses German citizenship. If only the father has German citizenship, the paternity must be recognised before the child attains 23 years of age, where it is necessary to establish the paternity according to German law;

- the child is born in Germany after 1 January 2000, and the parents are foreign nationals. One of the parents must have lived legally in Germany for at least eight years and have permanent resident permission or have had an unlimited residence permit for the previous three years.

Staatsangehörigkeitsgesetz came into force on 1 January 2000.
The German version of the Act is available at:
http://bundesrecht.juris.de/bundesrecht/rustag/
The English version of the Act is available at:
www.iuscomp.org/gla/.
The earlier version of the Act is available at:
www.legislationline.org index.php?country=17&org=0&eu=0&topic=4

[6] France still accepts dual nationality. A French national, who voluntarily acquires nationality of a foreign country does not lose French nationality for that reason. According to Article 23 of the *Code Civil*, the French national will only lose French nationality if they make a declaration to that effect. Accordingly, an alien who wishes to be granted French nationality does not have to renounce their present nationality. However, France has signed the Council of Europe Convention of 6 May 1963. Thus, a French national will lose French nationality when acquiring nationality of a country that has signed this convention. France thus accepts dual nationality but this is modified if it concerns signatory countries of the Convention. Denmark is one of these countries, and so a French national who acquires Danish nationality will automatically lose their French nationality. On the other hand, a French national who is granted Swedish nationality will not lose their French nationality, because Sweden accepts dual nationality and is not a signatory country. See www.legifrance.gouv.fr/html/codes_traduits/code_civil_textA.htm#CHAPTER%20I%20-%20GENERAL%20PROVISIONS

[7] Law 36/2002.

[8] Sweden is the largest Nordic country of immigration with about 20% of foreigners defined as a person who has either migrated themselves or has one parent with a migrant background (this includes migrants from other Nordic countries). About one third of this group are citizens from other Nordic countries (Ministry for Refugees, Immigration and Integration Affairs, 2004, p 231). Norway has 7.6%, Denmark 6% and Finland 2% of the population from third world countries outside the Nordic countries, the EU and North America. The number of migrants in Finland is only 100,000 and it is debatable whether it can be called a migrant country. Although the number of migrants grew during the 1990s the biggest group represent Finns who have been given the possibility to return to Finland after the breakdown of the Soviet Union (Brochmann and Hagelund, 2005, pp 68–70).

[9] Other requirements for naturalisation are: (a) requirement of spouses/ rules about family unification, (b) adequate accommodation (c) language requirements, (d) criminal offences, (e) overdue debt to public authorities, (f) declaration of allegiance and loyalty, and (g) renunciation of present nationality.

[10] Germany also has language requirements. Norway and Sweden represent the exception with no language requirements for naturalisation, but there have been policy proposals in both countries to adopt language requirements.

[11] One example is France where an alien or stateless person who contracts marriage with a French national may acquire nationality by declaration if some requirements are met (the marriage has lasted at least two years, they have sufficient French language skills and they have resided in France at least one year from the date of marriage). The spouse of a German national may be naturalised if they renounce their present citizenship provided that the person has lived legally in Germany for the last three years and has been married to the German spouse for at least two years and intends to conform to the German way of life.

[12] Denmark represents a special case since the adoption of four reservations to the Maastricht Treaty – on the Euro, the European army, EU citizenship and legal and interior matters – that allows for stricter rules concerning family unification than other member states are allowed under the EU Directive 2003/86 on family unification. See www.europakommissionen.dk/eupolitik

[13] This requirement does not apply if one of the spouses is a citizen of an EU country. EU citizens and individuals have the right to move freely within the territory of another member state, when the purpose is to apply for employment: a worker's family has derived rights to stay in the state in which the worker is employed.

[14] The official strategy to restrict the right to family unification started under the former coalition of the Social Democratic and Social Liberal Parties but the present amendment of the Aliens Act from July 2002 was adopted by the Liberal Conservative government after the election in November 2001 with the support of the right-wing populist Danish People's Party. The primary aim is to limit the number of immigrants and secondary goals include the prevention of forced marriages and to ensure 'the best possible base for a successful integration' (Grøndahl, 2003, p 186).

[15] Danish legislation on family unification has been criticised from a human rights perspective by the Danish Human Rights Institute (2004) (www.humanrights.dk)/nyheder/menneskerettighedskommisær) that finds that the age requirement together with the affiliation requirement will result in violation of the right to family life (European Convention of Human Rights, Article 8). Similar criticism has been voiced by the UN Committee on the Elimination of all forms of Discrimination against Women, in considering Denmark's report in 2002 (CEDAW, 2002, para 345) (Justesen, 2003, p 81) and the report of the Council of Europe's Commissioner of Human Rights' (Mr Alvaro Gil-Robles) visit to Denmark on 13-16 April 2004 (www.inm.dk). The government has dismissed the critique. Danes under the age of 24 marrying a non-EU citizen under the age of 24 have moved to Sweden and Germany and claimed that they have a right to bring their spouse back to Denmark according to the principle about the right for workers to move freely within the EU. The Danish government claims that only EU citizens who not only live abroad but also work abroad have the right to bring their spouse back to Denmark. Most recently the European Commission has stated clearly that the Danish government's interpretation is against the principle of the right of workers to move freely within the EU (Politiken, 28 May 2006). It is not yet clear how the government will respond to this.

[16] The United Nations High Commissioner for Refugees (UNHCR) has consistently advocated that gender-related persecution can constitute persecution for one of the five reasons set out in the 1951 Convention and therefore that claimants with a well-founded fear of such treatment should be recognised as refugees. This was also a claim made by black and migrant women's groups in the mid-1990s (Williams, 2003).

[17] Report in www.unhcr.org

[18] In the past, Spain has had a bilateral agreement for women fleeing domestic violence, but never refugee status under the 1951 Convention.

[19] The low grant to refugees first introduced by the government headed by the Social Democrats in 1999 was abandoned, because it did not have the intended effect of integrating refugees into the labour market (Ejrnæs, 2003, pp 224-5).

[20] The attempt to introduce local voting rights for foreigners on the Dutch model in Germany was deemed unconstitutional by the Federal Constitutional Court at the end of the 1980s but only a few years later the Court endorsed the extension of local- and European-level voting rights to EU citizens (Koopmans et al, 2005, p 44).

[21] Koopmans et al (2005, p 51) differentiate between two dimensions of citizenship: (1) an individual equality dimension that refers to equal treatment of the residents of the territory regardless of their race, ethnicity, religion, nationality, or cultural background, for example anti-discrimination rights, and (2) a cultural difference dimension that concerns differentiated rights based upon group membership. In this approach the cultural dimension is only about the right to cultural difference.

[22] Council Directive 2003/43/EC. For detailed information see the European Monitoring Centre on Racism and Xenophobia Annual Report, 2005, http://eumc.eu.int

[23] Modood (2006) noted that it was legal to discriminate against Muslims as Muslims because the courts did not accept Muslims as an ethnic group until December 2003 when religious discrimination became an offence but then only in relation to employment.

[24] UK legislation did, however, have a 'primary purpose rule' stating that a would-be immigrant spouse or fiancé(e) had to prove that a marriage was not entered into primarily to gain admission to the UK. This rule was abolished by New Labour. Prominent politicians, such as David Blunkett and Ann Cryer, have more recently expressed reservations about arranged marriages involving partners from the Indian subcontinent.

[25] However, Fauzia Ahmad (2006) observes within popular discourse a trend for the practices of both arranged and forced marriages to be presented as 'other' and 'traditional' as against 'modern' 'love' marriages.

[26] The Norwegian debate is based upon material from Anja Bredal (2006).

[27] The term *hijab* for headscarf is the most precise term since it makes it possible to differentiate between different forms of headscarves, like the *nijab* and the *burka* (the full veil). It is used by the European Court of Human Rights. In the following we use the English term 'headscarf' for the *hijab*.

[28] §13 in the Amsterdam Treaty forbids discrimination according to gender, 'race', ethnicity, religion, age and disability. The EU in 2000 agreed upon two anti-discrimination Directives: the Directive on Ethnic Equal Treatment (Council Directive 2000/43/EC) and the Directive concerning Discrimination on the Labour Market (Council Directive 2000/78/EC).

[29] In October 2006 Cabinet Minister Jack Straw made a public statement that if a female member of his constituency came to seek advice from him wearing a *niqab*, he would ask her to remove it as it was a barrier to communication. His view was subsequently supported by other members of the Cabinet.

[30] The European Court of Human Rights has, in two decisions (*Dahlab v Switzerland* (2001), on the teacher's right to wear the religious headscarf, and *Sahin v Turkey* (2004-05), on a student's right to wear the headscarf), ruled that such a right to religious manifestation can legitimately be restricted by member states (Skjeie, 2007: forthcoming).

[31] In a court case in Britain in March 2006, the court accepted the school's right to require a dress code against a girl who wanted to

wear a *nijab* for religious reasons (*The Guardian*, 23 March 2006). In October 2006, a British Muslim teacher who refused to remove her *niqab* in a primary school when male colleagues were present lost her discrimination test case against Kirklees Education Authority but won £1,100 for victimisation in the way the dispute was handled (*The Guardian*, 20 October 2006).

[32] www.elpais.es

FOUR

Gendered citizenship: the care of young children

Introduction

Since the 1990s, Western Europe has experienced a remarkable shift in political thinking about childcare. A profound politicisation of the relationship between the state and the family has generated renegotiations of the boundaries between public and private responsibilities in the care of young children. Parenting norms, parental responsibilities and relations are changing rapidly in many regions, while families and households are no longer expected to take full responsibility for the care of their children under school age. Policies aimed at reconciling paid work and childcare are accelerating these processes. With a special interest in the transformation of childcare – from private to shared collective responsibility and, in some welfare states, to a social right – this chapter takes as its starting point those policy shifts which are redefining access to various forms of childcare services and benefits as a social right of parents and children.

Within the European Union (EU) there is political agreement that childcare policies are essential in reducing gender inequalities and in changing the gendered nature of social and economic citizenship. This is most clearly evident in the Parental Leave Directive of 1996, the Recommendation on Childcare of 1992 and the targets set for the provision of childcare services at the European Council meeting in Barcelona in 2002. In fact, legislation and policy recommendations have redefined the young child's need for care as a responsibility of both the state *and* parents. Childcare policy reform has broadened the platform from which parents are entitled to make claims on the welfare state. The elaboration of public policies for the early childhood years is affecting the institutional arrangement between welfare states, families and labour markets, while childcare-related policies have added to the social and economic rights of mothers and fathers (Leira, 2002).

The transformation of childcare policies in Western Europe stands in stark contrast to the policy reforms since the early 1990s in those

Central and Eastern European welfare states known in the 1970s and 1980s for their massive public investments in provisions for preschoolers (see Kamerman and Kahn, 1978, 1991; UNICEF, 1999; Heinen and Portet, 2004). Since the 1990s, the dramatic decline in the public provision of childcare services and benefits has meant a shrinking of the childcare-related social and economic rights of parents. The following analysis of national policy reforms covers Denmark, Finland, France, Germany, the Netherlands, Norway, Spain, Sweden and the UK. With regard to Central and Eastern European countries, we refer only to specific aspects of the changes taking place.

In Western Europe, the pros and cons of increased welfare state responsibility for childcare have been debated, from different points of view, by parents, professionals, voluntary organisations, social partners and political parties, with various constellations of actors being important in different countries at different times. In all countries, increasing ethnic diversity and multiculturalism have revived the analysis of structures of class, gender, ethnicity and social rights. Generally, family and demographic changes have been important 'driving forces' in policy reform; in several countries an expansion of public involvement is considered part of population policy, triggered, for example, by declining birth-rates. Throughout Western Europe the rise in mothers' employment and dual-earner families, the growth in lone-parent families, often mother-headed, and the shrinking of informal care resources all generate a rising demand for extra-parental care arrangements. In the UK, one of the pressures behind recent policy change has been an attempt to increase the productivity of parents and to get single parents, in particular, off welfare and into work (Williams, 2004b).

In many countries, childcare policies are considered to be a means of furthering the social integration, participation and belonging of migrant children and children from different ethnic backgrounds. Childcare policy reform has also been advocated as beneficial to the development of young children and, more generally, as an instrument for reducing social inequalities among children. In recent years, growing state involvement in the early childhood years has been presented as an investment for the future and as in the interests of the whole of society (for example Esping-Andersen, 2002b).

Although EU work/family policy has set some common standards, it has to be borne in mind that the processes through which childcare is becoming a social right of parents and children take place within different national contexts; they are influenced by different political histories, with very different timescales, and are at very different stages.

National policy packages vary in, for example, the emphasis they put on mothers and fathers as workers and/or carers, as discussed further below. However, in some countries such as the UK, as a result of legislative changes and increased public involvement in different areas of childcare policy, the formal childcare-related social rights of the parents of young children have been strengthened. In other countries, such as Germany and Spain, wide-ranging policy reforms were being set in train by 2005 and early 2006.

Childcare policies are also influenced by different national and cultural models of motherhood, fatherhood and childhood. They may be considered as part of family policies, gender equality policies, labour market policies or all of these. In the following analysis of the childcare 'policy packages' of the nine countries mentioned above, we examine the reconceptualisation of traditional parental responsibilities, namely, economic provision (earning for short) and caring, nurturing and early socialisation (caring for short). Three sets of public policies are paramount in articulating the changes in the care-related social rights of parents of preschoolers in Western Europe:

- the institution of parental leave;
- the expansion of childcare services (sometimes referred to as early childhood education and care); and
- various cash benefits for childcare.

These policies are generally interpreted as assisting different family and parenthood models (Leira, 2002). *Parental leave* schemes support the mother or father as carer while *childcare services* support the mother or father as earner. In combination, these policies assist the parent who is both earner and carer in lone-parent families and in dual-earner, care-sharing families. The granting of *cash for parental care* generally presumes an economic provider who is not the carer, and is often interpreted as support for families adopting a more traditionally gendered division of labour.

In this chapter, 'citizenship' is understood conventionally as the relationship between the state and the individual parent-citizen (see also Part One of this book). 'Childcare-related social rights' refer to state-guaranteed welfare benefits and services. In focusing on national policy change, less attention is paid here to how individual parents experience, respond to or make use of childcare-related social rights in various countries (but see Chapter Five for a discussion of some of these aspects). The term 'parent' is used for an adult female or male who has parental responsibility for a child. The analysis of 'gender' is linked primarily to the discussion of the care-related social rights established for parents, and the different take-up and use of these entitlements among mothers and fathers. We include policies aimed at age groups 0 to 2 years and 3 years to school age (noting that age of school entry varies considerably across Europe). Public support of various forms of childcare has also recently been presented as the entitlement or right of children. While very important, this is referred to below but not examined in detail.

The remainder of the chapter, first, outlines the central theoretical perspectives on childcare, gender and social citizenship, and presents a framework for discussing childcare as a social right of parents. Second, we describe and compare the main components of the childcare policy packages of the nine European welfare states and briefly outline parents' take-up and use of the childcare-related rights available. Finally, in the conclusion, we return to the development of childcare-related social rights and their importance for the gendered differentiation of access to social and economic citizenship.

Childcare, gender and citizenship: theoretical perspectives

In the analysis of childcare, gender and citizenship, two theoretical approaches are of special importance: one examines the construction of *citizen as carer*, the other is represented in analyses of welfare states as *care regimes*. Both approaches reflect the necessity to link the citizenship discourse with the analysis of the gendered division of paid and unpaid work and care in society. Hence, both complement and correct mainstream welfare state research (for example Esping-Andersen, 1999; Korpi, 2000) in which unpaid care and the situation of carers have long been neglected. Feminist scholars have taken different stances when it comes to the question of childcare-related social rights. While some have advocated 'maternal thinking' and have come close to seeing the capability for childcare (and other forms of care) as an inherent female attribute, others have argued that capability for care-giving is a potential moral responsibility of all human beings.

Citizen as carer: childcare and citizenship

Central to the feminist analysis of citizenship is the theorising of what Carole Pateman (1988) termed 'Wollstonecraft's dilemma': whether women should be granted social and political rights based on their sameness with men or on their difference with respect to biological and social reproduction. (Wollstonecraft (1996/ 1792) tended towards the latter position, whereas Olympe de Gouges – see Chapter One and Gerhard, 2001 – before her argued the former.) More recently, feminist scholars have presented alternative theoretical models through which the masculine language of citizenship should not only be corrected but profoundly reconstructed. Yet, there is no theoretical agreement about the new feminist vocabulary of care and citizenship.

Nancy Fraser (1994) approaches the dilemma by formulating a tripartite access to citizenship. This involves: first, the 'universal breadwinner' model of the citizen, which takes men's working lives as the norm; second, the 'care parity model', which argues for making care 'costless' to the carer by providing care allowances and entitlements to social rights as carers; and third, the 'universal caregiver' model, inspired by Swedish policy statements of the early 1990s, which takes women's life pattern as the norm, and encourages men to take on more of the caring. (This strategy has been pursued in Scandinavia since the 1970s.)

From a perspective different from that of Fraser, European feminist policy research has raised a question about the articulation of care with citizenship (see, for example, Hernes, 1987; Leira, 1992; Knijn and Kremer, 1997; Daly and Lewis, 1998; Leira and Saraceno, 2002; Lister, 2003). The early conceptualisation of both paid and unpaid care for dependent persons as 'work' (but not just as work) (for example Wærness, 1978; Ungerson, 1990) highlighted the working conditions and social rights of unpaid care workers. Social policy analysts examined the basis of women's social rights as mothers, wives, daughters and/or wage-workers. Linking studies of social rights with the gendered division of labour in families opened the way for a consideration of the social rights accruing to mothers and fathers as earners and carers. Simple comparisons served to demonstrate the 'childcare penalties' (such as less income and weaker social rights) suffered by the parent who took up unpaid care for children, while postponing, reducing or terminating paid employment. Empirical research highlighted the gender differences in the access of parents to social and economic rights (for example Siim, 1987; Leira, 1992; Lewis, 1993; Lister, 2003).

Feminists have taken different policy approaches to the Wollstonecraft dilemma, with some arguing for mothers' wages or caring wages. Others have advocated the enhancing of women's rights to economic activity. A third position is taken by those who have promoted a redistribution of both economic and caring responsibilities in the family. (The three positions might perhaps be linked to the 'citizenship family tree', as maternalist, liberal and social democratic: see Introduction and Chapter

One.) The third position has been institutionalised in European parental leave legislation, starting in the Nordic countries in the 1970s. In principle, the EU, as mentioned above, has also endorsed policies that take fathers as well as mothers as capable of being both earners and carers.

However, national policies towards reconciling work and family have been coloured by the family ideologies of different care regimes. For example, in the Nordic countries, where the labour market participation of mothers rose rapidly in the 1960s and the welfare state expanded as 'caring states' (Leira, 1992), or as social service provider states (Siim, 1987; Sipilä, 1997), gender equality policies have promoted a more equal sharing of economic provision and childcare. In other welfare states, such as the UK, Germany, the Netherlands and some of the Southern European countries, up until the 1990s, policies supported family care or, rather, mothers' care, especially for the very young. However, in these countries, too, childcare-related policy reforms of more recent years have supported the reconciliation of work and family as an issue for both parents.

During recent years, demographic change and shortage of care labour have revived a different strand of care research in childcare, that is, as work performed by childminders, nannies and domestic workers, as discussed in Chapter Five. As European populations age and women increasingly join the labour market, the informal care labour reserves are shrinking, and formal services are insufficient to meet demand at affordable costs. Against this background, transnational – even transcontinental – migration into paid care work is becoming a heated policy issue, reopening the debate about remuneration and recognition of informal carers and domestic workers.

Care regimes

A significant amount of feminist research now exists which examines different models of welfare state and care service provision. Helga Maria Hernes (1987) introduced the term 'women-friendly welfare state' to refer to the way in which in the Nordic social democracies the state had assumed wide responsibility for reproductive activities such as the care of children. Mary Ruggie's (1984) comparative work revealed the contrast between Sweden and 'liberal' Britain, where the main responsibility for childcare was down to the family or individuals. Later, Anneli Anttonen and Jorma Sipilä (1996) argued that there were different social care models in Europe, which did not necessarily fit with the welfare regimes identified by Esping-Andersen (1990) in his celebrated study, *The Three Worlds of Welfare Capitalism*. As mentioned in the Introduction, Anttonen and Sipilä (1996) ended up with two distinct models: first, the *Nordic social care regime* with extensive public care services for both children and older people, and high female participation in paid labour; second, the *Southern European family care regime* in the Mediterranean countries, with its limited supply of care services and, in the early 1990s, a low proportion of women active in the labour force. According to the authors, other models were less distinct. In Britain, the state had assumed wide responsibility in health care and some responsibility in elder care, but much less in childcare. Continental Europe could again be split up into two regimes. Belgium and France had an extensive daycare and preschool system, while in Germany and the Netherlands the care of young children was mainly the responsibility of the family. At that time, Belgium and France had higher female labour market participation rates than Germany and the Netherlands, so generous service provision for children was closely related to women's rights as citizen-workers (Anttonen and Sipilä, 1996).

The work of scholars such as Daly (2001a, 2001b) and Bettio and Plantenga (2004) has further developed the care regime approach, consolidating the view that it is possible to identify. European care regimes. This care regime approach serves as a context that helps us in this chapter understand individual countries and their social policy institutions vis-à-vis care-related responsibilities and rights. However, placing European countries in clusters or regimes is more difficult today than it was at the beginning of the 1990s (see Anttonen and Sipilä, 1996). We would argue that in addition to the most distinctive care regimes – those of the Nordic caring states and the Southern European family care model – we can identify regimes that resemble the family care or the caring state regimes, to a greater or lesser degree, depending on the extensiveness of state-subsidised care arrangements and legal family obligations.

Now for the main concern of this chapter: it is clear that childcare is increasingly 'going public' in all Western European countries in the sense that it is leaving the informal and domestic world of the household and family to be managed and produced outside the home publicly by organisations, market and state sectors (see, for example, Bettio and Plantenga, 2004). Furthermore, going public has involved increasing state support for parental leave to care for children at home, and various cash grants and tax credits for childcare. Our intention here is not to present yet another classification of care regimes, but to use the care regime approach to serve as a theoretical framework through which to examine the recent changes in childcare policies in nine European countries and ask whether these countries should now be grouped in a different way. We return to this question in the conclusion.

By the early 2000s, the main issues in childcare research and policy related to three main trends: the redistribution of responsibility between the state and family; the redistribution of economic and caring responsibilities between mothers and fathers; and a transnational redistribution of care work (as discussed in Chapter Five). Each of these has important implications for gendered citizenship.

The welfare state and childcare

On an international scale, only very slowly has acceptance been won for the idea that responsibility for the care of very young children belongs to someone other than a family member, in particular, the mother. However, in many countries, protecting children 'at risk' predates the emergence of the modern welfare state and its childcare regimes: the responsibility for children in poverty and orphans, for example, was early on acknowledged as a matter for public intervention. Gradually since the 1960s and 1970s, and at different paces in different countries, some forms of childcare have come to be defined in terms of individual rights of parents *and* of children. Since the 1990s, these processes have gained ground across Western Europe.

Childcare: parental responsibilities and social rights

The need of a young child for tending, nurturing and everyday care has been – still is – considered to be met by parental responsibility to provide and care. However, childcare policy reforms of the recent past decades have introduced an expansion of welfare state responsibility in the early childhood years. The rise in state involvement has not meant a relinquishing of parental obligations or of the parental mandate with respect to children's upbringing. State subsidies do not mean that the state is the only provider of services and benefit. Childcare remains a responsibility of the individual parent even if parental care is supplemented by a 'collectivisation' of responsibility witnessed in publicly funded services, leave entitlements, subsidies and cash transfers. We are not arguing that state-subsidised care arrangements are necessarily of higher quality than non-subsidised arrangements. What *is* important when the state enters as a 'stakeholder' in childcare, however, is that it provides the possibility for affordability and quality control.

The political history of childcare illustrates what T.H. Marshall (1950) saw as a characteristic of welfare state development, namely the transformation of individual needs into social rights. In the formulation of Knijn and Kremer (1997), the *right to receive care* is a right of the young child, while *the right to give care* is the legal responsibility of the parent (even if not always articulated in the language of rights).

The meaning of state regulation of childcare vis-à-vis the parental mandate for a child's care has been a hot political topic in several countries: how much should or can the state finally regulate family life? Which family models, if any, should the welfare state support, by what means, and why? France and the Nordic countries have a long history of state intervention, while until more recently this has met with opposition in countries such as the Federal Republic of Germany, the Netherlands and the UK. Indeed, political and popular support for the growing state influence in childcare seems to have gathered ground in Western Europe since the early 1990s. In the Nordic countries, argues Leira (2002), childcare previously defined as a family affair now appears as a 'joint venture' between the state and parents. In the UK, too, parenting is projected as a partnership between parents and the state (Williams, 2004b). This all suggests that the processes of childcare 'going public' are at different stages, and follow similar and different trajectories at one and the same time.

Childcare as a right of the child

A different discourse attracting more attention focuses on childcare as a right of the individual child. The right of the child to be cared for by its parents is largely acknowledged in family law and welfare legislation. In some instances, parental leave legislation has been endorsed as being a right of the child *and* the parents, as have cash grants for parental childcare. In a strict sense, Finland is the only EU member state where a child's need for care is translated into a child's individual right to be cared for, either by parents or in state-subsidised daycare. In Sweden and Denmark, access to high-quality, state-subsidised childcare services has for decades been argued as a democratic right of the child and a supplement to parental upbringing. The recent 10-year National Childcare Strategy represents a shift in UK policies, argues Williams (2004c), in that childcare has been made a universal issue, if not a social right, as well as a strategy to fight child poverty. In nearly all European countries, a child's right to early childhood education and care, including preschool, is widely accepted for children over the age of three, often with strong educational motivations (Brannen and Moss, 2002). A number of European countries have established a childcare guarantee. All these developments represent a process through which childcare is becoming a social right of both parents and children much more strongly than earlier in the history of modern welfare states.

For decades, Europeans have argued over the conflicts that might arise from mothers' wish/need for employment and the child's need for care, and whether attending childcare services is good or harmful for young children. We do not argue that state-subsidised childcare services are 'good' per se; we do argue, however, that the experience of high-quality, well-staffed state-subsidised services at affordable prices is to the advantage of many children and their families. In some countries, the institution of cash benefits for parental childcare as an alternative to state-subsidised childcare services has raised the question of potential conflicts between the rights of the child and those of the parents. Financial incentives may keep at home children who could well benefit from attending services, for example by improving their language skills and expanding their opportunities for participation and belonging in society.

Childcare policy reforms: a framework

When does it make sense to speak of childcare as a social right? The childcare policy reforms discussed below include parental leave, childcare services and cash benefits for childcare. To varying extents these policies establish social rights of parents and children. Parental leave legislation institutes legal rights for working parents to give priority to childcare over the demands of their job. Some countries have legislated cash benefits for childcare as entitlements of parents who do not make use of publicly funded childcare services. It might be argued, too, that care-related rights include a right – or an opportunity – *not* to be the perpetual, full-time carer, through, for example, the provision of publicly funded childcare services. In this way, access to high-quality, state-subsidised childcare services, which are universally provided or available on demand and at affordable prices, takes on the character of a social right (Leira, 2002).

Since the 1990s, childcare-related reforms have aimed to support both mothers and fathers as both earners and carers. Policy reforms have therefore facilitated some forms of parental care as well as non-parental care. Parental leave policies support family-based parental care, especially when paid at a generous level, and thus promote '(re)familisation'. Publicly funded childcare services represent 'defamilisation' in the sense of providing extra-family childcare services. Moreover, in combination, both sets of policies facilitate parents' employment ('commodification') and, at the same time, set parents free from full-time employment ('decommodification') (Leira, 2002). Thus, childcare policies may serve to familise or defamilise childcare and to commodify or decommodify the labour of the parents (this is shown schematically in Figure 4.1).

Figure 4.1: Childcare-related rights: impact on parents' labour and care for children

		Care of children	
		Familised	Defamilised
Parents' labour	Commodified	Cash benefit for parental childcare	State-subsidised childcare services Cash benefit for private, extra-parental childcare
	Decommodified	Parental leave	

Source: From Leira (2002, Table 2.1, p 42)

Paid parental leave allows working parents to be full-time carers for an infant child. The parents' labour is decommodified and care is temporarily familised during the leave period. Prolonged leave with a modest or no cash benefit, however, might also lead to permanent refamilisation. Long childcare leave, in particular, can weaken women's position vis-à-vis the labour market. For a parent not previously employed, cash benefits for parental care represent a public payment for and recognition of care of one's own children. The parent's labour is commodified and the benefit supports familised care. In this situation state-subsidised childcare services facilitate the employment of both parents; childcare is defamilised and the labour of the parents is commodified.

Policy packages

We examine here three sets of childcare-related policy measures: (1) leave arrangements for parents (maternity, paternity and parental), (2) state-subsidised/approved childcare service provision for children under school age, and (3) cash benefits for childcare. In so far as these three main fields of childcare policy measures provide social rights for parents and children, they constitute important dimensions of social citizenship.

Within the EU, public responsibility for childcare has increased as a result of policy reforms facilitating the combination of employment of mothers and care for small children. The Maternity Leave Directive (1992) provides paid maternity leave of at least 14 weeks. The Directive on Parental Leave of 1996 stipulates a minimum of three months of unpaid leave for each parent to be used up to a given age of the child (to be defined by the member states). The implementation of EU policies on parental leave has been more successful than that of policies on childcare services. The European Commission Childcare Network in 1986 advocated a Directive on childcare, but it failed (Randall, 2000) and the eventual decision in 1992 was for a weaker policy instrument, a Recommendation. By 2002, the European Council meeting in Barcelona set new targets for childcare provision, with the aim of having by 2010 provisions in place for one in three of all children under the age of three and for 90% of children between three years and mandatory school age.

As Chapter Two explains, European Commission labour market policy has traditionally focused on paid workers and been less attentive to issues concerning care responsibilities. For example, in spite of the fact that in several countries, parents – mainly women – use part-time work as a way to reconcile paid work and childcare responsibilities, the EU Working Time Directive does not mention part-time employment as a strategy for parents to balance wage-earning and caring.[1] In what follows, we focus on those policies that aim to regulate arrangements for paid work and childcare.

European Union work/family policies have set some common standards for childcare policies, although in many countries national legislation actually provides more generous benefits, particularly where there were well-developed leave legislation and publicly funded childcare services in place decades before the EU legislation. However, as we discuss next, national childcare policy packages differ greatly.

Leave arrangements for parents

Parental leave policies guarantee parents the *time* to care for their young children, and, when leave is paid (in most countries at least some part is), *money* to exit from work for a certain period of time. Leave arrangements, as proposed earlier, therefore contribute to processes of decommodification and defamilisation. Leave legislation is particularly important for working mothers and fathers: universal access to leave establishes a right to care for their children, and for children a right to receive parental care. According to Deven and Moss (2002), the member states of the EU are unique because they all provide a statutory right to maternity and parental leave with a job guarantee that parents using these rights can return to the same or at least a similar position at work.

Table 4.1 sums up the main features of maternity, paternity and paternal leave rights in nine European countries in the early 2000s. (Note that reforms are planned in many countries.)

In the nine countries listed in Table 4.1, maternity leave varies between 14 and 52 weeks. Some countries guarantee only the EU minimum. The UK provides an exceptionally long maternity leave, a total of 52 weeks, but most of it is unpaid or is covered by a flat-rate allowance. However, there are plans for the entire 12-month period to be paid. In all other countries, maternity leave is paid leave with a high level of compensation for earnings. Sweden no longer has separate maternity leave; however, a period of 60 days of parental leave is reserved for mothers and 60 for fathers (daddy quota). This change in vocabulary indicates how far the ideology of shared parenthood has become accepted. France offers a longer leave period for mothers with several children. In most countries, mothers are entitled to the leave and benefit only if they are employed (or registered unemployed or students) and/ or are paying social security contributions (Bradshaw and Finch, 2002, p 104). Only Finland, Norway and Sweden pay a minimum benefit, or lump sum, to all mothers/parents on leave. Some countries pay 'maternity allowances' to mothers who are not covered by social insurance schemes. Often, however, these payments are means-tested and the level is not very high. Despite EU legislation, maternity leave arrangements in the nine countries are still rooted in different national models of motherhood and parenthood.

There is much more variation in parental and paternity leave arrangements, with the Nordic countries boasting the longest paid parental leave and also the longest paternity leave periods. In 2006, 'daddy quotas' existed only in Finland, Norway, Sweden and, more recently, Germany. A quota introduced in Denmark was abolished after only a few years. There is no paternity leave in Germany, and in the Netherlands and Spain paternity leave extends to two days. In Germany, an earnings-related parental payment of 67% of full pay for 14 months was introduced with a daddy quota of two months and a maximum of €1,800 per month. In Spain civil servants have recently won a right to 10 days' paternity leave, and a proposal of 10 days' paid paternity leave for *all* fathers is being put to the Parliament as part of

Table 4.1: The duration of maternity, paternity and parental leave and monetary benefits related to leave in nine countries, early 2000s

Country	Type of leave and maximum duration (in weeks, months, days)	Benefits: % of average wage/other benefits paid during leave
Denmark	maternity leave: 18 weeks paternity leave: 2 weeks parental leave: each parent 32 weeks until the child is 9 (the leave period can be extended to 40/46 weeks or to 64 weeks if parents work part time)	100%, maximum €431 per week rate as above rate as above (for 32 weeks to be shared by parents); if the leave period is longer the right to benefit is reduced so that it corresponds to 32 weeks at full rate of benefit
Finland	maternity leave: 18 weeks paternity leave: 18-30 days parental leave: each family 26 weeks + childcare leave until child is 3	66%, or minimum €15. 20 per day for all rate as above rate as above flat-rate benefit payment (universal with an income-tested supplement) until the child is 3 (max €462 per month)
France	maternity leave: 14/24 weeks (3rd child) paternity leave: 11 + 3 days parental leave: each family is entitled to full-time leave for one parent until child is 3	84%-100%, max €2,432 per month paid as above flat-rate benefit payment (the amount and period of payments vary according to the number of children and work history; max €485 a month)
Germany*	maternity leave: 14 weeks no paternity leave (see below) parental leave: 12 months + 2 months for the other parent (daddy quota); 14 months for lone mothers	100% 67%; max €1,800 per month, minimum €300 and flat-rate benefit of €300 for those without an income

Table 4.1: contd.../

Country	Type of leave and maximum duration (in weeks, months, days)	Benefits: % of average wage/other benefits paid during leave
Netherlands	maternity leave: 16 weeks	100% (max €165 per day)
	paternity leave: 2 days (also for partners)	unpaid (in some collective agreements leave is paid)
	parental leave: each parent 3 months (full-time) or 6 months (part-time leave) until the child is 8	rate as above
Norway	parental leave: 54 weeks (3 weeks before delivery and 9 weeks after are reserved for mother and 6 weeks for father(daddy quota) the rest is to be shared)	100% (44 weeks) or 80% (54 weeks), max €42,500 per year
	unpaid childcare leave: 12 months for each parent for child aged 12-36 months	cash benefit paid on condition that children do not use publicly funded daycare
	paternity leave: 2 weeks	unpaid (in some collective agreements leave is paid)
Spain	maternity leave: 16 weeks (6 weeks reserved for the mother; the rest can be shared)	100%, max €2,371 a month
	paternity leave: 2 days	100%
	parental leave: 3 years to be taken by either parent until child is 3	unpaid
Sweden	parental leave: 480 days, 60 reserved for mother and 60 for father (daddy quota)	80%, or minimum €20 per day for the first 390 days, thereafter a flat-rate allowance of €5.7 per day for all
	paternity leave: 10 days (+ see above)	rate as above
UK**	maternity leave: 26 (all) + 26 weeks (for eligible mothers)	90% (first 6 weeks), £106 per week (following 20 weeks), thereafter unpaid
	paternity leave: 2 weeks	flat rate as above
	parental leave: each parent 13 weeks until child is 5	unpaid

Notes: *Before the 2006 reform each family was entitled to full-time leave of 36 months or until the child reached 3 years (12 months could be postponed until the child was 8). The leave period was partly covered by an income-tested flat-rate benefit.

** From April 2007, flat-rate maternity pay is paid for 33 weeks. Further extensions of maternity pay and paternity leave are planned.

Sources: EIRO (2004); Fagan and Hebson (2006); Moss and O'Brien (2006); NOSOSCO (2004, p 46).

the new Law on Gender Equality drafted in 2006. Except for the Nordic countries, parental leave is either unpaid or covered by a low universal or means-tested flat-rate benefit. Finland, France, Norway and Spain represent different care regimes; however, these countries have extended the total leave period to approximately three years but long leaves are usually partly unpaid. Despite the variation in length, payment and flexibility of use, we argue that, through parental and paternity leaves, governments are now promoting the 'caring father' policy, at least symbolically. Many countries are planning to extend the parental or paternity leave period and/or improve the benefit system related to these leaves.

All in all, since the 1990s European countries have become more similar in relation to maternity leave arrangements and more generous in relation to paternity and parental leave benefits, even though there is still much variety in the length and payment of parental and paternity leaves. Importantly, paid leave for parents strengthens the social rights of mothers and fathers as economic providers *and* carers. However, leave legislation represents a complex set of rights. Entitlements are sometimes formulated as individual rights (such as the daddy quota in Sweden or parental leave in the Netherlands) and sometimes they are designed as family rights for families/parents to use at their discretion. Moreover, leave legislation can also include rights to reduced working hours when children are under a certain age.

Previous studies (for example Bruning and Plantenga, 1999; Bettio and Plantenga, 2004) show a huge gender gap in take-up rates in parental leave entitlements: in most countries, 95%-99% are taken up by women. However, where countries provide a separate paternity leave, fathers' take-up rates are relatively high. In 2000, 73% of Swedish fathers took the full 10 days of paternity leave, and roughly 40% of fathers claimed parental leave averaging 27 days in 2002. Of all parental leave days used during that year, fathers took up 16%. In Norway, in 2001, 81% of eligible fathers claimed their four-week non-transferable quota of parental leave, while 13% claimed over four weeks. Experiences from Sweden and Norway (and some other countries) support the notion that non-transferable parental leave is a major incentive for fathers (EIRO, 2004, p 20).

However, in most countries parental leave legislation has not brought about radical change in the division of care between mothers and fathers. In Spain and the UK, for instance, unpaid parental leave does not encourage working parents to take up the opportunity. In the UK in the early 2000s unpaid parental leave was taken up by only 3% of parents (EIRO, 2004, pp 20-21) and by very few fathers. Furthermore, high numbers of fathers taking leave days does not mean that fathers on average are long leave-takers. Even in Norway and Sweden, mothers generally appropriate a much greater share of the leave and often return to part-time work. Nonetheless, in the Nordic countries and elsewhere, it is the high rate of compensation for earnings and job security that makes it much easier to claim these rights.

Despite variations, the main trend in Western Europe is towards longer periods of leave, better benefit systems and less gender-segregated leave arrangements. Different trends can be identified in Central and Eastern Europe, where most governments have greatly reduced public spending. One consequence is that the notion of public care that existed under the communist regime has de facto disappeared from the political agenda. Central and Eastern European countries introduced paid maternity leave very early, and the possibility of returning to the same job after leave was one of the attractions of the communist social protection system. The number of women taking advantage of this possibility greatly decreased when more rigorous rules for re-entry to the labour market were introduced in the 1990s. In Poland, for example, family policy was reformulated in a totally new way with a strong pro-family emphasis with women as primary care-takers (Heinen, 2002; Pascall and Kwak, 2005).

Childcare services

Children are cared for at home by parents and kin; they are also cared for in different daycare institutions, including preschool, and they are cared for by childminders, au pairs, domestic workers and nannies. In this comparison, we only account for formal childcare services, referring to state-subsidised childcare in daycare institutions, preschool and those other childcare arrangements approved and registered by public authorities. Informal care is omitted from the analysis because of the paucity of comparable data. Nevertheless, formal care best illustrates the extent of public responsibility in childcare.

State-subsidised childcare services offer parents – predominantly mothers – opportunities for relief from full-time childcare and thus support the earning rather than the caring aspect of parenthood. The modernisation of motherhood with women taking on a greater wage-earning role in the family has rendered childcare a central political issue in every post-industrial society. However, there are different chronologies for this development: in those countries where mothers went into employment in the 1960s and 1970s (Denmark, Finland, France, Norway and Sweden), extensive state-subsidising of daycare services for children dates back to that time. An overview of childcare provision and maternal employment in nine European countries is presented in Table 4.2.

Welfare state involvement in providing childcare services (often referred to as early childhood education and care) differs greatly among countries in Europe (see also Bettio and Prechal, 1998; Bradshaw and Finch, 2002). Both Kamerman (2000) and Bradshaw and Finch (2002) show a significant difference in childcare provision for children over and for children under three years of age. In Denmark, France, the Netherlands and Spain, preschool or childcare services cover nearly all children in the age group three years and over. In all countries, nearly all children take part in universal preschool education, often publicly funded and delivered, for some period before compulsory school age, which varies from four (the Netherlands) to six/seven years of age in the Nordic countries.

Childcare services for children under the age of three reflect a slightly different developmental pattern. In countries where the educational dimension of childcare has been strong, care of the youngest children has been regarded as the responsibility of families and mothers. The dividing line between care and education has been especially tight in Germany, the Netherlands, Spain and the UK, where daycare service

Table 4.2: Childcare provision in the early 2000s and maternal employment rates in nine European countries, 2002

Country	Proportion of children using childcare services (low, medium, high)[a]		Maternal employment rates (%), age of youngest child (2002)[b]		
	children under 3	children 3 and over	under 3	3 to 5	6 to 14
Denmark	high	high	71	77	79
Finland	medium	medium	32	75	85
France	high	high	66	63	67
Germany	low	high	56	58	64
Netherlands	medium	high	74	68	70
Norway	medium	high	74	81	84
Spain	low	high	52	50	48
Sweden	high	high	73	82	77
UK	medium	high	57	57	67

Notes: [a] The proportion of children under 3 years in formal childcare: low = under 20%, medium = 20%-40% and high = over 40% of the age group in formal childcare. In the 3 and over age group: low = under 60%, medium = 60%-80% and high = over 80% of children in formal childcare. *Source:* Plantenga and Remery, 2005, Table A. 5, p 84.

[b] *Source:* OECD, 2005, Table SS4. 2, p 41; Norway: Centre for Gender Equality, 2001: age groups: under 3: 3-6; 7-10.

provision for the under-threes is low or has risen only recently (as in Spain and the UK). Denmark has the biggest share of children under three years attending state-subsidised childcare (about 60%) in Europe, followed by France and Sweden. However, now different European governments, such as Germany and Spain, have to respond to the new situation of maternal employment by providing more childcare, especially for children under the age of three. In the case of Germany and Spain, they plan to extend service provision in this age group.

The UK is a good example of a country with a childcare policy which has changed profoundly since the late 1990s (Lewis, 2003; Williams, 2005). Earlier, state-subsidised childcare was designed for children at risk, now the focus is on the needs of working parents. Among a number of policy measures adopted to encourage mothers' labour market participation are free part-time nursery care for children aged three to four years and the right to request flexible working hours. (For mothers in the most deprived neighbourhoods, daycare for the under-fours is free under the 'Sure Start' programme.)

Since the early 1990s, significant changes in childcare policy have taken place throughout Europe. In most Western European countries, childcare provision for the under- and over-threes has become both more comprehensive and more generous. Denmark, Finland and Sweden guarantee a childcare place for all children under school age: in Finland, parents and children have an individual right to a state-subsidised childcare place. Germany guarantees a half-day childcare place for children over three; and the UK has introduced a free nursery school place for children aged three and four. Strictly speaking, this childcare guarantee is not a legal right, but it might pave the way for a stronger acknowledgement of childcare as a basic social right of both parents and children.

It can be argued that care regimes have moved from a pattern of difference to one of similarity. In the Nordic countries and France, there are more services available and the state has assumed a wider responsibility in childcare. In all other Western European countries in our study, childcare service provision is on the increase, but it is too early to forecast what the new dividing lines between different care regimes will be. There is currently a great variety of ways in which childcare services meet the needs of working parents. In the Nordic countries, excepting Norway, daycare services for children aged both under and over three years are universally available for all children on a full-time basis. The same holds true in France. At the other end are Germany, the Netherlands and the UK, where early childhood education and care services operate mainly on a half-day basis and/or the preschool is not open every day. In the UK, for instance, in 2004, 97% of three- and four-year-olds took part in nursery education lasting only two-and-a-half hours a day. Thus, universal access to preschool does not mean that childcare needs are fully met. In Central and Eastern Europe, although childcare provision for three- to six-year-olds has held up reasonably well, many services for the under-threes have disappeared and women regret the loss of provision that was available when they were children (Pascall and Kwak, 2005).

If childcare services are to become real social rights, they have to be available for all parents during the time they are working, including evenings and weekends. Moreover, services have to be of high quality if parents are to trust them. It is not enough that governments in different countries are much more willing to invest in children and childcare than before: these investments have to acknowledge the diversified needs of parents and children. It is also important that services are relatively affordable. Universal access as such does not guarantee that all parents can avail themselves of childcare services: at the moment, service fees in Europe vary greatly, with parents paying anything between 0% and 70% of total costs. Hence, from a social rights perspective, there are still considerable problems attached to childcare services even in countries where state responsibility is fairly extensive.

Cash benefits for childcare

We have seen how mothers' entry into paid work has been facilitated by more public childcare facilities or supporting private childcare markets with tax credits and/or cash benefits. Paid parental leave arrangements are important for the working mother, but they also, to varying extents, promote fathercare. The third part of the childcare policy package, that of cash benefits, is much more ambiguous and may support parental as well as non-parental childcare. There are three types we look at here (excluding universal child benefit or family allowance):

- cash benefits (sometimes in the form of tax credits and vouchers) paid to parents to purchase services from for-profit or non-profit service providers (including private childminders);
- financial support from public authorities for employing a childcare worker in their homes;
- benefits paid to encourage parental care of children at home.

The first two types are designed to promote pluralism and consumer choice in service provision. In some countries, for instance the Netherlands, Spain and the UK, privately provided services have been predominant among children under the age of three years. Except for Denmark, Finland and Sweden, all the countries have some sort of tax credit scheme for parents purchasing childcare services at market rates. In the UK, working families within a certain income range can claim an income-related childcare tax credit of up to 80% off the costs of childcare. Included in this are costs for approved child carers, domiciliary workers or nurses from a registered agency who provide care at home (relatives are not included) (Williams, 2005). In Spain, families with three or more children can reduce their social security payments by 45% if they hire a childcarer or domestic worker. In France, there is also a tax-based support system for parents using registered childminders or employing a childcare worker to take care of their children at home. Offering tax credits is a measure taken by governments to discourage families from purchasing unregistered childcare services that might be of low quality and from using grey market labour.

There are also other types of support. In Germany, there are a limited number of subsidies for low-income parents using childcare centres or childminders approved by local authorities; and since 2006 there is a tax credit for all parents of two-thirds of all costs to buy childcare services of up to €4,000 per year. In Denmark, local government can subsidise the purchase of childcare from private providers or parent collectives. In Finland, a private care allowance is paid to all parents of preschool children who want to use private childcare services rather than municipal services. The allowance includes a flat-rate element paid to all parents and an addition paid according to family income, such that in principle all families, regardless of means, can make use of the benefit. In Spain, all working mothers with children under the age of three are entitled to a flat-rate allowance to be used for childcare purposes.

The third set of childcare benefits is based on the assumption that all parents have a right to care for their children and a right to economically secure parenthood irrespective of their position in the labour market. The motive is similar to advocating a basic income or social wage for all. When this focuses on women, it reproduces the discourse about mothers' wages and maternal citizenship that emphasises women's difference as mother-citizens whose care should be remunerated in monetary terms by recognising its social value. Against this background, some countries have introduced cash benefits for parents who take care of their children at home after or during the parental leave. Benefits for parental childcare are often attached to prolonged parental leave: this is the case in Finland, France, and Norway.

Following the paid parental leave in Norway, each of the parents is entitled to one year of unpaid leave. A cash benefit for childcare is instituted for children aged 12–36 months on condition that the child does not attend state-subsidised childcare services (reduced benefits are offered for those using part-time services). The cash benefit for childcare is to be used at the discretion of the parents, in support of either parental or extra-parental childcare.

Finland has the most distinctive cash benefit for childcare system. After parental leave, Finnish parents make a choice between using their individual right to a municipal daycare place and receiving a home-care allowance, which consists of a universal flat-rate element and a means-tested supplement. It is paid to one parent until the child reaches the age of three or attends a municipal daycare institution. Municipalities themselves also pay supplements to encourage parents to stay at home for several months.

In all countries, the majority of recipients of cash benefits for home-based care, offered as parental choice, are mothers. In most countries, students, the unemployed and women with low education or low salary are over-represented. It is important to remember that paid parental leave favours mothers with a regular work history. Mothers who have not yet entered the labour market, or have been long-term unemployed or in education, benefit very little, if at all, from parental leave rights. This is a further reason why alternative support systems have been developed. Also, national governments are worried about declining fertility rates and are trying to encourage women to produce more children and fathers to care more for them. In Germany, for example, the Merkel coalition government has approved a new programme of *Elterngeld* (parent's money) designed to address the low birth rate. This will provide mothers who take time off after childbirth with two-thirds of their take-home pay (up to a maximum of €1,800) for up to 12 months, with an additional two months paid leave for fathers (Caldwell, 2006).

The motives behind these new cash benefits for childcare vary from providing a mother's wage to allowing parental choice. However, parental choice with respect to the take-up of cash benefits has not encouraged fathers to spend more time on childcare. There are also economic reasons: it is cheaper, for example, for governments to pay low cash benefits rather than sponsor childcare services. However, the consequences are to cement gender divisions of labour and class divisions between women.

Conclusion: childcare and the gendering of citizenship

Feminist theorising on citizenship and care has led to a radical redefinition of social rights and social citizenship. The political reconceptualisation of *childcare* as a responsibility of both the welfare state and parents shows the growing importance of care in European thinking about social rights. In focusing on this transformation of childcare – from being a parental responsibility to the basis from which parents can make claims upon the welfare state – we have examined national childcare policy reforms in nine Western European welfare states. In stark contrast to the policy changes taking place in Central and Eastern Europe where generous childcare policy packages have been dismantled, in Western Europe, the main trend has been a strengthening of the formal childcare-related social rights of parents of young children.

Generally speaking, the change in policy approaches to the early childhood years should be interpreted as part of dramatic family and demographic change, labour market restructuring and redesign of the welfare state. In addition, increasingly multiethnic and multicultural societies with disparate demands have put new and more complex demands on the welfare state, and have revived the analysis of structures of class, gender, ethnicity and social rights. European families with young children are becoming increasingly diversified. There is a variety of parental partnerships, such as married parents, cohabiting parents, parents who live apart, parents of different cultural heritages, parents of the same sex, one or more parents, and a mix of reconstituted families with children from different partnerships. The declining birth rates in most European countries may result in new perspectives on childcare and citizenship. In one respect, however, 'the family' is converging through the massive entry of mothers into paid work. The extension of mothers' employment goes beyond the traditional European North/South divide; it has produced a profound transformation in the relations of family, work and care, and generated a rising demand for public policies. That said, it is still the case that national policy approaches to childcare vary widely across Western Europe. Some countries are now in a phase of expansion of childcare services, parental leave and other support systems, while others are in a phase of consolidation and reorganisation.

The gendering of citizenship is related to the renegotiation and redistribution of childcare responsibilities and this is particularly evident in two processes:

- the redistribution of responsibilities for childcare between the state and family, a process in which the public responsibility is increasingly being recognised;
- the renegotiation and redistribution of economic and caring responsibilities between mothers and fathers (or partners), reinterpreting and transcending the naturalisation of mothers as carers and fathers as economic providers.

Each of these processes has important implications for gendered citizenship, which we elaborate below. It should also be noted that the transnational redistribution of care work forces a rethinking of the global distribution of social rights and responsibilities, as discussed in Chapter Five.

Redistribution of responsibility between the state and family: changing care regime constellations?

In Western Europe, childcare is going public in the sense of increasing state involvement with various forms of support for care arrangements. Policy reforms assist in *defamilising* childcare, as illustrated in the expansion of childcare services, and in cash benefits for the purchase of extra-parental care. Public policies also facilitate *(re)familising* care, as witnessed in public regulation and funding of paid parental leave and the institution of cash benefits for parental care.

Increasing public responsibility and a willingness of governments to invest in the early years of childhood are changing the arrangement between welfare states and families. They thus necessitate a reconsideration of care regimes. In some respects, the differences between them are becoming less distinct, and new differences might be emerging (for instance, the extent and importance of migration into paid care work). The criteria for regime formation therefore require re-examination, as does the clustering of welfare states into care regimes. Still, the most distinctive care regimes are those of the Nordic caring state and the Southern European family care model respectively. In addition, based on the analysis of childcare policy packages and mothers' employment we would argue that, depending on the extensiveness of state-subsidised care arrangements and legal family obligations, welfare states do resemble either the family care or the caring state regime to a greater or lesser degree. For instance, a country such as Spain, earlier referred to as representing the family care regime, has seen a huge increase in mothers in employment and children in formal childcare. The Nordic countries, in turn, have consolidated their position as countries with high maternal employment rates and high proportions of children using state-subsidised childcare services. However, this regime too is becoming more diversified; in particular, in the adoption of different policy approaches to cash benefits, representing moves to refamilisation.

Redistribution of economic and caring responsibilities within the family: new models of the citizen carer?

The question of parenthood is a key issue for where gender equality policy meets with family and labour market policies. Childcare-related policy packages have been developed over time, by governments of different political persuasions, and make for different models of parenthood and citizenship. Social rights – in this case care-related social rights – are being extended to parents as citizen breadwinners, to parents as carers and to parents who are carers and breadwinners at the same time. All over Europe, earlier understandings of 'equality' and 'gender' are changing and influencing the policy discourse. Policies first targeted mothers' right to enter employment and only later fathers' right to care. When combined, the two sets of policies (leave policy combined with state-subsidised childcare services) point beyond the gendered divisions of paid work and unpaid care. They enhance, to varying extents, the notion that both parents – fathers as well as mothers – are citizens as both breadwinners and carers. Some countries also provide for a more traditional male breadwinner–female carer family, for example through the institution of cash grants for parental care.

Improving the formal childcare-related rights of parents does not mean that such rights are 'real' or effective in the sense of being universally available. Access to benefits and services may be restricted, for example, by eligibility criteria, availability and affordability. In countries where parental leave is unpaid, take-up and use of the leave is a class question. Where high-quality, state-subsidised childcare services are short in supply, or provided at high parental fees, access is not a real entitlement for parents and children. Moreover, new demands for recognition and belonging advocated by different minorities might lead to new kinds of childcare arrangements.

Especially relevant in the discussion of childcare and the gendering of social citizenship are questions relating to the effectiveness of policies in transcending the gendered division of labour and in 'equalising' the gendered responsibilities of parenthood. Thinking in terms of greater gender equality of participation in both paid work and childcare, it is important to observe that childcare-related policies may serve to reproduce, as well as to challenge, traditional gender divisions of breadwinning and caring responsibilities. Policies may also increase or reduce differences among mothers and among fathers. Mothers and fathers of different socio-economic, cultural and ethnic backgrounds may respond differently to the childcare-related rights available. The models of motherhood, fatherhood and parenthood preferred by mothers and fathers may not be the ones projected by policies to reconcile work and family. This again raises anew the question about which – if any – family forms the welfare state should support, by which means and why. These models are also closely linked to women's position as paid care workers, where most care workers are today still women.

Traditionally, and as overwhelmingly documented, responsibility for the provision of care for young children has been the responsibility of the family, and particularly the mother. This continues to render mothers less attractive as paid labour. For mothers, children may come to represent a 'cost', sometimes termed the 'childcare penalty', with the consequence of reduced income and weaker social rights over the life course. The institution of cash grants for parental childcare – used mainly by mothers only – does not really address the long-term social and economic costs of being the primary carer parent.

Mothers' entry into the labour market means increasing economic independence and protection from the risks of poverty that many – especially lone mothers – face. In addition, mothers gain access to employment-related social rights, and opportunities for participation and belonging in arenas beyond the family. Childcare policies also promote the carer aspects of parenthood in legislation on maternity, paternity and parental leave. Establishing a right for fathers to care, parental leave legislation is an innovative approach to challenge the tradition-bound gendered division of caring. The main trend in Western European policies is towards longer periods of leave, better benefit systems and less segregated gender arrangements. Several countries report more fathers making some use of the leave entitlement, particularly where there is a 'daddy quota', and also taking a bigger role in childcare and domestic work.

Nevertheless, in the practices of everyday life, changes in motherhood models have been far more profound than changes in fatherhood. Fathers are greatly underrepresented in the care of their own children, even though some change among fathers can be documented, for example in the Netherlands and the Nordic countries. However, the legislation offers many more opportunities for care sharing than are actually adopted. As citizen-earners, mothers and fathers are becoming more equal; as citizen-carers, the inequality remains pronounced. How to 'equalise' the social and economic rights of women and men as parents (and bearing in mind the interests of the child) remains a challenge for welfare states.

Recent policy reforms also demonstrate that the care of young children has become a very central issue in the social policies of Western Europe. Due largely to the rising employment of women there is now a widely shared political interest in facilitating the reconciliation of work and family. This situation creates a strong political platform for parents and other advocates of care-related social rights to make claims for better services and benefits. However, in parts of the population, so-called traditional family values remain strong. Yet new kinds of resistance and opposition might emerge, if all parents are expected to be full-time workers. In the early 2000s, it might still be the case that mothers' right to work is predominating in Southern Europe, while fathers' right to care is more to the forefront in the policies of the Nordic countries. The expansion of formal childcare-related social rights also shows new models of the citizen-parent emerging, although at different times in different countries. Increasingly, in most countries, legislation on leave and public sponsoring of childcare and preschool services do facilitate, to varying degrees, a new model of the citizen-parent, namely mothers and fathers who both combine both breadwinning and caring, even if, in practice, the division of responsibilities is still skewed. In some respects, national policies for reconciling paid work and childcare have become more common and more alike, in other respects more complex and differentiated, pointing to new configurations of welfare state caring regimes.

One aspect of this complexity, which contributes to new configurations, is the extent to which these regimes are drawing on migrant labour to solve their childcare needs. This is the subject of the following chapter.

Note

[1] The Directive lays down minimum safety and health requirements for the organisation of working time with full-time work as the norm. Part-time work has been looked upon as atypical. Increasingly in Europe, part-time work has led to difficulties in accommodating the relationship between family, welfare state and labour market. Definitions of and norms for part-time work vary across countries. In some countries, such as Sweden, 'long hours' part-time work has long been integrated into labour market policy, while in other countries, such as

the UK, 'short hours' part-time work has been an enduring feature of women's employment, but has been one of the main ways mothers have increased their economic activity in recent years. Problems relating to this are that part-time work is mainly women's domain with the service sector having the highest proportion of part-time workers. Discrimination in terms of pay and conditions is common. Until recently, many part-time workers did not have access to many of the statutory rights available to other employees, although now collective agreements are beginning to appear. Nevertheless, people on short part-time hours continue to have less access than full-timers to employment-related benefits, such as holidays and sick leave, and are less likely to be offered training and promotion. See www.eiro.eurofound.eu.int/2004/03/study/index_2.html

FIVE

Gendered citizenship and home-based childcare: transnational dynamics

Introduction

The previous chapters have examined changes in the perception and application of citizenship rights in relation to childcare provision and to migration and asylum. This chapter looks at what Chapter Four called the 'transnational redistribution of care work' – the ways migration and childcare intersect in the case of the private employment of migrant women as domestic and childcare workers in European households. This phenomenon has been referred to as 'the global care chain' (Ehrenreich and Hochschild, 2003) where women from poorer regions of the world migrate to care for the children and households of employed women in the West in order to support their own children who they leave in the care of female relatives in their countries of origin. Research on the care chain in Europe has exposed the highly oppressive nature of such work and the ways in which migration rules and regimes render women vulnerable, through lack of citizenship status, to work in the underpaid and undervalued grey economy of household labour (Phizacklea, 1998; Anderson, 2000; Kofman et al, 2000; Lutz, 2002; Cox, 2006). The chapter draws on empirical qualitative research in the UK, Spain and Sweden with both employers of migrant domestic/care workers and migrant women who carry out such work. While it reinforces some of the findings of research on domestic service, it seeks to focus more on the demand for childcare services and contextualise this in terms of wider social and policy changes. The chapter starts by looking at this context and outlines the many different and complexly connected dimensions of citizenship it invokes.

Domestic work is both a new and an old phenomenon. While such work had been commonplace in bourgeois homes in Europe up until the 1960s, it fell away with the mass use of domestic technology, with the increase of alternative work in the industrial and service sectors, as well as, in the Nordic social democratic countries, a repudiation on egalitarian grounds of the very idea of employing others to provide 'service'. By the 1990s it became evident in Western and Southern Europe that the demand for such work was on the increase again (for Britain, see Gregson and Lowe, 1994), and in the major cities it was in part migrant women from the poorer regions of the world who were meeting this demand (Anderson, 1997).

Migration into domestic and care work, and the employment of migrant workers, reveal the interconnections between policies and social changes happening at local, national, international and global levels (Williams, 2004a). There are three key dimensions of this that are relevant for this chapter: the changing regimes in different countries of welfare, of care and of migration, each of which involves different histories, policies, cultures and practices, combined with the international restructuring of labour markets and economies. These also contribute to the gendering of formal citizenship rights as well as the lived experience of citizenship (see Chapter One). First, as explained in the Introduction, changes in *welfare state regimes* in Europe have involved the replacement of the male breadwinner model with the 'adult-worker model' – or variations on this theme – where policies assume women's involvement in the labour market. In its turn, the increase in women's economic activity has created particular pressures to balance work and care responsibilities. For some women in some countries one strategy is to buy in services to cover care and household tasks (this includes all forms of household work, not only childcare and domestic cleaning, but elder care, home maintenance, gardening and catering too – Cancedda, 2001; Ungerson, 2003).

Second, the extent to which women in the West might do this further depends upon the nature of *care regimes*, that is, the different policy responses of countries to the need for childcare (and also for care of older people and disabled people – see Anttonen and Sipilä, 1996). This was the focus of discussion in Chapter Four, where it was noted that one important shift in a number of European countries has been the increasing provision of cash payments, tax credits or tax incentives to pay childminders, relatives, parents or domestic helps, for their services. In relation to child-related care, Britain, Finland, France, Italy and Spain have all introduced some form of cash provision to buy in help. These care regimes coexist with different 'care cultures' – practices and values about how best to combine work and care of children, such as full-time mothering, or surrogate mothering, intergenerational care, shared parental care, or professional daycare (see Duncan and Edwards, 1999; Kremer, 2002). However, how work and care are combined also depends upon the reach of family-friendly policies, and attempts to alter the gendered division of care and work within the home.

The lack of such policies is just as relevant for the countries from which migrant women come. Destruction of local economies, unemployment and poverty in many countries of Asia, South America and Africa have placed a growing pressure on women to assume the breadwinner role. The demand for women's work in both the formal and informal health and care sectors of the West means that it is women who increasingly take the initiative to migrate and send money back home to their family.[1] *Within* Europe, European Union (EU) enlargement, war and the effects of changes in Central and Eastern Europe on women's economic opportunities have also led to an increase in migration of women to Western Europe in search of work. How far this domestic and care work might be carried out by migrant workers in different countries further depends upon the third dimension in this analysis – *migration regimes* (see Chapter Three). These include the rules and regulations attending the movement of people into work, such as quotas for domestic workers and special entry permits for au pairs, working tourists or students. Cultures and practices around migration also have a bearing: the ways in which old trade links, colonialism, religious movements and refugee flights have carved historical migration paths across the world.

The intersection of the regimes of welfare, care and migration, along with the cultural practices associated with them, frame the different dimensions of citizenship caught up in this phenomenon. To begin with, the problem of the public–private dichotomy, which lies at the heart of the gendered critique of citizenship (see Lister, 2003), reveals itself in at least four ways. First, the strategy of employing domestic/ care labour in the home is an attempt to minimise the constraints attached to participating fully in the public sphere of paid work. However, it is a strategy that effectively collapses the public into the private, where home becomes work and work becomes home. As such, it generates a range of difficulties, not least because the home is not covered by the same employment protections afforded to the workplace. Second, the fact that the work also involves *affective* relations usually associated with close relationships also intensifies the confusion as to whether work practices are based upon informal obligation or upon contractual rights. Third, for the employees, this is further exacerbated by the fact that their migration status – for example, where they are waiting for visas, or where they have no recourse to public funds – makes them dependent upon an individual employer rather than able to sell their labour freely. Fourth, home-based work isolates the worker, makes the work invisible, and renders forms of collective mobilisation for rights more difficult.

Of course, both employers and employees who have children share the same problem of how to balance their care and work responsibilities. While the employee might exercise her rights to mobility, she may, at the same time, forfeit her own and her children's rights to family reunion, and the opportunity to see her children grow up, notwithstanding the efforts she will make to keep up contact and to ensure their care through a surrogate. At a wider level, trends in migration regimes also reveal new patterns of inclusion/exclusion. Changing boundaries of the EU, while effectively drawing a line between who is and who is not included as an EU citizen, coexist with rules in which skilled workers increasingly accrue more rights. These patterns are cut across by differences of employment: employees may provide housework or childcare or both; they may live in or live out; they may work a few or very long hours; they may be qualified yet designated as 'unskilled';[2] they may be a carer, cleaner or personal assistant for an older, frail person or a disabled person; they may be self-employed, or 'undeclared' or work for a private agency or local authority. As migrant workers, they may be working under a special permit or they may be undocumented. These differences are overlaid, as the case studies show, with racialised, ethnic or national stereotypes, which permeate the employment of these workers, giving them greater or lesser access to different types of work and payments.

The three case studies: Britain, Spain and Sweden

These three countries afford interesting comparison, not simply because they belong to three contrasting care regime types (see Table 4.2 in Chapter Four), but, as the case studies will show, because of differences in their histories, policies and practices for childcare, in female employment, and in practices of employing migrant workers as care workers and domestic workers in the home. As such, this brings a new dimension to the discussion in Chapter Four on types of care regimes. In Sweden, a social democratic women-friendly state, the employment of care and domestic workers in the home, whether migrant or home state, is the subject of intense *moral* disapproval; Spain, with rapid recent female employment, less available childcare provision but a subsidy for working mothers, has an explicit migration policy that favours such employment and an implicit normalisation of the practice for many working mothers. Britain, often labelled a 'liberal' welfare state, but in practice often mixing liberalism with elements of social democracy, lies somewhere in between, with a shift towards more available childcare in the mixed economy of care, childcare tax credits, a growing practice among middle-class dual-earning households favouring the buying in of care and domestic help, and migration policies that indirectly meet this demand. Reflecting these differences, Organisation for Economic Co-operation and Development (OECD) figures for the employment of 'foreigners' by sector in 2001-02 show that employment in households was 14.8% in Spain, 1.3% in the UK and statistically insignificant in Sweden (OECD, 2003). The case studies first contextualise their empirical data in terms of the different care and migration policies in Britain, Spain and Sweden; they then address the following issues: the employees' experience of migration; the reasons employers give for using this sort of care support; the relationship between employers and employees; and, where they have them, the employees' relationship with their own children.[3]

Migration and the commodification of childcare in Britain

Historically, Britain's post-war welfare state was built around a 'strong' male breadwinner model. However, by 2002, 69.6% of women aged 15-64 were in paid employment, although 60% of women with dependent children worked part time (Duffield, 2002). As discussed in Chapter Four, the New Labour administration has moved away from this model in terms of the acceptance and encouragement of women's employment, as well as the acknowledgement of the need for state childcare support, albeit mainly through the mixed economy with improvements in maternity entitlements, paternity leave and flexible working. Working families can claim an income-related childcare tax credit of up to 80% off the costs of childcare, and, interestingly, in 2005 this was extended to approved home-based nannies.[4] It does not include relatives. This is significant because in terms of childcare culture and practices, many women, especially working-class women, tend to work part time and to use informal care, particularly grandmothers or partners. Care work is generally low paid and there is a shortage of workers in this area. Figures show that all formal childcare use has been increasing, and by 2003 1.5% of working parents employed registered nannies/au pairs (Brewer and Shaw, 2004). The professional press (*Professional Nanny* and *Nursery and Childcare Market News*) claim that up to 25% increases in the average wages of nannies since 2005 reflect increased demand for their services.

A survey in the late 1990s showed, interestingly, that around 20% of mothers would ideally choose a daily or live-in nanny from the formal childcare options (Bryson et al, 2000, pp 90-4). A combination of the tradition of mother substitute preference, the increased use of unregulated paid domestic help in the home,[5] the positioning of mothers as consumers of services, and the reliance on the (expensive) private market and voluntary and informal sectors create in Britain the cultural and material conditions for the moral acceptance of the private employment of childcare workers in the home.

Immigration policies and migration paths are framed by Britain's imperial history and present EU enlargement. The current policy of 'managed migration' tends to differentiate between migrants more clearly in terms of skills, with greater rights for the greater skilled (Kofman et al, 2005). Crawley (2002) estimated 14,300 foreign domestic workers in the UK in 2000, mainly living out. The UK does not have a quota for domestic workers, but residents of EU member states are free to enter the UK as au pairs and there is an arrangement with the EU candidate countries (Bulgaria, Croatia, Romania and Turkey) along with Andorra, Bosnia-Herzegovina, Faroe Islands, Greenland, Macedonia, Monaco and San Marino for women aged 17-27 to become 'au pairs' to sponsoring families for two years as long as they do not have recourse to public funds[6] and for domestic workers who are accompanying named foreign nationals entering the UK. In addition, working holidaymakers between 17 and 30 years, who are citizens from the new Commonwealth, may enter the UK without an entry clearance.

Different migration paths and work experiences

Reflecting these migration rules, the research in London found that the most common types of migrant domestic/care workers were au pairs from Europe, particularly Central and Eastern European countries, domestic workers from non-EU countries, such as India, the Philippines and Sri Lanka, and nannies from Australia, New Zealand and South Africa. Domestic workers often came to Britain with their employer families and worked to support families back home because their earning potential was better than their male partners'. Au pairs saw the work as a stepping stone to learn English and move on into better work that meant they could live out. Some moved across different visa types (working holidaymaker to au pair). At the same time, migration often involved a step back. Ivana, a nanny and ex-au pair, was typical of this:

'I was a teacher of French and German in Romania. Now I'm back to zero being a servant. I came here because I thought I'd have an opportunity to find something else here after two years. Even as an au pair I'm paid better than as a teacher in Romania. I want to take a class and become a teacher in the UK.'

Generally, nannies saw themselves as childcare professionals who might move to a related profession or set up their own au pair/nanny business.

Insecurity of citizenship status, newness to the country, lack of regulation and lack of language skills placed all types of worker in a vulnerable situation, both when they first arrived and if they were trying to renew their visa, and all interviewees recounted stories of exploitation in their work. Those who had had satisfactory work placements regarded themselves as lucky. Domestic workers, who have to apply annually for a visa but after four years can apply for indefinite leave to remain with the prospect of better work, told of employers who illegally confiscated their passports so that they could not leave. This was compounded by the 'flexibility' of job descriptions where live-in au pairs and domestic workers would find themselves responsible for cleaning, cooking and childcare and almost permanently 'on call'. Even though agencies exist to set up employers and employees, many workers did not have, or see, formal contracts, so agreements around hours and pay could easily be reneged on. The household remains exempt from much employee protection including the 1976 Race Relations Act, and one agency interviewed estimated that over 90% of childcare and domestic work operated through the grey economy.

In May 2004, EU enlargement opened up migration from Central and Eastern Europe and paradoxically this may render those new migrants *more* vulnerable because they enter independently and set up their own employment placements. As one nanny/au pair agency manager said:

'This has changed the nanny world: they are willing to combine childcare with domestic work. The term nanny used to refer to a qualified childcarer, but it doesn't mean anything now. Girls come over as au pairs and stay. Now employers can get childcare and cleaning for less than £9 per hour – they love it!'

This was reflected by Carrie, an Australian nanny whose employer sacked both her and their cleaner, replacing them with

> 'someone to do all the cleaning and the nannying [and] she was living in the house as well, which meant she was working seven till seven and she was only being paid £200 a week I found out later whereas they were paying me £375 a week and their cleaner £240 a week.'

A further difference is the emergence of the male au pair, hired by mothers for sons or where there is no other male figure around. Many of the employees and employers interviewed had used or knew male au pairs who usually commanded higher wages than the women. Overall differences in rates of pay were further compounded by national/ethnic hierarchies often based upon racialised stereotypes. This is illustrated by Jennie, a Slovakian au pair:

> '... my friend was working for one family, she was from Slovakia and she was getting quite good money, she had about £60 a week. She worked about 30 hours or something like that, babysit twice a week and she asked me if I knew someone who could exchange with her and I knew about one girl who was looking for a job but she was from Thailand; she was a lovely girl and I brought her there for an interview and this lady required her to work 40 hours a week, do four babysitting [hours] a week for £45 and I said, like are you kidding me? Is that just because that person's from Thailand and that person was from Slovakia?'

One agency in London reported that employers' requests were based on national preferences with Filipinas at the top ('people think that Filipinas are from a different planet where everybody cares about children') and Africans at the bottom. Some employers felt that Latin Americans were more loving and expressive and Eastern Europeans more hard working, while Australians were seen as cheerful and flexible.

In terms of making claims to rights, domestic workers in Britain have important collective representation through the organisation Kalayaan. It lobbied, for example, for the rights of domestic workers to change employers, to renew their visas and apply for indefinite leave to remain and family reunification after four years. These were important in providing protection from abusive or exploitative employers. Nannies have PANN – the Professional Association of Nursery Nurses, which recently joined forces with the Association of Nanny Agencies to lobby for improved regulation and monitoring of agencies. However, in relation to domestic workers, recent proposals by the British government to 'control the borders' and restrict unskilled migrants' rights to renew employment visas, look set to undermine these hard-won rights.[7]

The employers' reasons for using migrant carers

When couples employed childcare workers in their homes, it was usually the mothers who managed the day-to-day negotiations with their childcarers and cleaners. The majority of the mothers interviewed were in employment, usually in full-time, traditionally male-dominated professions – accountancy, law, medicine, business – with partners often in similar fields. Employing care workers in the home was common among the networks and in the neighbourhoods where they lived; they passed au pairs on to families they knew from their children's schools, for example. While these households were relatively better off, their reasons were expressed as less to do with status or leisure and more about 'coping' or managing time and the stress of competing pressures: 'I get no more free time. We have a nanny 8 to 6pm, which is when I get home. I get time to change my clothes from work' (Cecile).

Nannies were often used for children under the age of two and mothers would move on to an au pair once the children started going to school or to preschool. Most of the London mothers interviewed had no available family support, but they preferred one-to-one care for young children for both practical and emotional reasons. This was seen as even more important when there was more than one child, as one child might be at nursery and another at home so there was all the collecting and dropping off to do, usually within working hours (see Skinner, 2005, on the spatial dimensions of childcare). For the most part, the workers were just one of the resources that were used for childcare, albeit a pivotal one.

There was also a concern to give children (and husbands) 'quality time': 'you're able to give the children a bit more individual attention rather than just being with three small ones all the time and feeding the baby' (Celine). Mothers also constructed this in terms of their own needs for self-esteem and contrasted the care qualities they and their employee could offer their children:

> 'They [mothers] might be very very good lawyers and they might be good at quality time at the weekend, but they know that during the week their nanny is probably going

to do many more activities than they would if they were looking after their children.' (Adrienne)

They similarly differentiated themselves from full-time mothers who they knew. Having a nanny/au pair was also seen as making children less 'clingy' and helping to prepare them for nursery.

Having a nanny/au pair from a different culture was also seen as educational for the children. This appreciation of cultural diversity co-existed in employers' accounts with the sorts of national stereotypes identified above, but, at the same time, some mothers rejected the idea of nationality as a basis of choice and spoke more in terms of age, skills and disposition, although class/educational background was sometimes implicit in these descriptions. Some of those mothers who came from minority ethnic groups preferred workers who shared their language or culture, and one mother with a mixed-race son spoke of her anxiety about racism in care and educational institutions. When it came to the issue of costs for care, those employing nannies felt that there was little saving as compared with a private nursery. However, those employing au pairs or domestic workers were very aware of the financial benefits of this option: 'some au pairs are very very good value for money but that makes me uncomfortable – the whole white slave trade thing' (Adrienne).[8]

The employer–employee relationship

A central tension in the employer–employee relationship was the dovetailing of private and public – home as a place of work, care as informal and intimate against care as paid work, sharing living space with your employers. These ambivalences in the family/work nexus created problems of boundaries for both employees and employers. The latter talked a great deal about the need to treat their employees properly, but also were aware of the difficulties:

> 'There's this big thing where they should be part of your family but they're just not, but you can't treat them like they are an employee because they're around when they're not working so I suppose I'd treat them with friendliness.' (Susanne)

It was cheaper to have a live-in au pair, but this involved an invasion of privacy and a lot of effort in keeping everyone happy ('Family relations take more effort' – Karen). In an attempt to keep hold of privacy, some mothers maintained more distant professional relationships, likening them to their employees at work. There was also an acute awareness of the need to recast the relationship away from traditional servitude. While employees defined their role in occupational terms ('nanny' and so on), mothers referred in public to their employees as 'help' or 'helper' to avoid this traditional connotation, and they insisted they used first names for each other. 'She feels uncomfortable about me saying to people that I'm her nanny, I'm just a friend who helps out kind of thing' (Carrie).

Employees had a different take on these matters. Many felt informality could be disempowering and struggled to maintain 'professional' distance. Others, especially those more dependent on their employers, felt an employer's distance to be demeaning. Either way, all expressed the need for trust and respect, which they felt had been lacking in many of their work placements. Ultimately, however, the balance of power lay in their care for their employer's child: 'It's like if you don't treat the children nicely then the family don't treat you nicely so it's like equal' (Johanna). Employees could invert this, too, by demonstrating greater understanding of the child in their care than the mother. Privately many held a moral high ground and felt it was wrong to leave a child with another person: 'I wouldn't want somebody else picking up my child's mess. I know I'm a nanny but I don't agree with having a nanny' (Lena).

The employees' own family and childcare cultures

The nannies and au pairs interviewed did not have children, but the domestic workers who did, left their children in their countries of origin, visiting them once every one or two years. What was interesting, however, was how 'being a good mother' meant different things for the different employees and the employers. For the domestic workers, being a good mother meant being a good provider, working to send money home so that their children might have better education. By contrast, many employers felt they were doing the right thing by going out to work, maintaining their self-esteem and being able to give their children 'quality time'; yet some of them disapproved of mothers who left their children behind in their country of origin. However, many of the nannies and au pairs tended to hold traditional ideas about the needs of young children for their mothers and, as mentioned above, privately disapproved of their employers' leaving their children in someone else's care. So while all these women shared the need to work and to fulfil their care responsibilities, they were divided not just by employer/employee status, and different positionings in relation to 'race', nationality and associated life chances, but also by their different views about what, in their circumstances, is right for children.

Immigration as a key resource for Spanish working mothers

Spain has been for centuries a country of emigration, whereas migration to Spain is a new phenomenon that has dramatically increased since 1995. Current data show that the rate of migration to Spain and the numbers of migrants are among the highest in Europe.[9] As with other Mediterranean countries such as Italy or Greece, this has been described as a shift of the 'migration frontier' from the Pyrenees and the Alps in the 1960s to the Mediterranean basin in the 1980s (King and Rybaczuk, 1993). Women no longer migrate for family reunion but, like men, to take up paid work (Izquierdo Escribano, 2000).[10] Similarly, working mothers' economic activity is a new phenomenon that has increased rapidly since the early 1980s. Both trends are related, partly because women immigrants, who represent almost half of the foreign population, have a high activity rate (Instituto Nacional de Estadística, 2003, p 249), partly because their care work is often necessary in dual-earner families.

In the context of few social policies for the reconciliation of work and home, resources for childcare are mainly based on mother substitutes, either grandmothers or paid domestic help. The former are the main resource for the first generation of working mothers and are more of a provisional solution for a transition period (Tobío, 2001), rather than a basic element of the Mediterranean welfare regime as conceptualised by authors such as Langan and Ostner (1991). In the old traditional family it is mothers, not grandmothers, who take care of their children. In this sense the strong mother–daughter relationship as a resource for care is a peculiar form of 'refamilisation' as it is precisely that which enables mothers to be in the labour market. Paid domestic help is another form of substitution of real mothers by other women, in this case based on economic compensation for care work. Maids and other domestic workers were part of middle-class lifestyles until the 1960s when the flow of young women from Spanish rural areas into big cities came to an end. By the end of the century, domestic service reappeared in response to care needs[11] both for children and for older people, as women in the family were rapidly becoming less available for this purpose.

Today among employed mothers some kind of paid domestic help is used in 28% of cases and this increases according to the number of hours mothers work, partnership and socioeconomic status. More than half of working mothers in highly skilled occupations hire domestic help; even 11.5% of those working in low-skilled jobs do so; these are often lone mothers without kinship support (Tobío, 2005, pp 178-9). When asked about the key resource to manage work and family responsibilities, 9% of employed mothers mentioned paid domestic work, compared to 37% who mentioned the family network, and 25% the husband or partner (Tobío, 2005, p 156).

There is a clear coincidence between the timing of Spanish women's involvement in paid work, the appearance of immigrant carers and the acknowledgement of family employment issues[12] as a social problem, beyond a family's private affair. Even if immigration is not explicitly presented as part of reconciliation policies,[13] several indicators suggest that *indirect* state support exists for this kind of childcare resource. These include the relative importance of an immigrant quota for domestic workers, which represents more than half the whole annual quota for all occupations (Secretaría de Estado de Inmigración y Emigración, 2003) and the €100 subsidy per month, which, since 2003, has been available to all working mothers with a child below the age of three.

The experiences of employers and employees discussed below hold a number of things in common. All are mothers, they share a strong involvement in paid work and are generational pioneers, most often the first females in the family to continue working after having children. Being employed is explained in the case of Spanish working mothers by a variety of factors, many of them related to a new desired identity as full citizens, such as through individual economic independence, professional development or fulfilment of personal aims, even though economic necessity for the family remains the main reason for them to have a job (Tobío, 2005, pp 25-41). In the case of migrants, the decision to leave their countries generally has to do with economic difficulties, but moving to a job often widens access to citizenship rights, even though they may be second-class citizens. In spite of both similarities and complementary needs between employers and employees, the specific situation that brings them together places them in opposite positions, in which tension and conflict are not absent.

The migratory project: paths and expectations

Survival is not usually the reason to migrate, even if countries of origin (in this case, Eastern Europe, Latin America and North Africa) are often touched by misery, hunger or insecurity. Those who act on such a decision are seldom in such an extreme situation. Building a future, particularly for their children, is a common theme, as is awareness of migration as the only alternative. Sometimes childbearing is postponed until a stable life is achieved in the new country. Some may plan to stay only a short time and then stay longer because of their own or their family's personal relationships, or simply because they get used to the Spanish way of life. In other cases, it has to do with unfulfilled expectations, such as not having saved enough money to invest back home.

Family and social networks play a crucial role in women's migration, providing information about employment and how to gain entry, generally through the tourist route, although this has lately been restricted for non-European immigrants. Women often come first because of better work opportunities, especially in domestic work, which they hear about through contacts who might even set up a job in advance. Jobs other than domestic service are difficult to find for newcomers in a country with a 14% unemployment rate for women (Instituto Nacional de Estadística, 2005). Demand for this domestic work has increased while the supply of indigenous labour for it has declined. In addition, it is an opaque sector, quite safe for undocumented workers with no residence or work permits. A live-in job allows a newly arrived migrant to adapt progressively, learn the language when necessary and be able to save most of her earnings, as costs for accommodation, food and transportation are minimal. Having settled, a woman might get her own place to live, especially if other members of the family have also migrated. Salaries and working conditions vary considerably, depending on individual negotiations between employer and employee. Their regulation by a specific labour relations norm[14] is much looser than other occupations, for example no written work contract is necessary and there are no unemployment benefits. In spite of this, the law is often bypassed, especially in terms of social security affiliation and number of working hours. Immigrants are often not aware of their rights as workers, nor of how and where to claim them; there are few organisations that advocate or mobilise collectively on this issue.

The cases of Raquel and Olga exemplify the wide variety of situations. The former works from 12am to 8pm six days per week and earns €360 per week. Of Spanish origin – her grandfather came from Asturias – she recently came to Spain from Cuba where she worked as a language teacher after having studied English Philology. While she is preparing her papers and documents to obtain the Spanish nationality to which she is entitled, she lives with relatives and works in cleaning, cooking and taking care of two small children. She knows her salary is ridiculously low, but thinks of her current job as transitional, leaving her free time in the mornings for the long and complicated administrative procedures she has to go through to become a Spanish citizen. Olga comes from Romania. She has been in Spain for five years. During the first couple of years she worked as a live-in maid. Then she changed to a full-time job, 10 hours a day with free weekends. For the last couple of years she has been working for a family with two teenage children, 15 hours per week, three hours per day from Mondays to Fridays, cleaning, cooking and ironing. She earns €350 per month plus social security (€110). In addition she works another 25 hours on a per hour basis (€10) for three other families.

Why do working mothers choose paid domestic help?

For upper-class mothers a full-time maid is the preferred option, possibly combined with other resources such as grandparents and crèches for a few hours to assure an early socialisation of their children. Hired domestic help means these mothers are fully available for their jobs, as men are. Flexibility is key. In addition, transferring practically all domestic tasks and a good deal of care work to another woman eliminates conflicts with husbands over the division of labour in the home. While upper-class working fathers are happy to pay for domestic service, they prefer not to be involved in any way. Pilar, a lawyer with three small children, says:

> 'I think most men do not even notice when the maid changes, they just take her for granted. They do not want to bother about supervising her or knowing anything about her. I look for them, choose them, I decide how much to pay them and tell them what to do and how to do it. My husband does not care.'

Hiring domestic help is quite different for lower middle-class working mothers. Here, it is limited to a small number of hours just to fill in gaps, like those between work and school opening hours, during children's long vacation or when they get ill, when relatives or friends are not available. It carries significant and deeply gendered calculations, often related to the opportunity cost of mothers' earnings and the importance of remaining in employment during those demanding years when children are small. It is a way to cope with the lack of care for the early years, and, as a form of maternal replacement, it is generally paid for out of the mother's wage, rather than the father's.

The employer–employee relationship

Workers are 'other' in different ways. Not just because they come from distant places, speak foreign languages or behave differently but also because of their blurred identities. They are doubles, duplicates as similar as possible to the real mother they have replaced. It is meant as a compliment that a maid, as one employer said, 'looks Spanish, she has been for a long time here, has our same customs. She does as I tell her, how I tell her and she has adapted perfectly. You would take her for Spanish'.

In the case of Latin American and Eastern European countries, there are similarities in how migrants see themselves, how they think employers see them and how employers actually see them, all compounding national and ethnic stereotypes. Care workers from South America are generally thought to be gentle, warm and tender with the children, but less efficient in cleaning and organising domestic work. Immigrants from Poland, Romania or Ukraine are considered to be extremely intelligent and good workers but distant with the children. Moroccans generate greater misunderstandings and contradictions. Moroccan employees interviewed considered that the ethics of Muslim women made them especially fit for care work, a job based on trust, in spite of being aware of initial barriers such as the language and cultural differences related, for example, to food or clothes. However, most of the employers declared explicitly that they did not trust Muslim women, and because of cultural differences particularly around gender, they did not want them taking care of their children.[15]

Beyond a pure market relationship, a salary in exchange for services, something else is expected of domestic servants, something enveloped with feminine mystique. Surrogate mothers are expected to love the children they care for, thus compensating for the 'abandonment' of the real mother, a latent feeling often tinged with guilt. Paid carers can even be better mothers than real ones, an issue around which tension emerges. Workers elaborate a rich and self-gratifying discourse on differential competences and results in children's education between them and mothers:

> 'I have been with them since they were born and they are used to my way. They behave very well. The lady [the mother] says 'Norma, I don't know what you do to make

them eat', because with her they do not want to eat. When she comes home they misbehave, not with me. The mother comes and they begin to cry, not with me.'

Being 'part of the family' is a common yet ambiguous idea. On the one hand, it means that the worker shares time and space with the family, especially when they live in. Workers necessarily perceive and feel the family mood and know a lot about it; on the other hand, as one employer put it 'of course my family is my family but if you have a person living in your home 24 hours a days, six days per week, it cannot be as if you have a lamp on a table'. Another interviewee made the difference between 'being part' of the family and just 'being' in the family.[16] But the relationship is not symmetrical. The employee is one way or another within the family as a sheer fact or even beyond, as she is often expected to be personally involved in the problems or the needs of the persons she works for. She is expected to care, in the double meaning of the term. In spite of that, the employer does not generally reciprocate; she is not expected to be concerned about her employee's personal problems. Employers usually prefer not to know much about them, even if they are aware of their difficult, even tragic lives.

Who takes care of the maid's children?[17]

Employees sometimes take their children with them when they migrate, or they leave them to be taken care of by older siblings or, when no other resource is available, leave them alone at home (see also Romero's [1997] account for the US). Sometimes domestic workers as low-paid workers can access means-tested public childcare for small children, an issue that is creating tension with Spanish families in some working-class neighbourhoods. But the more common way of organising care is to leave them behind in their countries of origin to be taken care of by grandparents, husbands or other relatives. Even when children are aged three and go to public school it is difficult to make schedules compatible with women's jobs, exactly the same problem faced by Spanish working mothers when they decide to hire domestic help if they can afford it. Leaving their children back home is a difficult decision, often taken because there are no other feasible alternatives.

'My child stayed with my mother in Ecuador for two years. I suffered too much, I had never been separated from him, and the first month I spent all my wages on the telephone.'

'The same happened to me.'

'I used to cry every day.'

'I left my three children. It was terrible. Their life changed. My daughter called me and said: "Please, mummy, come home" and my son … he was not well taken care of [by the former husband and his new wife]. He called me and told me: "I do not get enough to eat, I cannot go to school because they do not give me money for the bus, my shoes are worn out." (Discussion group with domestic workers from South America)

Care, along with raw materials and handicrafts, has become part of the global exchange of goods and services perpetuating inequalities between the centre and the periphery. While some children accumulate mothers and carers in the global core (Ehrenreich and Hochschild, 2003), other children are destined to share theirs in the hope of a better future.

Migrant domestic workers and moral debate in Sweden

As discussed in Chapter Four, Sweden has a long history of policies enabling family and work reconciliation, encouraging women's participation in the labour market, and has one of the highest rates (76%) of female labour force participation in the EU (Bergqvist and Jungar, 2000, p 160; Stark and Regner, 2001, p 167). Public childcare has been a widespread practice and care ideology in Sweden since the 1960s, and the provision of childcare is considered a shared responsibility between parents, society and employers (Björnberg, 2002a, p 96). Nevertheless, especially in the private sector, unreconstructed gender relations still leave women with the main responsibility for children and household work (Björnberg, 2002b; Cousins and Tang, 2004), and the number of men who take advantage of parental rights remains low even though it has increased slightly and is greater than in other EU countries (Björnberg, 2002b, p 40). Thus, despite high social provision, the demand for private domestic services is increasing in Sweden for a number of reasons: filling the gaps between daycare and work schedules, shifting priorities into more family time/leisure, as well as cutbacks in the provision of quality services (de los Reyes, 2002; Platzer, 2003). However, women's struggles to get rid of the 'double shift' by turning to the informal sector of migrant female workers clashes with feminist and social democratic ambivalence around the hierarchical implications of domestic work.

In Swedish public discourse there has been a century-old discussion known as the *pigdebatten* ('maid debate'), where employment of domestic workers is considered an upper-class privilege and employees are compared to servants and maids of the 1800s (Öberg, 1999). The concept of a private domestic worker creates social democratic and feminist dilemmas because of the way it conveys sensitive historical images of the exploitation of working-class and migrant women (Öberg, 1999; Platzer, 2003).[18] 'Who does domestic work for the domestic worker?' is a recurring question (Olsson, 2005). So far, proposals for subsidies or tax exemptions for domestic services have been widely debated since the mid-1990s and were resuscitated by the New Moderate Party, which took power in 2006 (see note 18). However, the voices of the 'maids' themselves are conspicuously absent in the 'maid debate' (de los Reyes and Mulinari, 2005, p 102).

In contrast to Spain and Britain, it is not common in Sweden to employ private childcare; also grandmothers or other family members are less likely to be available for informal childcare. In 2005, 65% of one- to five-year-olds were in municipal preschool, 13% in private (subsidised) preschool care, 6% in family-run daycare and 16% in 'other' care (which includes children looked after at home) (Statistics Sweden, 2006, p 42). Those who do employ help in the home usually hire cleaners through the informal market; there are also families who employ au pairs and so-called '*barnflickor*' (young Swedish women from small towns or rural areas working as live-ins for about a year after high school) to complement publicly subsidised daycare services. For the present study, au pairs and their host families constitute the main interviewees. Au pairs are a transitional group migrating as part of particular study/exchange programmes, and their employers[19] tend to be well-paid professionals in sectors with a high demand for flexibility and availability. Thus, according to one agency interviewed, these groups are just the tip of the iceberg of a large informal/ unregistered market of household services increasingly demanded by, and available to, the average Swede (*medelsvensson*). Numbers are difficult to find, but in 1996 the National Tax Board of Sweden estimated that 93,000 households hired the services of the unregistered market for domestic work (cited by Platzer, 2003, p 271). Dominated by the companies 'HomeMaid' and 'Hemfrid', the formal/registered market for domestic work has been estimated at a value of 150 million crowns per year (€16 million), with these two organisations having approximately 2,000 and 3,500 clients respectively (Rappe and Strannegård, 2004, p 57).

Swedish politics is an interesting contrast to Britain and Spain because of the resistance through high taxation and general ideological opposition to the development of a private sector for domestic work. Further, in relation to migration, as pointed out in Chapter Three, Sweden has introduced some liberal policies, such as the allowance of dual citizenship, while also, since 1972, cutting back on the immigration of workers. Sweden does not have migration quotas or regularisation policies for migrant domestic workers, and only issues temporary permits for high-demand jobs, international exchange and for family reunion rights (Ecotec, 2001). The only way for domestic workers to enter legally is through the au pair system, which, some argue, is being used by employers as a way to get cheap labour (Platzer, 2003).

Why employees choose to work in this sector

Most domestic work takes place in the informal/unregistered sector in Sweden, since formal/registered domestic work is heavily taxed. Since the mid-1980s, live-in au pairs have been in demand in Sweden (Platzer, 2003). The most common origins of au pairs are Eastern European countries (such as Estonia, Latvia, Lithuania, Poland, Romania, Russia and Ukraine), Finland, Germany, but also Morocco, the Philippines and the US. Until 2002, there were about 1,000 au pair applications per year in Sweden (Platzer, 20023, p 35). Although au pair working conditions are formally regulated, they are not connected to controls or sanctions (Platzer, 2003, p 49). There seems to be a general 'career' pattern among migrant domestic workers and *barnflickor*/au pairs in Sweden to start out in the informal sector and then move into study or work in the formal labour market. Working for domestic work agencies is one step into the formal labour market for migrants who start out in the informal/unregistered market, according to one representative of such an agency. Another way to get into the formal/registered labour market is to start your own business with the help of a work permit/visa and a network in the informal market. Workers who used to come on tourist visas from countries such as Poland for three months at a time have been able to work legally in Sweden since EU expansion. As a result, Swedish domestic service agencies worry that foreign-owned businesses that previously operated on the informal market will now enter the formal market legally, and offer services at lower prices.

However, domestic work is not necessarily a means into the formal/

registered labour market. For instance, there are au pairs who say they prefer being au pairs even though they have other options. Some au pairs in Sweden prefer to stay with a family and work for very little pocket money as opposed to going through the trouble of getting their own apartment and a formal job. Some au pairs and *barnflickor* see their job as a learning experience and an opportunity to study the language and experience a foreign culture. According to some observers, such as the staff at a language school for au pairs, Eastern European au pairs are more likely to have the intention of staying to live and work in Sweden than Western Europeans and are more likely to see au pairing as a way to make money (as opposed to a study break/cultural exchange). However, this observation was not reflected in interviews with au pairs, many of whom resisted what they saw as a prejudice among employers that Eastern European au pairs come from 'poor families'. For instance, Maria, a Czech au pair, said 'they [the employers] really like the feeling that they are helping the poor of Eastern Europe so they are having a Polish cleaning lady and a Czech au pair'. None of the au pairs (whether from non-EU or EU countries) interviewed for this study expressed an original intention to stay in Sweden and none of them said they saw au pairing as a good way to make money – quite the opposite.

Why do employers use this sort of care?

Services in the formal/registered market are the most expensive but at the same time considered the most 'moral'. According to two representatives at a domestic work agency, public figures prefer to use domestic services from the formal labour market for fear of scandal, but ordinary Swedes turn to the cheaper informal labour market. When representatives from domestic work agencies talk about the increasing demand for domestic work, they mostly refer to the demand for cleaning. In the words of one agency representative; 'daycare is [a standard] taken for granted, but cleaning is a service you can [opt to] purchase'. Employers interviewed for this project all used subsidised daycare in combination with privately hired domestic work (sometimes both a cleaner and an au pair or *barnflicka*) and most seemed happy with public daycare services. It was mainly women who managed the employment of their employees. When it came to the type of au pair/ *barnflicka* employers preferred, they mentioned language, age, experience, 'personal chemistry' and independence. Those who had preferences in terms of nationality had particularly strong views about Swedes (who they thought were more independent and adjusted to

'Swedish' egalitarian work relations), Eastern Europeans (who were considered hard working but also tougher negotiators and more desperate for money) and Filipinas (whom some preferred because they thought they were willing to work hard and worked well).

All domestic work agencies in Sweden who contributed to this project spoke of an increasing demand for domestic services in both the formal/registered and the informal/unregistered markets, which has recently spread more widely in class terms and reflects a shifting set of priorities. Interviewees from two different agencies said that younger generations are more likely to buy domestic services than older ones. According to one agency representative, some people now choose to use their money for these services instead of a night out at the pub. Another agency representative said that many people work a lot and prioritise leisure time: 'there's a lot of golf'. Cutbacks in state provision of childcare seem to be another factor contributing to the increasing demand for private domestic services. For instance, Helena said that her options are very restricted because: 'large groups of children in daycare due to the cutbacks make me less willing to have my children go there'. Another benefit employers identify from having au pairs and *barnflickor* is more time for family members.

Preferring shorter hours at daycare for their children was one major reason employers gave for wanting an au pair or *barnflicka*. These employers were in a socioeconomic position where they could buy flexibility to combine work and care. Most employers interviewed for this study worked long hours as chief executive officers, specialist managing directors, business managers, professors, IT consultants and lawyers. Some of these preferred not to use benefits to stay home with sick children even though they were entitled to this option.

The relationship between employers and employees

Employers of domestic workers in Sweden often address the moral discourses of the 'maid debate' by seeking to legitimise their own practices and 'employer morality'. It was not uncommon for Swedish employers to pride themselves on egalitarian standards in the way they treated employees and attribute this to notions of Swedishness. For instance, one employer said that Swedish employers and Swedish employees have more egalitarian relationships than those in other countries and are more accustomed to treating each other with respect. She said that her foreign colleagues at work have a more authoritarian relationship towards their au pairs and that Sweden is unique in its egalitarianism. Employers said, for example: 'We haven't hired a person as cheap household help to use them to the max', 'we've made a deal between two equal parties' and 'it's important that they like it so it doesn't turn into an upstairs/downstairs mentality'. When asked whether they use first names both ways between employer and employee, Kristina exclaimed: 'Well God yes! This is Sweden goddammit!!' Furthermore, two employers expressed moral indignation over the 'global care chains' idea that a person would leave her own children behind in order to take care of theirs.

The majority of au pairs and *barnflickor* interviewed for this project said that they were generally happy with their Swedish employers, but they were still critical about working relationships. For instance, Natalje, an au pair from Russia, said that host families seek out au pairs from poor countries, overwork them and expect these 'poor girls' to be grateful. One common problem among *barnflickor* and au pairs in Sweden is having a hard time saying 'no' to extra and unpaid work for employers. Isolation is another major problem identified by au pairs and *barnflickor* in Sweden, being confined to working and living in private homes in the suburbs with minimum social interaction. According to the experiences of some au pairs, employers apply pressure when negotiating working hours and conditions by refusing to cover (as they are supposed to) the costs of public transport, and some employers also refuse to pay for language classes. Thus, these au pairs have difficulties creating social networks and communicating in Swedish. Furthermore, for au pairs who are not EU citizens and who did not come through an agency, social insurance may be an issue up for individual negotiation with the host family.

However, despite the problems involved in living with employers, many au pairs preferred family-like relations. Some au pairs complained that relations with host families were too impersonal; they wanted more social interaction and wanted their host parents to take more interest in them as persons – not treat them as invisible and exchangeable workers. Au pairs/*barnflickor* did, however, point out the disadvantages of not having a professional type of relationship, such as lack of a clear timetable and time off. All Swedish employers except for two (who preferred a professional relationship) said they preferred a combination of a personal and professional relationship. Most of them do not seem to feel that they have a choice if the au pair/*barnflicka* lives in their home.

The relations between au pairs and their employers are not subject to clear definition, although these groups are quite specific in the larger context of domestic work sectors[20] and it is important to point out that cleaners in the informal market have not been a major focus for interviews for this chapter. The stories of migrant domestic workers without papers in the informal/unregistered market might be quite different from those of au pairs and *barnflickor*, and quite significant to the general picture. One also needs to take into account that employers' rationalisations and their practices may sometimes be contradictory, in that employers may not feel able to live up to expectations of 'employer morality'.

What about the employee's family?

Since young and childless au pairs and *barnflickor* constitute the majority of domestic workers undertaking private childcare in Sweden, issues concerning employees' own families do not apply as they do in Britain and Spain. When it comes to social and political networks of domestic workers in Sweden, invisibility is the key. There are limited possibilities for employees to negotiate with employers or to make their voices heard in public discussions. This is due to the transitional and vaguely defined nature of au pairing, the invisibility of the informal/unregistered labour market and the lack of organisations or mobilisation for domestic workers in Sweden. As one coordinator for a social centre for au pairs said, 'it's difficult to negotiate over people and workplaces that supposedly do not exist'. Herein lies a major paradox: the continuing invisibility and lack of voice of one group of workers because of the way the 'maid debate' has constructed egalitarianism as central to Swedishness. Since not everyone is willing or able to live up to Swedish 'employer morality', the rights of Swedish women to reconcile work and care are uncomfortably pitted against socioeconomic, ethnic and racial inequalities between women with asymmetric access to citizenship, labour market rights and representation.

Conclusion

These three case studies reveal common issues faced by working women from different regions of the world: the rights, aspirations and needs to take up paid work compared to the constraints in meeting their work and care responsibilities created by the organisation of work, the limitations of publicly available childcare provision, and unreconstructed gender relations in the home. At the same time, the case studies show two important areas of divergence. First is the extent to which different societies in Europe may come to depend upon migration as a way of reconciling these constraints. Care cultures that prefer mother substitution for care, care regimes that encourage the commodification of care and domestic labour, and migration regimes that facilitate the movement of migrant women into this area of work, all predispose countries such as Spain and, to a lesser extent, Britain to this as a partial solution to the 'care deficit'. In fact, in this area of private childcare, it is probably only Spain that fully fits the notion of the 'global care chain' where the majority of women migrants have left their own children behind to care for others' children. Sweden's traditions of public childcare provision, a culture of moral disapproval of domestic service and few special migration arrangements militate against this form of childcare resource, even though there may be signs in *all* three countries that private domestic/care work is on the increase.

The second divergence lies in the way changing geopolitical relations, at both a regional level (Central/Eastern, Southern and Western Europe) and a global level (richer and poorer worlds), give rise to different manifestations of gendered citizenship. For the migrant workers, crossing continents to earn money provides an important opportunity, but it is an opportunity to enter a world in which migration rules construct limited and different rights to social, economic, political and intimate citizenship compared to their employers'. Furthermore, these limitations give rise to the likelihood of women entering the often unregulated world of domestic and care work in the home, whose conditions perpetuate the devaluation and invisibility of the private domain and its subservience to the public world. In addition, when home becomes work, and workers become 'part of the family' then all three case studies show the tensions and power relations that ensue, articulated in racialised stereotypes and hierarchies and competing moralities about what is best for the child. It is here that the 'lived experience' can reveal more than a comparison of different citizenship regimes. It is where the unequal relations of global interdependence become translated into the unequal relations of personal interdependence. As Anderson and O'Connell Davidson (2003, p 33) point out in their survey of domestic work in Europe, 'the introduction of market relations into the private home can be experienced as deeply disturbing by employers'.

If the Swedish case reveals better access to social rights by Swedish women, it also shows how the very discourse of 'egalitarianism' can work two ways: to defend those rights, but also to render unheard the articulated needs of both employers and employees of domestic labour. The use of domestic labour in Sweden can be read as simply the actions of a minority and unrepresentative elite exercising their economic power, or alternatively as a warning that the journey from 'adult-worker' to the 'universal care-giver' model of society, where men and women have not only equal rights to work but equal responsibilities for care, is still far from complete. It involves much more than the public provision of care to deal with the gendered divisions of labour in the household.

The issue raises difficult dilemmas about the future of the adult-worker model across Europe. At one level, regularising care and domestic work, improving migrants' rights of citizenship (including family reunion, rights to contracts, training and so on) is urgent. This needs to be accompanied by policies that ensure that workers are treated with respect and as citizens, not simply as units of labour quotas or as inferiorised others. But it is also about seeking strategies to rebalance the subservience of the private world of care to the public world of work in ways that do not also reinforce the subservience of poorer countries to richer ones.

Notes

[1] In some countries, emigration is encouraged by governments as a form of 'export'; for example, since the 1960s the Philippines has promoted female emigration to improve the economy (Mozière, 2004).

[2] The Italian government has promoted the immigration of *badanti* (someone who 'keeps an eye on' another – an attendant) which explicitly deskills and devalues the nature of care work (Scrinzi, 2004).

[3] The case studies are drawn from two separate projects and have been pulled together to tell different stories with common themes, rather than being case studies sharing the same methodologies. They are based on interviews in the capital cities of the three countries with those migrant workers who reflected the main employment groups and migrant groups, as well as, in the case of Stockholm and London, representatives from domestic work/nanny organisations/agencies. Using theoretical sampling, the material for the Swedish and British contributions is based on ethnographic fieldwork in Stockholm and London, conducted by Anna Gavanas, Marie Curie Intra-European Fellow, for the project 'Migrant Domestic Workers in European Care Regimes', working with Fiona Williams at the University of Leeds. We are grateful for funding from the European Community's Sixth Framework Programme (ref MEIF-CT-2003-502369). The methods used were recorded, semi-structured and recorded and unrecorded informal interviews, as well as participant observation. These were carried out in London between July and September 2004, and included

16 employees, 10 employers and eight organisations. Of the 16 employees, six were domestic workers, seven were nannies and three were au pairs, recognising that the line between different employee groups is fuzzy. They came from Australia, Central and Eastern Europe, East and South Africa, New Zealand and South-east Asia. Of the domestic workers, three had children who were living in their countries of origin and one had children who were living in Britain. In Stockholm the interviews were carried out between September and December 2004, and included 17 employees, 10 employers and eight organisations. Of the employees, 12 were au pairs, three were domestic workers, and two were *barnflickor* (see p 155). Of the domestic workers, one had her child with her and one had children who were living in her home country. The employees came from Africa, the Baltic Republics, Central and Eastern Europe, Croatia, Germany and Russia. The Spanish study is based on data from two discussion groups held in Madrid in June 2002 with Spanish working mothers who employ migrants to take care of their children, and three discussion groups with migrant domestic workers from different regions in the world (Latin America, North Africa and Eastern Europe). One group of employers comprised nine Spanish mothers aged 33-42 working in middle-lower-class occupations; the other comprised eight mothers aged 34-45 who worked in high-skilled occupations. The group of Latin American women comprised eight migrants, all of them over 37 years of age and having lived in Spain between three months and nine years. The North African group was formed of nine Moroccan women and one from Algeria, aged 25-35 and with big differences in the time they had been living in Spain, between a few months and 15 years. The Eastern European group was composed of 10 women from Bulgaria, Poland and Romania. They were aged 22-39, having lived in Spain between two months and seven years. The whole sessions were recorded, transcribed and analysed with NVivo. For more information on the methodology used and the results, see Tobío and Díaz Gorfinkiel (2003).

[4] This was not available in 2004 when fieldwork was carried out in London.

[5] Gregson and Lowe's (1994, p 41) study found that over a third of middle-class dual-career families in the early 1990s employed some sort of domestic help, often on an undeclared 'cash-in-hand' basis.

[6] At a recommended payment of £55 per week for five hours' work a day for five days, plus board and lodging.

[7] See the debate in the House of Commons, 10 May 2006, where in response to a question raised over this issue, the Parliamentary Under-secretary of State for the Home Office said that, 'If employers want to employ low-skilled domestic staff on a long-term basis they can look to the resident and EU labour market' (*Hansard*, 2006).

[8] It should be said that by the very process of selection the employers interviewed were probably 'good' employers, and that a better cross-section is represented by the comments of the agencies and the employees.

[9] In 2001, there were 231,700 immigrants in Spain, a figure which is smaller only than the number in Germany and a rate of 5.7 per thousand, smaller only than that of Ireland (Instituto Nacional de Estadística, 2003, p 240).

[10] As, for example, in Bohning's (1984) migratory regime model, based on four stages, the first the migration of young single men and the last characterised by the immigration of wives and children.

[11] One in four dual-earner households hire domestic workers but only 6% on a full-time basis (Tobío, 2005, pp 178-91). The number of work permits given to immigrants in domestic service has multiplied by three between 1993 and 2000. In 2000 this represented 26% of all work permits (Instituto Nacional de Estadística, 2004).

[12] To some extent related to the assimilation of European policies and recommendations, such as those included in the European Commission Framework Strategy on Gender Equality 2001-05 or in the Directive 92/85/EC on maternity leaves and in the Directive 96/34/EC on parental leave.

[13] See, for example, the 1999 law on reconciling family and employment (Ley para la Conciliación de la Vida Laboral y Familiar de las Personas Trabajadoras), which focuses mainly on unpaid parental leaves.

[14] R.D. 1424/1985 on labour relations in the domestic service sector.

[15] The interviews were carried out before the Madrid bombings (11 March 2004), which might have increased negative perceptions towards Moroccan domestic workers.

[16] Expressed in Spanish as the difference between '*ser de la familia*' and '*estar en la familia*'.

[17] The term 'maid' is commonly used in Spain; in Britain it is used far less often and refers to a position of cleaner/cook in a wealthy household. In Sweden, the debate about domestic service uses the term 'maid' and the wealthy use this term, but it is generally regarded, as in Britain, as connoting unacceptable servitude.

[18] At the time of the fieldwork for this project (the latter part of 2004), there was yet another heated debate around the idea of the state facilitating the employment of domestic workers (Norrlander and von Sydow, 2004). Every now and then, scandals hit the Swedish media when employers are caught hiring domestic workers from the informal market. In 2003, six middle-class women in the Gothenburg area were caught hiring Eastern European domestic workers (Gustavsson, 2003). October 2006 saw the Swedish 'Nannygate' when two female ministers in the recently elected New Moderate government were forced to quit for hiring private childminders and not paying tax. A third male minister's future hung in the balance for the same offence. According to AFP Sweden, Prime Minister Reinfeldt has 'come out and said what no other politician has dared to say publicly before: that in a gender equality society like Sweden, where the vast majority of women hold jobs, families sometimes need to hire home help'. He said, 'If I were to pass judgement on every parent in this country who paid cash for a babysitter's help ... I don't know what kind of snowball that would start'. The government intends to lower taxes for low and middle wage earners in an attempt to end the large unregulated domestic service economy (AFP, 19 October 2006, www.sweden.se).

[19] For simplicity's sake, host parents of au pairs are here referred to as employers although they are not in a formal employer–employee relationship.

[20] However, there are au pairs who work 'on the side' in the informal domestic work sector and there are au pair/*barnflicka* employers who also hire other domestic services, such as cleaning from the formal and informal markets.

Conclusion

We have had two main objectives in writing this volume. The first, which originated in our longstanding collaboration in the research field of gendered citizenship, has been to explore the key challenges facing those who study citizenship in a cross-national context. The second has been to illustrate some of these challenges through an analysis of two important dimensions of gendered citizenship, which tend to be treated separately – care and migration – and to do so within a global context. In this brief conclusion we pull together a number of threads and raise some general issues for future research and policy making. The first part reflects on the challenges and the second expands on the fresh perspectives we believe our study offers to understandings of gendered citizenship in Europe.

Challenges

Our analysis throws up four key challenges in studying gendered citizenship in a cross-national context. These derive from: citizenship's contextual nature; the perspectives of 'lived citizenship'; the inadequacy of existing cross-national data for our purposes; and the need to study the gender culture within which policy packages are enacted, together with their differential usage across gender, class and ethnic lines, in order to understand the policies' meanings for and impact on gendered citizenship.

As we explained in the Introduction and Part One, context matters when understanding citizenship both as an academic and political concept and as lived experience. Vocabularies of citizenship may appear superficially similar in different countries but the meanings attached to the words are not always the same (Bellamy, 2004). Contemporary understandings of citizenship are the product of different historical and legal traditions and institutional and cultural complexes (frequently articulated in terms of welfare, care, gender, citizenship and migration regimes). They also reflect the processes by which citizenship rights came to be established – whether as the product of struggle from below or of anticipatory state action from above or a combination of both (Turner, 1990).

These statements are made on the basis of political and theoretical writings about citizenship. However, an even greater challenge faces us as we try to understand the lived experience of citizenship in a cross-national context. The notion of 'lived citizenship' is about 'the meaning that citizenship actually has in people's lives and the ways in which people's social and cultural backgrounds and material circumstances affect their lives as citizens' (Hall and Williamson, 1999, p 2). It is about how individuals understand and negotiate the three key elements of citizenship: rights and responsibilities, belonging and participation. This volume does no more than point to the rich insights that might be gained from a more holistic cross-national study of citizenship, which combines analysis of citizenship regimes 'from above' with study of the cultural, social and political practices that constitute lived citizenship 'from below'. Chapters Three and Five, in particular, offer some insights into how women negotiate 'majority' and 'minority' cultural practices and the responsibilities of paid work and childcare in the context of different migration, welfare, care and gender regimes.

As explained in the Introduction, these different forms of regime do not neatly map onto each other to form distinct clusters of countries. We have therefore used the notion of regimes not as a way of classifying the countries studied but to throw light on particular institutional patterns and policy logics. Their heuristic value lies in capturing these patterns in a still frame at a time when so much is in flux both in Western and in Central and Eastern Europe. As illustrated by our policy studies in Part Two, citizenship, welfare, care, gender and migration regimes are shifting – sometimes converging, sometimes diverging – as they respond to a range of challenges including globalisation, migration, multiculturalism, falling birth rates and a growing care gap.

There has been remarkably little empirical analysis of lived citizenship in comparison with the volume of theorising about citizenship in individual member states of the European Union (EU), never mind cross-nationally. This is particularly the case with regard to citizens' own understandings of citizenship's meaning.[1] What little there has been indicates that citizenship can have a range of meanings for the citizens of individual nation states (see, for instance, Lister et al, 2003). We can therefore expect an even greater diversity of understandings across nation states.

With the exception of Chapter Five, the present study is not based on new empirical data. This has posed its own methodological challenges, particularly in relation to childcare (see also Bradshaw and Hatland, 2006). Cross-national studies of social citizenship rights tend to use quantitative data. The data available on childcare provision in member states of the EU proved inadequate to the task of analysing this key dimension of gendered social citizenship. It is therefore welcome that the European Commission is developing a methodology for harmonising childcare statistics in the future (Ruxton, 2005). However, even if this proposed methodology is successful in providing more comparable data, our work suggests that quantitative data need complementing with more qualitative understandings of the nature of childcare provision in order to understand the role it plays as a key plank of social citizenship in the lives of women, men and children. It is this that we have tried to provide from our knowledge of debates around childcare in our respective countries. The available data on migration are also deficient because definitions of, for instance, foreigners or au pairs vary between countries.

Childcare has not traditionally been regarded as a citizenship issue. It is only with the advent of feminist analyses that care has been acknowledged as of relevance to citizenship. Despite welfare state retrenchment, childcare is one dimension of social citizenship rights that has been strengthened in most Western European welfare states in recent years (although there has been a parallel weakening in Central and Eastern Europe). Gradually during the 20th century, responsibility for childcare came to be seen as a public as well as a private familial responsibility and in some, although by no means all, countries it is now to a certain extent articulated as a right of both parents and children. Policy packages vary in the balance of support they provide for maternity and parental leave, cash benefits for home childcare and provision of collective childcare services and in the extent to which they encourage fathers to share responsibility for childcare. To understand the implications of these provisions for gendered citizenship again poses a two-level challenge. At one level it is necessary to look behind the policies at the gender regimes within which they operate, for similar policies can vary in their effects according to dominant gender cultures (Morgan and Zippel, 2003). At another, related, level, the impact of various policy packages depends on the use made of them by both women and men of different social classes and ethnic groups.

Fresh perspectives

In addition to pointing the way to the potential of a more holistic approach to the cross-national study of citizenship – and the challenges it poses – our study offers a fresh perspective on the study of gendered citizenship by bringing together the issues of childcare, migration and global relations. This has involved connecting concepts and literatures, which are usually kept separate, and has benefited from the very different approaches taken in the various chapters. The analysis has also placed emphasis on the agency of women and other social actors in the development of citizenship both historically and today.

The combination of childcare, migration and global relations complicates the gendered citizenship puzzle; throws new light on aspects of the meanings of citizenship; reveals the contradictory impact of regimes and the policies developed within them on people's lives; and poses a number of questions in relation to some of the issues raised in the Introduction. These questions concern, in particular, the adult-worker model; the intersections of gender, 'race' and class in a global context; citizenship's emancipatory and disciplinary tension; and its multilayered construction.

The development of the adult-worker model is contradictory in its impact. It offers women a place in the labour market, which is critical to full and equal citizenship in contemporary welfare states, without significantly altering men's role (see also Bradshaw and Hatland, 2006). The model is presented as the solution to problems of demographic change, economic competitiveness and future pensions entitlements in much of the policy documentation of the EU and Organisation for Economic Co-operation and Development (OECD). Yet, because it pays insufficient attention to the care gap to which it contributes, the adult-worker model poses as many problems as solutions. Despite the development of childcare provision as a public responsibility to a greater or lesser extent and as a social right of citizenship (at least in some countries) across Western Europe (discussed in Chapter Four), the movement of a growing number of women into the labour market has left a deficit of care resources. This gap has not in most cases been filled by men, for men's practices on the private side of the gendered division of labour have not changed as fast as women's on the public side (see also Finch, 2006). There is only very limited recognition of the significance of this for gender equality at EU level (Lewis, J., 2006a; Lombardo and Meier, 2006). Nevertheless, public policy in some European countries is now acknowledging that fathers' role is critical to the equitable development of gendered citizenship and we have seen in Chapter Four that some policy steps are being taken to encourage more active fathering. However, mothers and fathers are being squeezed between two processes of intensification: on the one side, in the labour market and on the other, in the nature of parenting itself as greater demands are made of parents in the interests of the healthy development and education of their children.

Migration offers an apparent solution to shortages of labour power within both the labour market and the home, particularly in the context of inadequate public childcare provision. In the home (explored in

Chapter Five), it is a privatised solution negotiated by individual parents – in practice mothers – but increasingly it is a solution that has the support of the state. Although the migration of care providers is only a small part of a much larger global movement of migrant workers, it is of particular significance for gendered citizenship yet is generally less visible than migration into the formal labour market.

The implications for gendered citizenship are mixed. A growing number of Western European women are able to access employment-based citizenship, thereby strengthening their social citizenship rights. New opportunities and forms of belonging are opened up for migrant women, including those from the global South. As their families' breadwinners, they function as wage-earning citizens whose remittances also make an important contribution to the economy of their country of origin and this is recognised explicitly in the emigration policies of some of those countries.

Yet these new opportunities are built on relationships of inequality and sometimes exploitation. First, the employment of migrant domestic workers makes it easier for men to continue to absent themselves from care and housework, particularly in countries such as Spain where the gendered division of labour in the domestic sphere remains fairly rigid. Even in Britain, where our research found that the division of labour is subject to more negotiation, it is the mothers who carry the responsibility as employers of the domestic workers.

This gendered responsibility, in turn, underlines a second set of inequalities. Study of the transnational dynamics of care (global care chains) exposes in stark form the inequalities of resources and power between women derived from their social class, ethnicity and location in the global economy. The reliance of some mothers on other women to provide informal care for their children so that they can combine motherhood with wage-earning citizenship is not new. Nor are '"domestic" encounters across ethnicity' and continents totally new in that they occurred previously as part of 'the European colonial project' in the global South (Lewis, G., 2006, p 98). However, what is relatively new is that such encounters are taking place within Europe, as mothers are increasingly using *migrant* labour in order to enter paid employment themselves. Moreover, EU enlargement means that this labour is now recruited from the accession countries of Central and Eastern Europe as well as the global South. The paradox is that Central and Eastern European women, who have suffered a reversal in terms of the social citizenship rights they used to enjoy, are now working as second-class citizens in Western Europe, thereby facilitating Western

European women's access to employment-based social citizenship rights.

For the migrant women, the global care chain can mean that the strengthening of their position as wage-earning citizens is at the expense of their role as immediate carers of their own children. Further down the care chain in the women's countries of origin, other women – for example grandmothers and sisters – and also older children themselves may, unrecognised, be filling some of the care void left behind (Nieuwenhuys, 2005). Moreover, as migrant workers without the citizenship rights enjoyed by their employers and isolated in the private sphere of their employers, the women lack security and their ability to participate as political citizens is weakened. Their position calls for both recognition and redistribution (as discussed in Chapter Two).

The intersection of gender and ethnicity also emerges as a key dimension of the multicultural challenge posed by migration more generally. Minority ethnic women carry much of the strain created by the tensions of multiculturalism (see also Gupta, 2003). This is illustrated in Chapter Three with the examples of forced and arranged marriages and the headscarf debate. Moreover, as illustrated in Chapter Five, these tensions are played out in the domestic sphere of families who employ migrant domestic workers where the latter often have to deal with cultural stereotyping and childcare cultures different from their own.

For minority ethnic women, lived citizenship often involves negotiating a complex of changing gender and family cultures as they move between minority and majority communities. One conclusion reached in Chapter Three is the need for their voices to be heard within democratic arenas so that they are not lost in translation, when mediated by others – feminists and non-feminists. The debate on multiculturalism has also had the effect in some countries of positioning gender equality as a key element of citizenship and European culture, to be protected against non-European 'others'; where this is the case it offers an example of how feminist arguments can be deployed by non-feminists in exclusionary ways. Moreover, as acknowledged in Chapter Three, feminists themselves are divided as to the implications of multiculturalism for women.

The complicated relationship between multiculturalism and gender equality illustrates the point, made in the Introduction, that citizenship operates simultaneously as an inclusionary and exclusionary force and that the processes of exclusion within and at the borders of nation states intersect. Chapter Three at the same time shows how policies, designed to encourage the integration of immigrants, exemplify gendered citizenship's double-edged emancipatory and disciplinary quality. The examples discussed are the implications for women migrants of the introduction of language tests as a condition of naturalisation, and policies concerning forced and arranged marriages and the wearing of the headscarf. More generally, Chapter Two points to how contemporary developments in citizenship have strengthened both its disciplinary face (as in the growing emphasis in many countries on citizenship obligations) and its emancipatory potential (as in the extension of sexual citizenship rights for gay men and lesbians).

The volume also contributes to our understanding of the multilayered nature of citizenship. Not only do the spaces of citizenship stretch from the intimate to the global, as noted in the Introduction, but the intimate and the global are interwoven through the global care dynamics discussed in Chapter Five (see also Plummer, 2003). A complex web of wage-earning and care is spun by migrant women stretching from the intimate private sphere of their citizen employers to their countries of origin, with implications for the citizenship of all those connected through the global care chain. The chain links 'the domestic' as the intimate/household sphere to 'the domestic' as 'site of the nation(al)', highlighting the racialised and gendered character of both (Lewis, G., 2006, p 100). Migrant women have to negotiate new ways of belonging within the disjunction between home and homeland (Williams, 2004a).

Global care dynamics also support the case made by a number of theorists for a global or cosmopolitan citizenship, which draws on elements of both liberalism and civic republicanism but beyond the confines of the nation state (see, for instance, Hutchings and Dannreuther, 1999). Various international human rights treaties can be understood as representing instruments of global citizenship (Linklater, 2002). As illustrated in Chapters Two and Three, the discourse of human rights can be used to strengthen gendered citizenship claims but there are also tensions between citizenship exclusionary boundaries and the internationalist promise of human rights. From the perspective of citizenship as a practice, international campaigns – for example for access to employment and social rights for home-workers – are helping to forge an embryonic global citizenry practising citizenship at a global level.

At the same time, the artificiality of the kind of fixed public–private divide that underpins traditional understandings of citizenship, as discussed in the Introduction, is thrown into relief. One family's private sphere becomes part of the public sphere of migrant women who are severed from their own private sphere. In other words, the workplace

– typically part of the public sphere – of these migrant women is here the private sphere of their employers, while the migrant women are unable to live in their own private sphere. Market relations are tangled up with intimate family relations, creating tensions and racialised power relations. Childcare remains hidden within the private domain and unregulated by the state.

Between intimate and nation state citizenship on the one side and global citizenship on the other stands the EU. The EU constitutes a community of law, the regulatory powers of which have been important to the development of gendered citizenship in individual member states, particularly in the areas of employment and family leave (see Chapters Two and Four). Some observers have suggested that the extension of regulatory powers in relation to social rights can be interpreted as the emergent 'contours of a European social citizenship' (Johansson and Hvinden, 2006, p 13). However, both gendered citizenship in particular and social citizenship more generally remain subordinate to the dictates of European economic competitiveness (Lewis, J., 2006a). This is the lens through which both childcare and migration policies are filtered. Some of the consequences for women's lived citizenship can be seen in the policy studies in Part Two. Nevertheless, as made clear in Chapter Two, the EU also represents 'a site of engaged feminist politics' (Ferree, 2004, p 1) and a space for citizenship practice: women and other marginalised groups can unite across national boundaries to contest exclusionary policies and fight for stronger and more extensive social rights such as childcare. An example is the European Network of Migrant Domestic Workers' Organisations (RESPECT) established by Kalayaan and Solidar to campaign for domestic workers' rights, combining a politics of recognition and redistribution.

Finally, the interconnections that we have demonstrated between the growing dominance of an adult–worker model across Europe, childcare policies and migration in a global context have implications for policy within individual member states, at EU level and beyond through global institutions such as the United Nations and the International Labour Organisation. They point to the need for a more integrated policy approach. This would, on the one hand, use the power of the state to address the care deficit created by the adult–worker model through the creation of a more comprehensive public infrastructure of care and the promotion of care as citizenship responsibility for men as well as women. It would also, on the other hand, strengthen the citizenship rights and status of immigrant women and men in general and domestic workers in particular. Individual indicative policy areas, to which the analysis in earlier chapters points, include childcare, leave and employment provisions that take account of the reality of women's lives and of the specific needs of particular groups of women and which recognise and actively promote men's care responsibilities; social protection extended to the home as workplace; training and accreditation opportunities for care workers and open to migrant workers; and social rights for women workers in the countries at the other end of the global care chain. Such policies have to operate in tandem. They also need to ensure that social and employment rights are effective, particularly for marginalised groups. A holistic approach of this kind is crucial to the development of a more inclusive model of gendered citizenship in Europe.

Note

[1] A rare example of such analysis by Conover et al (1991) was confined to the US and Britain and is already over a decade old. More recent relevant British studies are reported in Dwyer (2000); Home Office Research, Development and Statistics Directorate (2004); Pattie et al (2004); and Almond (2005).

References

Afshar, H., Aitkin, R. and Franks, M. (2005) 'Feminisms, Islamophobia and identities', Paper given at the ESRC Social Justice and Public Policy Seminar, 'Social justice and multiculturalism: tensions and possibilities', 24 November 2005, York CVS.

Ahmad, F. (2006) 'The scandal of 'arranged marriages' and the pathologisation of BrAsian Families', in N. Ali, V.S. Kalra and S. Sayyid (eds) *A Postcolonial People: South Asians in Britain*, London: Hurst and Company, pp 272-88.

Almond, M. (2005) 'An investigation into the meanings of good citizenship, PhD thesis, unpublished, Loughborough University.

Anderson, B. (1997) 'Servants and slaves: Europe's domestic workers', *Race and Class*, vol 39, no 1, pp 37-49.

Anderson, B. (2000) *Doing the Dirty Work*, London: Zed Press.

Anderson, B. and O'Connell Davidson, J. (2003) *Is Trafficking in Human Beings Demand Driven? A Multi Country Pilot Study*, Geneva: International Organization for Migration.

Andreassen, R. (2005) 'The mass media's construction of gender, race, sexuality and nationality: an analysis of the Danish news media's communication about visible minorities 1971-2004', PhD thesis, Department of History, University of Toronto.

Anttonen, A. and Sipilä, J. (1996) 'European social care services: is it possible to identify models?', *Journal of European Social Policy*, vol 6, no 2, pp 87-100.

Banks, O. (1986) *Faces of Feminism: A Study of Feminism as a Social Movement*, Oxford: Basil Blackwell.

Barton, L. (1996) 'Citizenship and disabled people: a cause for concern', in J. Demaine and H. Entwistle (eds) *Beyond Communitarianism: Citizenship, Politics and Education*, Basingstoke: Macmillan, pp 179-92.

Bell, S. G. and Offen, K. (1983) 'Olympe de Gouges', in S.G. Bell and K. Offen (eds) *Women, the Family, and Freedom: The Debate in Documents*, vol 1, Stanford: Stanford University Press, pp 104-9.

Bellamy, R. (2004) 'Introduction: the making of modern citizenship', in R. Bellamy, D. Castiglione and E. Santoro (eds) *Lineages of European Citizenship*, Basingstoke: Palgrave, pp 1-12.

Bellamy, R. and Warleigh, A. (eds) (2001) *Citizenship and Governance in the European Union*, London and New York: Continuum.

Bergqvist, C. and Jungar, A.-C. (2000) 'Adaptation or diffusion of the Swedish gender model?', in L. Hantrais (ed) *Gendered Policies in Europe*, Basingstoke and New York: Macmillan and St Martin's Press, pp 160-79.

Berkovitch, N. (1999) *From Motherhood to Citizenship: Women's Rights and International Organizations*, Baltimore, MD, and London: The Johns Hopkins University Press.

Bettio, F. and Plantenga, J. (2004) 'Comparing care regimes in Europe', *Feminist Economics*, vol 10, no 1, pp 85-113.

Bettio, F. and Prechal, S. (1998) *Care in Europe: Joint Report of the 'Gender and Employment' and the 'Gender and Law' Groups of Experts*, Medium-term Community Action Programme on Equal Opportunities for women and men (1996-2000), Brussels: European Commission.

Beveridge, W. (1942) *Social Insurance and Allied Services*, Cmnd 6404, London: HMSO.

Björnberg, U. (2002a) 'Working and caring for children: family policies and balancing work and family in Sweden', in A. Carling, S. Duncan and R. Edwards (eds) *Analyzing Families: Morality and Rationality in Policy and Practice*, London and New York: Routledge, pp 93-100.

Björnberg, U. (2002b) 'Ideology and choice between work and care: Swedish family policy for working parents', *Critical Social Policy*, vol 22, no 1, pp 33-52.

Bleijenbergh, I. (2004) *Citizens who Care: European Social Citizenship in EU Debates on Childcare and Part-time Work*, Amsterdam: Dutch University Press.

Blom, I. (2001) 'Demokratie, Wohlfahrt und Feminismus in Norwegen', in U. Gerhard (ed) *Feminismus und Demokratie. Europäische Frauenbewegungen der 1920er Jahre*, Königstein/Ts: Ulrike Helmer, pp 38-63.

Blunkett, D. (2003) *Civil Renewal: A New Agenda*, London: Home Office.

Bock, G. (1995) 'Weibliche Armut, Mutterschaft und Rechte von Müttern in der Entstehung des Wohlfahrtsstaats, 1890-1950', in G. Duby and M. Perrot (eds) *Geschichte der Frauen*, vol 5, Frankfurt/M. and New York: Campus, pp 427-62.

Bock, G. and Thane, P. (eds) (1994) *Maternity and Gender Policies: Women and the Rise of European Welfare States 1880s-1990s*, London and New York: Routledge.

Bohning, W. (1984) *Studies of International Migration*, London: Macmillan.

Bradshaw, J. and Finch, N. (2002) *A Comparison of Child Benefit Packages in 22 Countries*, Department for Work and Pensions Research Report No 174, Leeds: Corporate Document Services.

Bradshaw, J. and Hatland, A. (eds) (2006) *Social Policy, Employment and Family Change in Comparative Perspective*, Cheltenham: Edward Elgar.

Brannen, J. and Moss, P. (2002) *Rethinking Children's Care*, Buckingham: Open University Press.

Bredal, A. (2005) 'Tackling forced marriages in the Nordic countries: between women's rights and immigration control', in L. Welchman and S. Hossain (eds) *Honour Crimes: Paradigms and Violence against Women*, London: Zed Books, pp 482-509.

Bredal, A. (2006) *'Vi er jo en familie': Arrangerte ekteskap, autonomi og fellesskap blant unge norsk-asiater*, Institutt for Samfunnsforskning, Norway (ISF), Oslo:Unipax.

Brewer, M. and Shaw, J. (2004) *Childcare Use and Mothers' Employment: A Review of British Data Sources*, DWP Working Paper No 16, London: HMSO.

Brinkmann, C. (1959) 'Citizenship', in E.R.A. Seligman and A. Johnson (eds) *Encyclopaedia of the Social Sciences*, vol 3, New York:The Macmillan Company, pp 471-4.

Brochmann, G. and Dölvik, J.E. (2004) 'Is immigration an enemy of the welfare state? Between human rights and realpolitik in European immigration policies', in D. Papademetriou (ed) *Managing Migration: A Policy Agenda for Economic Progress and Social Cohesion*, Washington, DC: Migration Institute, pp 155-79.

Brochmann, G. and Hagelund, A. (2005) *Innvandringens Velferdspolitiske Konsekvenser: Nordisk Kunnskapsstatus (The Welfare Political Consequences of Migration)*, Copenhagen: Nordic Council of Ministers.

Brubaker R. (1994) *Staats-Bürger: Frankreich und Deutschland im Historischen Vergleich*, Hamburg: Junius.

Bruning, G. and Plantenga, J. (1999) 'Parental leave and equal opportunities: experiences in eight European countries', *Journal of European Social Policy*, vol 9, no 3, pp 195-209.

Bryson, C., Budd, T., Lewis, J. and Elam, G. (2000) *Women's Attitudes to Combining Paid Work and Family Life*, London: The Women's Unit, Cabinet Office.

Bussemaker, J. (1998) 'Vocabularies of citizenship and gender: the Netherlands', *Critical Social Policy*, vol 18, no 56, pp 333-54.

Bussemaker, J. and Voet, R. (eds) (1998) *Participation, Citizenship and Gender: Contributions from the Netherlands*, Aldershot: Avebury.

Caldwell, C. (2006) 'Germany's truce with feminism', *Financial Times*, 17 June.

Cancedda, A. (ed) (2001) *Employment in Household Services*, Dublin: European Foundation for the Improvement of Living and Working Conditions.

Cantó, P. (2003) *Mujeres de dos Mundos: Ciudadanía Social de las Mujeres Latinoamericanas*, Madrid: Dirección General de la Mujer, Comunidad de Madrid.

Center for ligestillingsforskning ved Roskilde Universitetscenter (2003) *Tvangsægteskaber i en europæisk kontekst. Rapport om best practices i England, Norge og Tyskland (Forced Marriages in a European Context. Report on Best Practices in the UK, Norway and Germany)*, Roskilde: Roskilde University.

CEDAW (2002) (www.un.org/News/Press/docs/2002/WOM1345.doc.htm).

Chauvière, M. (2000) 'Le familialisme face à l'homoparentalité', in M. Gross (ed) *Homoparentalité, état des lieux, Parentés et différences des sexes*, Vaucresson: ESF, pp 95-108.

Closa, C. (2004) 'Spanish citizenship: democracy-building and plural nationhood in the European context', in R. Bellamy, D. Castiglione and E. Santoro (eds) *Lineages of European Citizenship*, Basingstoke and New York: Palgrave Macmillan, pp 130-47.

Comité des Sages (1996) *For a Europe of Civic and Social Rights*, Luxembourg: Office for Official Publications of the European Communities.

Commaille, J. (2001) 'Les injonctions contradictoires des politiques publiques à l'égard des femmes', in J. Laufer, C. Marry and M. Maruani (eds) *Masculin-Féminin: Questions pour les sciences de l'homme*, Paris: PUF, pp 129-88.

Commission on Citizenship (1990) *Encouraging Citizenship*, Report of the Commission on Citizenship, London: HMSO.

Conover, P. J., Crewe, I. M. and Searing, D.D. (1991) 'The nature of citizenship in the United States and Great Britain: empirical comments on theoretical themes', *Journal of Politics*, vol 53, no 3, pp 800-32.

Cornish, W. R. (1982) 'England', in H. Coing (ed) *Handbuch der Quellen und Literatur des Neueren Europäischen Privatrechtsgeschichte: Das 19: Jahrhundert*, vol 3, München: Beck, pp 2217-79.

Cousins, C.R. and Tang, N. (2004) 'Working time and work and family conflict in the Netherlands, Sweden and the UK', *Work, Employment & Society*, vol 18, no 3, pp 531-49.

Cox, R (2006) *The Servant Problem: Domestic Employment in a Global Economy*, London: I. B. Tauris.

Crawley, H. (2002) *Refugees and Gender: Law and Process*, London: Jordans and Refugee Women's Legal Group.

Daly, M. (ed) (2001a) *Care Work: The Quest for Security*, Geneva: International Labour Office.

Daly, M. (2001b) 'Care policies in Western Europe', in M. Daly (ed) *Care Work: The Quest for Security*, Geneva: International Labour Office, pp 33-55.

Daly, M. (2004) 'Changing conceptions of family and gender relations in European welfare states and the third way', in J. Lewis and R. Surender (eds) *Welfare State Change: Towards a Third Way?*, Oxford: Oxford University Press, pp 135-54.

Daly, M. and Lewis, J. (1998) 'Introduction: conceptualising social care in the context of welfare state restructuring', in J. Lewis (ed) *Gender, Social Care and Welfare State Restructuring in Europe*, Aldershot: Ashgate, pp 1-24.

Daly, M. and Rake, K. (2003) *Gender and the Welfare State*, Cambridge: Polity Press.

de los Reyes, P. (2002) 'Vem tar hand om barnen? Könsarbetsdelning och offentlig barnomsorg ur ett ekonomiskt-historiskt perspektiv', in L. Andersson-Skog and O. Krantz (eds) *Omvandlingens Sekel: Perspektiv på Ekonomi och Samhälle i 1900-Talets Sverige*, Stockholm: Studentlitteratur, pp 257-80.

de los Reyes, P. and Mulinari, D. (2005) *Intersektionalitet: Kritiska Reflektioner över (O)jämlikhetens Landskap*, Malmö: Liber.

Del Valle, T. (1997) 'El género en la construcción de la identidad nacionalista', *Ankulegi: Revista de Antropología Social*, no 11, pp 4-17.

Deven, F. and Moss, P. (2002) 'Leave arrangements for parents: overview and future outlook', *Community Work and Family*, vol 5, no 3, pp 237-55.

Dietz, M. (1985) 'Citizenship with a feminist face: the problem with maternal thinking', *Political Theory*, vol 13, no 1, pp 19-39.

Dixon, M. and Margo, J. (2006) *Population Politics*, London: Institute for Public Policy Research.

Dübeck, I. (1987) 'Dänemark', in H. Coing (ed) *Handbuch der Quellen und Literatur der Neueren Europäischen Privatrechtsgeschichte: Das 19: Jahrhundert*, vol 3, Vieter Teilband, München: Beck, pp 21-174.

Duhet, P.-M. (1971) *Les femmes et la révolution 1789-1794*, Paris: Julliard.

Duffield, M. (2002) 'Trends in female employment', *Labour Market Trends*, November, London: ONS.

Duncan, S. and Edwards, R. (1999) *Lone Mothers, Paid Work and Gendered Moral Rationalities*, Basingstoke: Macmillan

Dwyer, P. (2000) *Welfare Rights and Responsibilities: Contesting Social Citizenship*, Bristol: The Policy Press.

Dwyer, P. (2004) *Understanding Social Citizenship*, Bristol: The Policy Press.

EC (European Commission) (2003) *Council Directive 2003/86/EC*, Brussels: EC.

EC (2006) *Towards an EU Strategy on the Rights of the Child*, MEMO/06/266, Strasbourg: EC.

Ecotec (2001) 'Admission of third country nationals for paid employment or self-employed activity', (www.ecotec.com).

Ehrenreich, B. and Hochschild, A.R. (2003) 'Introduction', in B. Ehrenreich and A.R. Hochschild (eds) *Global Women*, New York: Metropolitan Books, pp 1-13.

Einhorn, B. (2006) *Citizenship in an Enlarging Europe*, Basingstoke: Palgrave.

EIRO (European Industrial Relations Observatory) (2004) 'Family-related leave and industrial relations', (www.eiro.eurofound.eu.int/2004/03/study/index_2.html).

Ejrnæs, M. (2003) 'Andenrangsborgere fra begyndelsen' ('Second-class citizens from the start'), in C. Fenger-Gørn, K. Qureshi and T. Seidenfaden (eds) *Når du strammer garnet – et opgør med mobning af mindretal og ansvarsløs asylpolitik*, Aarhus: Aarhus Universitetsforlag, pp 212-34.

Elshtain, J.B. (1981) *Public Man, Private Woman: Women in Social and Political Thought*, Princeton, NJ: Princeton University Press.

Esping-Andersen, G. (1990) *The Three Worlds of Welfare Capitalism*, Cambridge: Polity Press.

Esping-Andersen, G. (1999) *Social Foundations of Post Industrial Economies*, New York: Oxford University Press.

Esping-Andersen, G. (ed) (2002a) *Why We Need a New Welfare State*, Oxford: Oxford University Press.

Esping-Andersen, G. (2002b) 'A child-centred social investment strategy', in G. Esping-Andersen (ed) *Why We Need a New Welfare State*, Oxford: Oxford University Press, pp 26-67.

Fagan, C. and Hebson, G. (2006) *'Making Work Pay', Debates from a Gender Perspective: A Comparative Review of Some Recent Policy Reforms in Thirty European Countries*, Co-ordinators' synthesis report prepared for the Equality Unit, European Commission, Final Report, Luxembourg: Office for Official Publications of the European Communities.

Fagnani, J. (2001) *Un travail et des enfants: petits arbitrages et grands dilemmes*, Paris: Bayard.

Fassin, E. (2002) 'La parité sans théorie: retour sur un débat', *Politix*, no 60, pp 19-32.

Faulks, K. (2000) *Citizenship*, London and New York: Routledge.

Ferree, M. (2004) 'Introduction', *Social Politics*, vol 11, no 1, pp 1-3.

Finch, N. (2006) 'Gender equity and time use: how do mothers and fathers spend their time?', in J. Bradshaw and A. Hatland (eds) *Social Policy, Employment and Family Change in Comparative Perspective*, Cheltenham: Edward Elgar, pp 255-81.

Finlayson, A. (2003) *Making Sense of New Labour*, London: Lawrence and Wishart.

Fraisse, G. (1995) *Geschlecht und Moderne: Archäologie der Gleichberechtigung*, Frankfurt/M.: Fischer.

Fraser, N. (1985) 'What's critical about critical theory? The case of Habermas and gender?', *New German Critique*, vol 35, pp 97-131.

Fraser, N. (1994) 'After the family wage: gender equity and the welfare state', *Political Theory*, vol 22, no 4, pp 591-618.

Fraser, N. (1997) *Justice Interruptus: Critical Reflections on the 'Postsocialist' Condition*, London and New York: Routledge.

Fraser, N. (2003) 'Social justice in the age of identity politics: redistribution, recognition, and participation', in N. Fraser and A. Honneth (eds) *Redistribution or Recognition? A Political-philosophical Exchange*, London and New York: Verso, pp 1-109.

Frevert, U. (1995) *'Mann und Weib und Weib und Mann': Geschlechterdifferenzen in der Moderne*, München: Beck.

García Guitián, E. (1999) 'Ciudadanía y género: posibilidades de análisis desde la teoría política', in M. Ortega, C. Sánchez and C. Valiente (eds) *Género y Ciudadanía: Revisiones desde el Ámbito Privado*, Madrid: Ediciones de la Universidad Autónoma de Madrid, pp 53-62.

García Indo, A. and Lombardo, E. (2002) *Género y Derechos Humanos*, Huesca: Mira.

Gaspard, F. (2006) 'Le foulard et la dispute', in D. Fougeyrollas-Schwebel and E. Varikas (eds) *Cahiers du Genre, numéro hors série: Féminisme(s). Recompositions et mutations*.

Gaspard, F. and Khosrokhavar, F. (1995) *Le foulard et la République*, Paris: La Découverte.

Gerhard, U. (1988) 'Sozialstaat auf kosten der frauen: einleitung', in V. Slupik, U. Gerhard and A. Schwarzer (ed) *Auf Kosten der Fraue: Frauenrechte im Sozialstaat*, Weinheim: Beltz, pp 11-37.

Gerhard, U. (1997) 'Grenzziehungen und überschreitungen: die rechte der frauen auf dem weg in die politische öffentlichkeit', in U. Gerhard (ed) *Frauen in der Geschichte des Rechts: Von der frühen Neuzeit bis zur Gegenwart*, München: Beck, pp 509-46.

Gerhard, U. (2000) 'Legal particularism and the complexity of women's rights in nineteenth-century Germany', in W. Steinmetz (ed) *Private Law and Social Inequality in the Industrial Age: Comparing Legal Cultures in Britain, France, Germany and the United States*, Oxford: Oxford University Press, pp 137-55.

Gerhard, U. (2001) *Debating Women's Equality: Toward a Feminist Theory of Law from a European Perspective*, New Brunswick, NJ: Rutgers University Press.

Gerhard, U. (2006) 'European citizenship: a political opportunity for women?', in S. K. Hellsten, A. M. Holli and K. Daskalova (eds) *Women's Citizenship and Political Rights*, Basingstoke: Palgrave, pp 37-52.

Giddens, A. (1983) 'Klassenspaltung, klassenkonflikt und bürgerrechte', in R. Kreckel (ed) *Soziale Ungleichheiten*, Göttingen: Schwartz, pp 15-33.

Gordon, L. (ed) (1990) *Women, the State and Welfare*, Madison, WI: University of Wisconsin Press.

Gosewinkel, D. (2001) *Einbürgern und Ausschließe: Die Nationalisierung der Staatsangehörigkeit vom Deutschen Bund zur Bundesrepublik Deutschland*, Göttingen: Vandenhoeck und Rupprecht.

Gregson, N. and Lowe, M. (1994) *Servicing the Middle Classes: Class, Gender and Waged Labour in Contemporary Britain*, London: Routledge.

Grøndahl, M. (2003) 'Familiesammenføring – fra verdensrekord til verdensrekord' ('Family unification – from world record to world record'), in C. Fenger-Gørn, K. Qureshi and T. Seidenfraden (eds) *Når du Strammer Garnet – et Opgør med Mobning af Mindretal og Ansvarsløs Asylpolitik*, Aarhus: Aarhus Universitetsforlag, pp 184-211.

Gupta, R. (ed) (2003) *From Homebreakers to Jailbreakers: Southall Black Sisters*, London and New York: Zed Books.

Gustafson, P. (2005) 'International migration and national belonging in the Swedish debate on dual citizenship', *Acta Sociologica*, vol 48, no 1, pp 5-19.

Gustavsson, T. (2003) 'Det var rena slavarbetet: rika familjer i jättehärva – hyrde svart städhjälp', *Aftonbladet*, 4 May.

Habermas, J. (1989) *The Structural Transformation of the Public Sphere: An Inquiry into a Category of Bourgeois Society*, Cambridge, MA: MIT Press.

Habermas, J. (1992) *Faktizität und Geltung: Beiträge zur Diskurstheorie des Rechts und des Demokratischen Rechtsstaates*, Frankfurt/M.: Suhrkamp.

Habermas, J. (1996) 'Three normative models of democracy', in S. Benhabib (ed) *Democracy and Difference: Contesting the Boundaries of the Political*, Princeton, NJ: Princeton University Press, pp 21-30.

Hall, T. and Williamson, H. (1999) *Citizenship and Community*, Leicester: Youth Work Press.

Hansard (2006) House of Commons Debates, Westminster Hall, 10 May, col 101WH, (www.publications.parliament.uk) [cm200506].

Hansen, N.E. (2003) 'Diskrimination på arbejdsmarkedet' ('Discrimination in the labour market'), in C. Fenger-Gørn, K. Qureshi and T. Seidenfraden (eds) *Når du Strammer Garnet – et Opgør med Mobning af Mindretal og Ansvarsløs Asylpolitik*, Aarhus: Aarhus Universitetsforlag, pp 235-53.

Hantrais, L. (ed) (2000) *Gendered Policies in Europe: Reconciling Employment and Family Life*, London: Macmillan.

Harris, J. (2004) 'Nationality, rights and virtue: some approaches to citizenship in Great Britain', in R. Bellamy, D. Castiglione and E. Santoro (eds) *Lineages of European Citizenship: Rights, Belonging and Participation in Eleven Nation States*, Basingstoke and New York: Palgrave Macmillan, pp 73-91.

Hausen, K. (1997) 'Arbeiterinnenschutz, Mutterschutz und gesetzliche Krankenversicherung im Deutschen Kaiserreich und in der Weimarer Republik: Zur Funktion von Arbeits- und Sozialrecht für die Normierung und Stabilisierung der Geschlechterverhältnisse', in U. Gerhard (ed) *Frauen in der Geschichte des Rechts: Von der frühen Neuzeit bis zur Gegenwart*, München: Beck, pp 713-43.

Heater, D. (2004) *A Brief History of Citizenship*, New York: New York University Press.

Heinen, J. (1997) 'Public/private, gender, social and political citizenship in Eastern Europe', *Theory and Society*, vol 26, no 4, pp 577-97.

Heinen, J. (2002) 'Children collective keeping in Poland, yesterday and today', in S. Michel and R. Mahon (eds) *Child Care and Welfare State Restructuring: Gender and Entitlement at Crossroads*, New York: Routledge, pp 126-42.

Heinen, J. (2003) 'L'Union européenne face aux inégalités sociales de genre', *Contretemps*, no 9, pp 158-67.

Heinen, J. (2004) 'Genre et politiques familiales', in C. Bard, C. Baudelot and J. Mossuz-Lavau (eds) *Quand les femmes s'en mêlent. Genre et pouvoir*, Paris: La Martinière, pp 283-99.

Heinen, J. (2006) 'Clashes and ordeals of women's citizenship in Central and Eastern Europe', in J. Lukic, J. Regulska and D. Zavirsek (eds) *Women and Citizenship in Central and East Europe*, Aldershot: Ashgate, pp 95-114.

Heinen, J. and Portet, S. (2002) 'Social and political citizenship in Eastern Europe: the Polish case', in M. Molyneux and S. Razavi (eds) *Gender Justice, Development and Rights*, Oxford University Press, pp 141-69.

Heinen, J and Portet, S. (eds) (2004) 'Genre et politiques socials en Europe de l'Est, *Numéro de Transitions*, vol XLIV, no 1, pp 5-14.

Hernes, H.M. (1987) *Welfare State and Women Power: Essays in State Feminism*, Oslo: Norwegian University Press.

Hernes, H.M. (1998) 'Scandinavian citizenship', *Acta Sociologica*, vol 31, no 3, pp 199-215.

Hobsbawm, E.J. (2000) 'Introduction', in E.J. Hobsbawm and T. Ranger (eds) *The Invention of Tradition*, Cambridge: Cambridge University Press, pp 1-14.

Hobson, B. (2002) *Making Men into Fathers: Men, Masculinities, and the Social Politics of Fatherhood*, Cambridge: Cambridge University Press.

Hobson, B. and Lister, R. (2002) 'Citizenship', in J. Lewis, B. Hobson and B. Siim (eds) *Contested Concepts in Gender and Social Politics*, Cheltenham: Edward Elgar, pp 23-54.

Hoffman, J. (2004) *Citizenship Beyond the State*, London: Sage Publications.

Holthöfer, E. (1982) 'Zivilgesetzgebung Frankreich', in H. Coing (ed) *Handbuch der Quellen und Literatur der Neueren Europäischen Privatrechtsgeschichte: Das 19: Jahrhundert*, vol 3, München: Beck, pp 863-1068.

Home Office Research, Development and Statistics Directorate (2004) *2003 Home Office Citizenship Survey: People, Families and Communities*, London: Home Office.

Hutchings, K. and Dannreuther, R. (eds) (1999) *Cosmopolitan Citizenship*, Basingstoke: Macmillan.

Instituto Nacional de Estadística (2003) *Tendencias Demográficas Durante el Siglo XX en España*, Madrid: INE.

Instituto Nacional de Estadística (2004) *Anuario Estadístico de España*, Madrid: INE.

Instituto Nacional de Estadística (2005) *Encuesta de Población Activa, Nota de Prensa*, Madrid: INE.

Izquierdo Escribano, A. (2000) 'El proyecto migratorio de los indocumentados según género', *Papers*, no 60, pp 225-40.

Jenson, J. and Phillips, S.D. (2001) 'Redesigning the Canadian citizenship regime: remaking the institutions of representation', in C. Crouch, K. Eder and D. Tambini (eds) *Citizenship, Markets and the State*, Oxford: Oxford University Press, pp 69-89.

Jenson, J. and Sineau, M. (1995) *Mitterrand et les Françaises*, Paris: Presses de Sciences Po.

Jenson, J. and Sineau, M. (eds) (1998) *Qui doit garder le jeune enfant? Modes d'accueil et travail des mères dans l'Europe en crise*, Paris: LGDJ.

Johansson, H. and Hvinden, B. (2006) 'Opening citizenship in European welfare states: a framework for capturing the emergent dynamics of social citizenship', Paper given at the conference 'Globalization and the political theory of the welfare state and citizenship', Aalborg, 4–5 May,.

Jones, E. and Gaventa, J. (2002) *Concepts of Citizenship: A Review*, Brighton: Institute for Development Studies.

Justesen, Pia (2003) 'International kritik. Den nationale arrogance' ('The international criticism. The national arrogance') in C. Fenger-Gørn, K. Qureshi and T. Seidenfaden (eds) *Når du strammer garnet – et opgør med mobning af mindretal og ansvarsløs asylpolitik*, Aarhus: Aarhus Universitetsforlag, pp 69-86.

Kamerman, S.B. (2000) 'Early childhood education and care: an overview of developments in the OECD countries', *International Journal of Educational Research*, 33, pp 7-29.

Kamerman, S.B. and Kahn, A.J.K. (eds) (1978) *Family Policy: Families and Government in Fourteen Countries*, New York: Columbia University Press.

Kamerman, S.B. and Kahn, A.J.K. (1991) *Childcare, Parental Leave and the Under 3s: Policy Innovation in Europe*, New York and London: Auburn House.

Kangas, O. and Palme, J. (2005) *Social Policy and Economic Development in the Nordic Countries*, Basingstoke: Palgrave.

Kant, I. (1793/1922) *Die Metaphysik der Sitten*, Leipzig: Wigand.

Kastoryano, R. (2006) 'French secularism and Islam: French headscarf affair', in T. Modood, A. Triandafyllidou and R. Zapata-Barrero (eds) *Multiculturalism, Muslims and Citizenship: A European Approach*, London: Routledge, pp 57-69.

Kaufmann, F.X. (1994) 'Staat und wohlfahrtsproduktion', in H.U. Derlien (ed) *Systemrationalität und Partialinteresse*, Baden Baden: Nomos, pp 357-380

Kiernan, K., Land, H. and Lewis, J. (1998) *Lone Motherhood in Twentieth-Century Britain: From Footnote to Front Page*, Oxford: Oxford University Press.

King, R. and Rybaczuk, K. (1993) 'Southern Europe and the international division of labour: from mass emigration to mass immigration', in R. King (ed) *The New Geography of European Migration*, London: Bellhaven, pp 175-206.

Klausen, J. (2006) *The Islamic Challenge: Politics and Religion in Western Europe*, Oxford: Oxford University Press.

Klein, V. (1971) *The Feminine Character: History of an Ideology*, London and New York: Routledge.

Klinkhammer, G. (2003) 'Moderne Formen Islamischer Lebensführung: Musliminnen der zweiten generation in Deutschland', in M. Rumpf, U. Gerhard and M.M. Jansen (eds) *Facetten Islamischer Welten: Geschlechterordnungen, Frauen und Menschenrechte in der Diskussion*, Bielefeld: Transkript, pp 257-71.

Knijn, T. and Komter, A. (eds) (2004) *Solidarity between the Sexes and the Generations*, Cheltenham, UK, and Northampton, MA: Edward Elgar.

Knijn, T. and Kremer, M. (1997) 'Gender and the caring dimension of welfare states: towards inclusive citizenship', *Social Politics*, vol 4, no 4, pp 328-61.

Kofman, E., Raghuram, P. and Merefield, M. (2005) *Gendered Migrations: Towards Gender Sensitive Policies in the UK*, Asylum and Migration Working Paper No 6, London: Institute for Public Policy Research.

Kofman, E., Phizacklea, A., Raghuram, P. and Sales, R. (2000) *Gender and International Migration in Europe: Employment, Welfare and Politics*, London: Routledge.

Koopmans, R. and Statham, P. (eds) (2000) *Challenging Immigration and Ethnic Relations Politics: Comparative European Perspectives*, Oxford: Oxford University Press.

Koopmans, R., Statham, P., Giugni, M. and Passy, F. (2005) *Contested Citizenship: Immigration and Cultural Diversity in Europe*, Minneapolis, MN, and London: University of Minnesota.

Korpi, W. (2000) 'Faces of inequality: gender, class and patterns of inequalities in different types of welfare states', *Social Politics*, vol 7, no 2, pp 127-91.

Koselleck, R. (1975) *Preußen zwischen Reform und Revolution. Allgemeines Landrecht, Verwaltung und soziale Bewegung von 1791-1848*, Stuttgart: Klett.

Koven, S. and Michel, S. (1993) *Mothers of a New World*, London and New York: Routledge.

Kremer, M. (2002) 'The illusion of free choice: ideals of care and childcare policy in the Flemish and Dutch welfare states', in S. Michel and R. Mahon (eds) *Child Care Policy at the Crossroads: Gender and Welfare State Restructuring*, London: Routledge, pp 113-42.

Kymlicka, W. (1999) 'Liberal complacencies', in S.M. Okin, J. Cohen, M. Howard and M. C. Nussbaum (eds) *Is Multiculturalism Bad for Women?*, Princeton, NJ: Princeton University Press, pp 31-4.

Laborde, C. (2004) 'Republican citizenship and the crisis of integration in France', in R. Bellamy, D. Castiglione and E. Santoro (eds) *Lineages of European Citizenship: Rights, Belonging and Participation in Eleven Nation States*, Basingstoke and New York: Palgrave Macmillan, pp 46-72.

Landes, J. B. (1988) *Women and the Public Sphere in the Age of the French Revolution*, Ithaka, NY: Cornell University Press.

Landes, J. B. (1996) 'The performance of citizenship: democracy, gender, and difference in the French Revolution', in S. Benhabib (ed) *Democracy and Difference: Contesting the Boundaries of the Political*, Princeton, NJ: Princeton University Press, pp 295-313.

Langan, M. and Ostner, I. (1991) 'Gender and welfare', in G. Room (ed) *Towards a European Welfare State?*, Bristol: SAUS publications, pp 127-50.

Lawson, N. and Leighton, D. (2004) 'Blairism's agoraphobia: active citizenship and the public domain', *Renewal*, vol 12, no 1, pp 1-12.

Leca, J. (1992) 'Questions on citizenship', in C. Mouffe (ed) *Dimensions of Radical Democracy*, London: Verso, pp 17-32.

Leira, A. (1992) *Welfare States and Working Mothers*, Cambridge: Cambridge University Press.

Leira, A. (1998) 'Caring as social right: cash for childcare and daddy leave', *Social Politics*, vol 5, no 3, pp 367-78.

Leira, A. (2002) *Working Parents and the Welfare State: Family Change and Policy Reform in Scandinavia*, Cambridge: Cambridge University Press.

Leira, A. and Saraceno, C. (2002) 'Care: actors, relationships and contexts', in J. Lewis, B. Hobson and B. Siim (eds) *Contested Concepts in Gender and Social Politics*, Cheltenham: Edward Elgar, pp 55-83.

Lépinard, E. (2007: in press) *L'égalité introuvable. La parité, les féministes et la République*, Paris: Presses de Sciences Po.

Lewis, G. (2006) 'Imaginaries of Europe: technologies of gender, economies of power', *European Journal of Women's Studies*, vol 13, no 2, pp 87-102.

Lewis, J. (1991) 'Models of equality for women', in G. Bock and P. Thane (eds) *Maternity and Gender Policies: Women and the Rise of European Welfare States 1880-1990*, London and New York: Routledge, pp 72-92.

Lewis, J. (1992) 'Gender and the development of welfare regimes', *Journal of European Social Policy*, vol 2, no 3, pp 159-73.

Lewis, J. (ed) (1993) *Women and Social Politics in Europe: Work, Family and the State*, Aldershot: Edward Elgar.

Lewis, J. (1994) 'Gender, the family and women's agency in the building of "welfare states": the British case', *Social History*, vol 19, no 1, pp 37-55.

Lewis, J. (1997) 'Gender and welfare regimes: further thoughts', *Social Politics*, vol 4, no 2, pp 160-77.

Lewis, J. (2003) 'Developing early years childcare in England, 1997-2003: the choices for (working) mothers', *Social Policy and Administration*, vol 37, no 3, pp 219-38.

Lewis, J. (2006a) 'Work/family reconciliation, equal opportunities and social policies: the interpretation of policy trajectories at the EU level and the meaning of gender equality', *Journal of European Public Policy*, vol 13, no 3, pp 420-37.

Lewis, J. (ed) (2006b) *Children, Changing Families and Welfare States*, Cheltenham: Edward Elgar.

Limbach, J. (2001) 'Constitutional reform and gender mandates', in J. Klausen and C.S. Maier (eds) *Has Liberalism Failed Women?*, Basingstoke and New York: Palgrave Macmillan, pp 177-81.

Linklater, A. (2002) 'Cosmopolitan citizenship', in E.F. Isin and B.S. Turner (eds) *Handbook of Citizenship Studies*, London: Sage Publications, pp 317-32.

Lister, R. (1997) 'Citizenship: towards a feminist synthesis', *Feminist Review*, vol 57, pp 28-48.

Lister, R. (1998) 'Vocabularies of citizenship and gender: the UK', *Critical Social Policy*, vol 18, no 3, pp 309-31.

Lister, R. (2002) 'Sexual citizenship', in E.F. Isin and B.S. Turner (eds) *Handbook of Citizenship Studies*, London: Sage Publications, pp 191-207.

Lister, R. (2003) *Citizenship: Feminist Perspectives* (2nd edition), Basingstoke: Palgrave.

Lister, R. (2004) 'The third way's social investment state', in J. Lewis and R. Surender (eds) *Welfare State Change: Towards a Third Way?*, Oxford: Oxford University Press, pp 157-81.

Lister, R. (2007) 'Citizenship', in G. Blakeley and V. Bryson (eds) *Just Something for the Girls? The Impact of Feminism on Political Concepts and Debates*, Manchester: Manchester University Press.

Lister, R., Smith, N., Middleton, S. and Cox, L. (2003) 'Young people talk about citizenship: empirical perspectives on theoretical and political debates', *Citizenship Studies*, vol 7, no 2, pp 235-53.

Locke, J. (1970/1690) *Two Treatises of Government*, London and New York: Cambridge University Press.

Lombardo, E. and Meier, P. (2006) 'Gender mainstreaming in the EU: incorporating a feminist reading?', *European Journal of Women's Studies*, vol 13, no 2, pp 151-66.

Lutz, H. (2002) 'At your service madam! The globalization of domestic service', *Feminist Review*, vol 70, pp 89-104.

Macpherson, C. B. (1964) *The Political Theory of Possessive Individualism: Hobbes to Locke*, Oxford: Clarendon Press.

Marks, D. (2001) 'Disability and cultural citizenship: exclusion, integration and resistance', in N. Stevenson (ed) *Culture and Citizenship*, London: Sage Publications, pp 167-79.

Marquand, D. (2004) *Decline of the Public*, Cambridge: Polity Press.

Marques-Pereira, B. (1998) 'Reproduction et citoyenneté', *Sextant*, vol 8, pp 169-79.

Marshall, T.H. (1950) *Citizenship and Social Class*, Cambridge: Cambridge University Press.

Meehan, E. (1993) *Citizenship and the European Community*, London: Sage Publications.

Melby, K., Pylkkänen, A., Rosenbeck, B. and Carlsson Wetterberg, C. (2006) 'The Nordic model of marriage', *Women's History Review*, vol 15, no 4, pp 651-61.

Ministry for Refugees, Immigration and Integration Affairs (2003) *Regeringens Handlingsplan for 2003-2005 om Tvangsægteskaber og arrangerede ægteskaber* (*The Government's Action Plan for 2003-2005 on Forced, Quasi-forced and Arranged Marriages*), Copenhagen: Ministry for Refugees, Immigration and Integration Affairs, 15 August.

Ministry for Refugees, Immigration and Integration Affairs (2004) *Udlændinge- og integrationspolitikken i Danmark og udvalgte lande - Baggrundsrapport* (*Migration and Integration Legislation in Denmark and Selected Countries*), Tænketanken om udfordringer for integrationsindsatsen i Danmark i samarbejde med Socialforskningsinstituttet (The Think Tank for Challenges to Integration Policies in Denmark in cooperation with the Institute for Social Research), Copenhagen: Danish Ministry for Refugees, Immigration and Integration.

Modood, T. (2006) 'British Muslims and the politics of multiculturalism', in T. Modood, A. Triandafyllidou and R. Zapato-Barreo (eds) *Multiculturalism, Muslims and Citizenship*, London: Routledge, pp 37-56.

Moeller, R. G. (1998) 'The 'remasculinization' of Germany in the 1950s: introduction', *Signs: Journal of Women in Culture and Society*, vol 24, no 1, pp 101-6.

Moghadam, V.M. (2005) *Globalising Women: Transnational Feminist Networks*, Baltimore, MD, and London: John Hopkins University Press.

Molyneux, M. and Razavi, S. (eds) (2002) *Gender Justice, Development and Rights*, Oxford: Oxford University Press/UNRISD.

Morgan, K.J. and Zippel, K. (2003) 'Paid to care: the origins and effects of care leave policies in Western Europe', *Social Politics*, vol 10, no 1, pp 49-85.

Morissens, A. and Sainsbury, D. (2005) 'Migrants' social rights, ethnicity and welfare regimes', *Journal of Social Policy*, vol 34, no 4, pp 637-60.

Morris, J. (2005) *Citizenship and Disabled People*, London: Disability Rights Commission.

Moss, P. and O'Brien, M. (eds) (2006) 'International Review of Leave Policies and Related Research', *Employment Relations Research Series No 57*. London: Department of Trade and Industry, pp 95-9 (www.dti.gov.uk) [Reference 11.10.2006].

Mouffe, C. (ed) (1992) *Dimensions of Radical Democracy: Pluralism, Citizenship, Community*, London: Verso.

Mozière, L. (2004) 'Des domestiques philippines à Paris: un marché mondial de la domesticité défini en termes de genre?', *Journal des Anthropologues*, no 96-97, pp 291-320.

Nash, M. (2004) 'The rise of the women's movement in nineteenth-century Spain', in S. Paletschek and B. Pietrow-Ennker (eds) *Women's Emancipation Movements in the 19th Century: A European Perspective*, Stanford, CA: Stanford University Press, pp 243-62.

Nelson, B. (1990) 'The origins of the two-channel welfare state: workmen's compensation and mother's aid', in L. Gordon (ed) *Women, the State and Welfare*, Madison, WI, and London: University of Wisconsin Press, pp 123-51.

Neumann, F. L. (1978/1935) Die gewerkschaften in der demokratie und in der diktatur, in F.L. Neumann (ed) *Wirtschaft, Staat und Demokratie*, Frankfurt/M.: Suhrkamp, pp 145-222.

NIACE (National Institute of Adult Continuing Education) (2006) *More Than a Language ...*, Final report of the NIACE Committee Inquiry on English for Speakers of other Languages (ESOL), Leicester: NIACE.

Nieuwenhuys, O. (2005) 'The wealth of children: reconsidering the child labour debate', in J. Qvortrup (ed) *Studies in Modern Childhood*, Basingstoke: Palgrave, pp 167-83.

Norrlander, I. and von Sydow, T. (2004) 'Ompröva synen på hushållstjänster', *Dagens Nyheter*, 17 November.

Norway: Centre for Gender Equality (2001) *Minifacts on Equal Rights*, Oslo: Centre for Gender Equality.

NOSOSCO (Nordic Social-Statistical Committee) (2004) *Social Protection in the Nordic Countries 2002: Scope, Expenditure and Financing*, NOSOSCO 24:2004, Copenhagen: NOSOSCO.

Nowicka, W. (2004) 'L'avortement en Pologne: une loi contraire au bon sens', in J. Heinen and S. Portet (eds) *Egalité des sexes en Europe centrale et orientale: Entre espoirs et déconvenues, Transitions*, vol XLIV, no 1, pp 145-52.

Öberg, L. (1999) 'Ett socialdemokratiskt dilemma: Från hembiträdesfrågan till pigdebatt', in C. Florin, L. Sommerstad and U. Wikander (eds) *Kvinnor mot Kvinnor: Om systerskapets svårigheter*, Stockholm: Nordstedts, pp 159-99.

OECD (Organisation for Economic Co-operation and Development) (2003) *Trends in International Migration*, SOPEMI Report, Paris: OECD.

OECD (2005) *Society at a Glance: OECD Social Indicators 2005 Edition*, Paris: OECD (www.oecd.org).

Offen, K. (2000) *European Feminisms 1700-1950: A Political History*, Stanford, CA: Stanford University Press.

Okin, S. M. (1999) 'Is Multiculturalism Bad for Women?' in Okin, S.M., Cohen, J., Howard, M. and Nussbaum, M. C. (eds) (1999) *Is Multiculturalism Bad for Women? Susan Moller Okin with respondents*, Princeton, NJ: Princeton University Press, pp 9-24.

Oliver, D. and Heater, D. (1994) *The Foundations of Citizenship*, Hemel Hempstead: Harvester Wheatsheaf.

Olsson, K. (2005) 'Kvinnorna måste befrias från obetalt arbete', *Dagens Nyheter*, 19 August.

Ong, A. (2006) 'Mutations of citizenship', *Theory, Culture & Society*, vol 23, no 2-3, pp 499-505.

Orloff, A. S. (1993) 'Gender and the social rights of citizenship: state policies and gender relations in comparative perspective', *American Sociological Review*, vol 58, no 3, pp 303-28.

Ostner, I. and Lewis, J. (1995) 'Gender and the evolution of European social policies', in S. Leibfried and P. Pierson (eds) *European Social Policy: Between Fragmentation and Integration*, Washington, DC: The Brookings Institution, pp 159-93.

Ostrogorskij, M. J. (1897) *Die Frau im Öffentlichen Recht: Eine Vergleichende Untersuchung der Geschichte und Gesetzgebung der Civilisierten Länder*, Leipzig: Wigand.

Pakulski, J. (1997) 'Cultural citizenship', *Citizenship Studies*, vol 1, no 1, pp 73-86.

Paletschek, S. and Pietrow-Ennker, B. (eds) (2004) *Women's Emancipation Movements in the 19th Century: A European Perspective*, Stanford, CA: Stanford University Press.

Pascall, G. and Kwak, A. (2005) *Gender Regimes in Transition in Central and Eastern Europe*, Bristol: The Policy Press.

Pascall, G. and Lewis, J. (2004) 'Emerging gender regimes and policies for gender equality in a wider Europe', *Journal of Social Policy*, vol 33, no 3, pp 373-94.

Pateman, C. (1988) *The Sexual Contract*, Stanford, CA: Stanford University Press.

Pattie, C., Seyd, P. and Whiteley, P. (2004) *Citizenship in Britain: Values, Participation and Democracy*, Cambridge: Cambridge University Press.

Pfau-Effinger, B. (2002) 'Changing welfare states and labour markets in the context of European gender arrangements', in J.G. Andersen and P.H. Jensen (eds) *Changing Labour Markets, Welfare Policies and Citizenship*, Bristol: The Policy Press, pp 235-56.

Pfau-Effinger, B. (2005) 'Culture and welfare state policies: reflections on a complex interrelation', *Journal of Social Policy*, vol 34, no 1, pp 3-20.

Phillips, A. (1991) *Engendering Democracy*, Cambridge: Polity Press.

Phillips, A. (1995) *The Politics of Difference*, Cambridge: Polity Press.

Phillips, A. (2003) 'Recognition and the struggle for political voice', in B. Hobson (ed) *Recognition Struggles and Social Movements*, Cambridge: Cambridge University Press, pp 263-73.

Phillips, A. and Dustin, M. (2004) 'UK initiatives on forced marriage: regulation, dialogue and exit', *Political Studies*, vol 52, no 3, pp 531-52.

Phizacklea, A. (1998) 'Migration and globalization: a feminist perspective', in K. Koser and H. Lutz (eds) *The New Migration in Europe*, London: Macmillan, pp 21-38.

Plantenga, J. and Remery, C. (2005) *Reconciliation of Work and Pprivate Life: A Comparative Review of Thirty European Countries*, EU Expert Group on Gender, Social Inclusion and Employment (EGGSIE), European Commission, Directorate-General for Employment, Social Affairs and Equal Opportunities Unit G.1, Luxembourg: Office for Official Publications of the European Communities (www.beruf-und-familie.de).

Platzer, E. (2003) 'Genuskontrakt och social differentiering: om karriärfamiljers efterfrågan på hushållstjänster', in D. Mulinari, S. Kerstin and E. Schömer (eds) *Mer än Bara Kvinnor och Män: Feministiska Perspektiv på Genus*, Lund: Studentlitteratur, pp 249-70.

Plummer, K. (2003) *Intimate Citizenship*, Seattle, WA, and London: University of Washington Press.

Politiken (2006) 28 May (http://www.politiken.dk).

Portalis, J. E. M. (1844) *Discours: rapports et travaux inédits sur le Code civil*, Paris: Joubert.

Preuß, U. K. (2004) 'Citizenship and the German nation', in R. Bellamy, D. Castiglione and E. Santoro (eds) *Lineages of European Citizenship: Rights, Belonging and Participation in Eleven Nation States*, Basingstoke and New York: Palgrave Macmillan, pp 22-45.

Pudrovska, T. and Ferree, M. (2004) 'Global activism in "virtual space": the European Women's Lobby in the network of transnational women's NGOs on the web', *Social Politics*, vol 11, no 1, pp 117-43.

Randall, V. (2000) 'Childcare policy in the European states: limits to convergence', *Journal of European Public Policy*, vol 7, no 3, pp 346-68.

Rappe, E. and Strannegård, L. (2004) *Rent Hus: Slaget om den Svenska Dammråttan*, Stockholm: Nordstedts.

Regner, N. and Hirschfeldt, J. (1987) 'Dritter Teil: Schweden', in H. Coing (ed) *Quellen und Literatur der Neueren Europäischen Privatrechtsgeschichte: Das 19: Jahrhundert*, vol 3, München: Beck, pp 235-373.

Richardson, D. (1998) 'Sexuality and citizenship', *Sociology*, vol 31, no 1, pp 83-100.

Richardson, D. (2000) 'Constructing sexual citizenship', *Critical Social Policy*, vol 20, no 1, pp 105-35.

Riedel, M. (1975) 'Gesellschaft, bürgerliche', in O. Brunner, W. Conze and R. Koselleck (eds) *Geschichtliche Grundbegriffe*, vol 2, Stuttgart: Klett, pp 719-800.

Rochefort, F. (2004) 'The French feminist movement', in S. Paletschek and B. Pietrow-Ennker (eds) *Women's Emancipation Movements in the 19th Century: A European Perspective*, Stanford, CA: Stanford University Press, pp 77-101.

Romero, M. (1997) 'Who takes care of the maid's children? Exploring the costs of domestic service', in H.L. Nelson (ed) *Feminism and Families*, New York and London: Routledge, pp 151-72.

Rousseau, J.-J. (1947) *The Social Contract*, New York: Hafner Publishing Company.

Rousseau, J.-J. (1963) *Emile oder über die Erziehung*, Stuttgart: Reclam.

Ruddick, S. (1989) *Maternal Thinking: Towards a Politics of Peace*, New York: Ballantine Books.

Ruggie, M. (1984) *The State and Working Women: A Comparative Study of Britain and Sweden*, Princeton, NJ: Princeton University Press.

Rupp, L. (1998) *Worlds of Women: The Making of an International Women's Movement*, Lawrenceville, NJ: Princeton University Press.

Rupp, L. and Taylor, V. (1990) *Survival in the Doldrums: The American Women's Rights Movements 1945 to the 1960s*, Columbus, OH: Ohio State University Columbus.

Ruxton, S. (2005) *What About Us? Children's Rights in the European Union, Next steps*, Brussels: The European Children's Network.

Saharso, S. (2007: forthcoming) 'Headscarves: a comparison of public thought and public policy in Germany and the Netherlands', *Critical Review of Social and Political Philosophy*, vol 10, no 4.

Sainsbury, D. (1996) *Gender, Equality and Welfare States*, Cambridge: Cambridge University Press.

Sales, R. (2002) 'The deserving and the undeserving: refugees, asylum seekers and welfare in Britain', *Critical Social Policy*, vol 22, no 1, pp 456-78.

Sánchez Muñoz, C. (2003) 'Ciudadanía y derechos humanos', in P. Díaz Cantó (ed) *Mujeres de dos Mundos: Ciudadanía Social de las Mujeres Latinoamericanas*, Madrid: Comunidad de Madrid, Consejería de Trabajo, pp 15-34.

Sandel, M.J. (1982) *Liberalism and the Limits of Justice*, Cambridge: Cambridge University Press.

Sandvik, G. (1987) 'Norwegen', in H. Coing (ed) *Handbuch der Quellen und Literatur der Neueren Europäischen Privatrechtsgeschichte: Das 19: Jahrhundert*, vol 3, München: Beck, pp 375-425.

Saraceno, C. (1997) 'Reply: citizenship is context-specific', *International Labor and Working-Class History*, vol 52, pp 27-34.

Sarvasy, W. (1994) 'From man and philantropic service to feminist social citizenship', *Social Politics*, vol 1, pp 306-25.

Sarvasy, W. and Siim, B. (1994) 'Gender, transitions to democracy and citizenship', *Social Politics*, vol 1, pp 249-55.

Schmidt, G. and Jacobsen, V. (2004) *Pardannelse Blandt Etniske Minoriteter i Danmark (Marriage among Ethnic Minorities in Denmark)*, Kbh: SFI, 04:09.

Scholz, J.-M. (1982) 'Kodifikation und gesetzgebung des allgemeinen privatrechts: Spanien', in H. Coing (ed) *Handbuch der Quellen und Literatur der Neueren Europäischen Privatrechtsgeschichte: Das 19: Jahrhundert*, vol 3, München: Beck, pp 397-686.

Schlosser, J.G. (1970) *Briefe über die Gesetzgebung überhaupt und den Entwurf des preußischen Gesetzbuchs insbesondere* [zuerst Frankfurt/M: Fleischer, 1789] Glashütten: Auvermann.

Scott, J.W. (1995) 'Die arbeiterin', in G. Duby and M. Perrot (eds) *Geschichte der Frauen*, vol 4, Frankfurt/M. and New York: Campus, pp 451-80.

Scott, J.W. (1996) *Only Paradoxes to Offer: French Feminists and the Rights of Man*, Cambridge, MA: Harvard University Press.

Scott, J.W. (2005) *Parité! Sexual Equality and the Crisis of French Universalism*, Chicago, IL: University of Chicago Press.

Scrinzi, F. (2004) '"Ma culture dans laquelle elle travaille": les migrantes dans les services domestiques en Italie et en France', in *Cahiers du Cedref no 10*, 'Genre, travail et migrations en Europe', Paris: Publications universitaires Denis-Diderot/Cedref, Série 'Colloques et travaux', pp 137-62.

Secretaría de Estado de Inmigración y Emigración (2003) *Anuario de Migraciones 2002*, Madrid: Ministerio de Trabajo y Asunto Sociales, pp 289-95.

Sevenhuijsen, S. (1998) *Citizenship and the Ethics of Care: Feminist Considerations on Justice, Morality and Politics*, London and New York: Routledge.

Sevenhuijsen, S. (2000) 'De plaats van zorg. Over de relevantie van de zorgethiek voor social beleid', Utrecht, inaugural lecture, 18 May.

Siim, B. (1987) 'The Scandinavian welfare states: towards a sexual equality or a new kind of male domination?', *Acta Sociologica*, vol 3-4, pp 255-70.

Siim, B. (2000) *Gender and Citizenship: Politics and Agency in France, Britain and Denmark*, Cambridge: Cambridge University Press.

Siim, B. (2003) *Medborgerskabets Udfordringer: Belyst ved Politisk Myndiggørelse af Etniske Minoritetskvinder* (*The Challenges to Citizenship: Political Empowerment of Ethnic Minority Women*), Århus: Århus Universitetsforlag.

Siim, B. (2007: forthcoming) 'The challenge of recognizing diversity from the perspective of gender equality', *Critical Review of International Social and Political Philosophy,* vol 10, no 4.

Siim, B. and Skjeie, H. (2004) 'The Scandinavian model of citizenship and feminist debates', in R. Bellamy, D. Castiglione and E. Santoro (eds) *Lineages of European Citizenship: Rights, Belonging and Participation in Eleven Nation States*, Basingstoke and New York: Palgrave Macmillan, pp 148-66.

Sipilä, J. (ed) (1997) *Social Care Services: The Key to the Scandinavian Welfare Model*, Avebury: Aldershot.

Skjeie, H. (2007: forthcoming) 'Religious exemptions to equality', *Critical Review of International Social and Political Philosophy*, vol 10, no 4.

Skinner, C. (2005) 'Coordination points: a hidden factor in reconciling work and family life', *Journal of Social Policy*, vol 34, no 1, pp 99-119.

Skocpol, T. (1992) *Protecting Soldiers and Mothers: The Political Origins of Social Policy in the United States*, Cambridge, MA: Belknap Press.

Southall Black Sisters (2001) *Forced Marriage: An Abuse of Human Rights – One Year After, A Choice by Right*, Interim report, London: Southall Black Sisters.

Soysal, Y. (1997) *Limits of Citizenship: Migrants and Post-national Membership in Europe*, Chicago, IL: University of Chicago Press.

Stark, A. and Regner, Å. (2001) *I vems händer? Om Arbete, Genus, Åldrande och Omsorg i Tre EU Länder (Cared for by Whom? On Work, Gender, Ageing and Care in Three EU Countries)*, Linköping: Linköping Universitet.

Statistics Sweden (2006) *Women and Men in Sweden 2006*, Stockholm: Statistics Sweden Forecasting Institute.

Staunæs, D. (2004) *Køn, Etnicitet og Skoleliv (Gender, Ethnicity and School Life)*, Fredriksberg: Samfundslitteratur.

Stevenson, N. (2003) *Cultural Citizenship*, Maidenhead: Open University Press.

Stratigaki, M. (2000) 'The European Union and the equal opportunities process', in L. Hantrais (ed) *Gendered Policies in Europe: Reconciling Employment and Family Life*, London: Macmillan, pp 27-48.

Stuurman, S. (2004) 'Citizenship and cultural difference in France and the Netherlands', in R. Bellamy, D. Castiglione and E. Santoro (eds) *Lineages of European Citizenship, Rights, Belonging and Participation in Eleven Nation States*, Basingstoke: Palgrave, pp 167-85.

Tamm, D. (1987) 'Einführung: Skandinavien als selbständiger Rechtskreis', in H. Coing (ed) *Handbuch der Quellen und Literatur des Neueren Europäischen Privatrechtsgeschichte: Das 19: Jahrhundert*, vol 3, München: Beck, pp 3-18.

Thane, P. (1993) 'Women in the British Labour Party and the construction of the welfare states', in S. Koven and S. Michel (eds) *Mothers of the World: Maternalist Politics and the Origins of the Welfare State*, New York and London: Routledge, pp 343-77.

Therborn, G. (1995) *European Modernity and Beyond: The Trajectory of European Societies, 1945-2000*, London: Sage Publications.

Tobío, C. (2001) 'Working and mothering: women's strategies in Spain', *European Societies*, vol 3, no 3, pp 339-71.

Tobío, C. (2005) *Madres que Trabajan: Dilemas y Estrategias*, Madrid: Cátedra.

Tobío, C. and Díaz Gorfinkiel, M. (2003) *Las Mujeres Inmigrantes y la Conciliación de la Vida Familiar y Profesional*, Madrid: DGM-CAM.

Togeby, L. (2003) *Fra Fremmedarbejdere til Etniske Minoriteter* (From Immigrant Workers to Ethnic Minorities), Århus: Århus University Press, Magtudredningen.

Torpe, L. (2003) 'Social capital in Denmark: a deviant case?', *Scandinavian Political Studies*, vol 26, no 1, pp 27-48.

Turner, B. S. (1990) 'Outline of a theory of citizenship', *Sociology*, vol 24, no 2, pp 189-217.

Turner, B. S. (1992) 'Outline of a theory of citizenship', in C. Mouffe (ed) *Dimensions of Radical Democracy, Pluralism, Citizenship, Community*, London and New York: Verso, pp 33-62.

Turner, B. S. (1993) 'Outline of a theory of human rights', in B. S. Turner (ed) *Citizenship and Social Theory*, London: Sage Publications.

Ungerson, C. (1990) (ed) *Gender and Caring: Work and Welfare in Britain and Scandinavia*, New York: Harvester Wheatsheaf.

Ungerson, C. (2003) 'Commodified care work in European labour markets', *European Societies*, vol 5, no 4, pp 377-96.

UNICEF (United Nations Children's Fund) (1999) *Women in Transition*, Regional Monitoring Report No 6, Florence: UNICEF.

UNRISD (United Nations Research Institute for Social Development) (2005) *Gender Equality: Striving for Justice in an Unequal World*, New York and Geneva: United Nations.

Voet, R. (1998) *Feminism and Citizenship*, London: Sage Publications.

Vogel, U. (1990) 'Zwischen privileg und gewalt: die geschlechterdifferenz im Englischen common law', in U. Gerhard, M. Jansen, A. Maihofer, P. Schmid and I. Schulz (eds) *Differenz und Gleichheit: Menschenrechte haben (k)ein Geschlecht*, Frankfurt/M.: Ulrike Helmer, pp 217-23.

Vogel, U. (2000) 'Fictions of community: property relations in marriage in European and American legal systems of the nineteenth century', in W. Steinmetz (ed) *Private Law and Social Inequality in the Industrial Age*, Oxford: Oxford University Press, pp 91-122.

von Zahn-Harnack, A. (1928) *Die Frauenbewegung: Geschichte, Probleme, Ziele*, Berlin: Deutsche Buch-Gemeinschaft.

Vovelle, M. (1982) *Die Französische Revolution: Soziale Bewegung und Umbruch der Mentalitäten*, München: Oldenbourg.

Wærness, K. (1978) 'The invisible welfare state: women's work at home', *Acta Sociologica*, vol 21, pp 193-207.

Walby, S. (2004) 'The European Union and gender equality: emergent varieties of gender regime', *Social Politics*, vol 11, no 1, pp 4-29.

Weber, M. (1907) *Ehefrau und Mutter in der Rechtsentwicklung*, Tübingen: Mohr.

Weeks, J. (1998) 'The sexual citizen', *Theory, Culture and Society*, vol 15, no 3-4, pp 35-52.

Wesel, U. (1997) *Geschichte des Rechts: Von den Frühformen bis zum Vertrag von Maastricht*, München: Beck.

Wieacker, F. (1967) *Privatrechtsgeschichte der Neuzeit unter Berücksichtigung der Deutschen Entwicklung*, Göttingen: Vandenhoeck und Ruprecht.

Wiethölter, R. (1972) 'Art: Zivilrecht', in A. Görlitz (ed) *Handlexikon zur Rechtswissenschaft*, Darmstadt: Wissenschaftliche Buchgesellschaft, pp 545-6.

Williams, F. (1995) 'Race, ethnicity, gender and class in welfare states: a framework for comparative analysis', *Social Politics*, vol 2, no 1, pp 127-59.

Williams, F. (2001) 'In and beyond New Labour: toward a new political ethic of care', *Critical Social Policy*, vol 21, no 4, pp 467-93.

Williams, F. (2003) 'Contesting 'race' and gender in the European Union: a muti-layered recognition struggle', in B. Hobson (ed) *Recognition Struggles and Social Movements: Contested Identities, Power and Agency*, Cambridge: Cambridge University Press, pp 121-44.

Williams, F. (2004a) 'Trends in women's employment, domestic service, and female migration: changing and competing patterns of solidarity', in T. Knijn and A. Komter (eds) *Solidarity Between the Sexes and Generations: Transformations in Europe*, Cheltenham: Edward Elgar, pp 210-18.

Williams, F. (2004b) *Rethinking Families*, London: Calouste Gulbenian.

Williams, F. (2004c) 'What matters is who works: commentary on the Green Paper Every Child Matters', *Critical Social Policy*, vol 24, no 3, pp 406-27.

Williams, F. (2005) 'New Labour's family policy', in M. Powell, L. Bauld and K. Clarke (eds) *Social Policy Review 17*, Bristol: The Policy Press with Social Policy Association, pp 289-302.

Wollstonecraft, M. (1996/1792) *A Vindication of the Rights of Women*, London: Constable.

Young, B. (1999) *'Triumph of the Fatherland': German Unification and the Marginalization of Women*, Ann Arbor, MI: University of Michigan.

Young, I.M. (1990) *Justice and the Politics of Difference*, Oxford: Princeton University Press.

Young, I. M. (2000) *Inclusive Democracy*, Oxford: Oxford University Press.

Yuval-Davis, N. (2007: forthcoming) 'Intersectionality, Citizenship and Contemporary Politics of Belonging' in *Critical Review of International Social and Political Philosophy*, vol 10, no 4.

Zippel, K. (2004) 'Transnational advocacy networks and policy cycles in the European Union: the case of sexual harassment', *Social Politics*, vol 11, no 1, pp 57-85.

Index

Note: Page references for notes are followed by *n*